and Pomegranates

An explanation of the culture and
beliefs of a Greek island community

Maria Broadley

Photography by Costas Andreou

Published by Travelleur

First published in 2013 by
Travelleur
96 Thorpes Avenue
Denby Dale
Huddersfield HD8 8TB
UK

ISBN 978-0-9576115-1-1

Printed and bound by CPI Group (UK) Ltd, Croydon, CR0 4YY

For my parents, Margaret and Ray; and Peter and Marge, my husband's parents; all sadly no longer with us in body, but always with us in spirit.

And for families and friendship, everywhere.

Contents List

Introduction

Scenery, seaside, sunshine and sightseeing: postcard prettiness and villages consisting of labyrinthine staircase alleys scaling the flanks of hillside and bay. This appears to be the essence of Skopelos, one of the most beautiful of all the Greek islands.

No visitor to the island can fail to notice, as they sail into harbour, the typically picturesque scene: the wide leafy waterfront promenade, yacht masts swaying against a red and white wall of tile-roofed houses interrupted by the turrets and towers of over a hundred Churches, terminating abruptly on its northern side with a cliff wall where a series of beautiful chapels is perched above the sea like battlements along the ramparts.

But Skopelos isn't just a pretty two dimensional postcard: it is a living, breathing community, existing all year round, not just wheeled out for the duration of the tourist season. It is an island with picturesque bays, some excavations, local tavernas... and a place to enjoy the small pleasures of life: a friendly shopkeeper; a baker on the corner; children playing till late in the evening; and Greek women sitting on small chairs talking about daily worries. In other words, this is the real Greece - a world full of special people, with their own stories, their own habits and a way of life - from which you can learn a lot.

Though an island, Skopelos is also very much a rural community, and as such, its inhabitants tend to be more conservative, strongly resisting any change. As they have inherited the land and the language, many have also inherited the beliefs and customs of the past and it is therefore possible not only to observe acts and usages, but also to enquire as to their significance. Although some customs will undoubtedly be found either to be mere survivals of which the meaning has long been forgotten, or even to have been subjected to new and false interpretations, yet others, still rooted in and nourished by an intelligent belief, may be vital documents of Greek life and thought reaching back to Ancient Greece itself.

At the heart of all lies the Orthodox Church, the beliefs and customs of which - although it exists in many countries of the world - many people are unfamiliar: in fact, many are unclear about whether it is a Christian religion at all. They hear services broadcast over loudspeakers early in the morning on Skopelos and wonder if they are in Turkey, listening to the Islamic call to prayer!

Therefore we need to look beyond the language, the tremulous singing, the black clothes and the headscarves of the nuns and the older village women, to the religion of Greece itself: Orthodox Christianity. At the same time, we will discover that usually the form of worship is older than the religion itself, and the application of the ritual is more universal, because the pathways through which religious feelings and awe are provoked are limited: in other words, that tradition and custom and religion and ritual are often inextricably bound together in the lives of ordinary people.

The essence of Skopelos, its way of life and its system of beliefs, stretches back over thousands of years. It consists not only of Churches and chapels; religious celebrations and processions; icons, crosses and religious rites; but also of traditions and customs; legends, superstitions and old wives' tales. These secular beliefs play a much greater part in the lives of the people than has been seen in many other countries for at least fifty years – if not a century. They informally govern the community – not just of islanders, but of Greeks everywhere; giving a unity of existence and a collective pride that has withstood the people of Greece through centuries of endurance, war and hardship and ensured the survival of their religion, their language and their country. For this reason, although this book takes Skopelos as its starting point, it is hoped that anyone who wants to know more about the Greeks and their faith will find answers to their questions here.

It is the intention that this guide will help you to a small understanding of the people and culture of your holiday destination, so that you take away with you not just souvenirs and memories, but also a little of the soul of Greece when you leave.

Welcome to Skopelos, the island of bells and pomegranates!

Fast Facts on Greek Orthodoxy

Founder: Jesus Christ through the Apostles; primarily Andrew

Place founded: Metropolitan Sees in Thessaloniki, Corinth, Nicopolis, Philippi and Athens

Primate and Headquarters: Ieronymos II; Archbishop of Athens and All Greece.

Bartholomew I; the Ecumenical Patriarchate of Constantinople

Type of theism: One God - a Trinity of Father, Son and Holy Spirit

Sacred texts: There is no 'Bible' in the Orthodox Church. The various service books are located on the Altar , or at the Chanter's Stand.

Holy Books :

The Septuagint: the official version of the Old Testament

The New Testament

The Gospels (Matthew, Mark, Luke and John) a single volume placed on the Altar

The Apostolos: the *Epistles*, found at the Chanter's Stand.

The Menaion (twelve volumes) the **Triodion** and **Pentekostarion**, also found on the Chanter's Stand

Religious professionals: Deacon; Priest; Bishop; Archbishop; Patriarch

Houses of worship: chapel, Church, cathedral – also called the Metropolis

How to live: Have faith in God and Christ's resurrection; participate in the Sacraments

Afterlife: The resurrection of body and soul and eternal heaven or hell

Religious symbols: Cross, dove, anchor, fish, alpha and omega, chi rho

Major religious holidays:

Good Friday (last Friday before Easter) and Easter (date varies)

Dormition of Mary (Aug. 15)

Advent (Nov. 30 - Dec. 24) and **Christmas** (Dec. 25)

Epiphany (Jan. 6); and **Lent** (40-day period prior to Easter)

Date of declared Independence from Constantinople: 1833

Date of Recognition: Autocephaly 1850.

A Brief History of Orthodoxy

The true orthodox way of thought has always been historical, has always included the past, but has never been enslaved by it. . . [for] the strength of the Church is not in the past, present, or future, but in Christ.

-Fr. Alexander Schmemann

Orthodox worship is invariably also a witness to history: it recalls, in its rich diversity, particular historical events not only from the earthly life Jesus, the heart of the faith; but alsofrom the life of the Church, its saints, ascetics, martyrs, and theologians. Every liturgy, every feast, is at once a celebration of time and of the *eschatological* reality – eschatology being the branch of theology that is concerned with the end of the world or of humankind - an anticipation of the 'world to come', of what is beyond history - as well as a remembrance of a concrete historical past.

But history likewise lies at the root of Orthodoxy's conviction that it is the true Church of Christ on earth. It is actually because of its possession of an uninterrupted historical and theological continuity that it is able to make this claim at all. The Church, as we should expect of any historical phenomenon, has changed and developed through the centuries. True enough. Still, the Church in its essential identity and spiritual continuity remains substantially coextensive with the Church of the Apostles. It is, in effect, the living continuation in time and space of the Primitive Church in Jerusalem. In a full theological sense it believes itself to be the one Orthodox Catholic Church in all its fullness and plenitude.

The Early Christian Church

Historical Roots

Christian Priesthood originally issued from being at one with the Chriot, the one true Priest ot the New Testament, having the right by His sacrifice and His very nature to stand before God, to mediate for men.

1

Christ then gave the Apostles the following powers in the new Church:

♦ *to teach the truths of the Faith to all nations on earth;*

♦ *to perform the Sacraments of Baptism and Communion;*

♦ *to administer the Church and to govern the faithful in the paths of Christian living.*

After granting these powers to the Apostles, Christ also promised them *energeia*; a c*omforter—the Spirit of Truth* who would be with them until the end of the World. This Holy Spirit came to them on the day of Pentecost, in the form of fiery tongues; and the Twelve received instructions to begin the work of the Church. It was then that the Orthodox Church was born - today the second largest organized body of Christians in the world. Only then were they able to fully understand the mystery of Easter, that God had raised Jesus from the dead, and begin their mission. Their task was to ordain successors to inherit their Apostolic powers, even until the end of the world and they baptised thousands of people at a time.

Doctrine was also particularly important in this new form of Judaism, a Jewish cult turned into a world-wide movement, because it was not culturally bound, as were Judaism and the Graeco-Roman religions of the time. *Right living* flowed from *right belief*, not from cultural values: it was therefore necessary to have authoritative teachers, as well as administrators of common property. Soon the Church grew to a point where it was no longer possible for the Apostles to minister alone. The Christian community therefore granted the right of authority to various people who were appointed to further the mission of the Church.

The Sacrament of Holy Orders

The Apostles did this everywhere they established Churches by the rite of *Cheirotonia*, the *laying on of hands*, setting up an official Priesthood to ensure the continuation of the service of the Lord in the Church. This power of ordination is called the *Apostolic Succession* and can be traced in both the Orthodox and the Roman Catholic Church to the present in an unbroken line. The Eastern Orthodox Church considers **ordination,** the laying on of hands, to be a *Sacred Mystery* (what in the West is called a Sacrament).

This evolved into a hierarchy of Overseers (*Episkopoi* - Bishops) and assistants (*Deaconoi* - Deacons and Deaconesses) to preside over the Christian communities so that the Apostles themselves might continue their preaching. The Apostles gave Bishops the right to teach in the Church: the power and grace to perform the Sacraments; and the right to administer and govern the Holy Orthodox Church.

After establishing the hierarchal structure of the *Sacrament of Holy Orders*, the Apostles commanded of the faithful obedience to the teaching and respect for the office of the Deacons, the later Priests, and Bishops: the individual shortcomings of any pastor do not lessen the effects of any Sacraments performed by him; his actions are separated from himself and are transformed by the power of the rite.

Episkopoi

Historically, only Bishops received the full graces and became replacements of the Apostles. Only Bishops could ordain Deacons, Priests, and other Bishops as the need arose. Beside the power to ordain, Bishops also received power from the Apostles to judge Deacons and Priests: to rebuke sinners; to honour the worthy; and reject heretics. These are their responsibilities even today.

However, the unique function of a Bishop is *teaching*: he is the one who declares the final word about a disputed matter of faith. He does this not as an individual but as a member of the *Holy Episcopal Synod*, which decides what is orthodox and what is heretical teaching.

The Greek term *hairesis* simply means 'choice' or 'path' (such as choosing to follow a particular career or adhere to a particular philosophical school of thought), but by the time of Justin, the term had taken on inherently negative connotations: it was now seen as 'bad choice'. Those groups or individuals who were labelled *heretics* were seen as innovators of novel ideas rather than adhering to established truths, that is, those set down by the Apostles as understood by the Church Fathers; and as parasitical entities that preyed upon the True Church.

Each Bishop has a territory (*See*) over which he governs. His main duty is to make sure the traditions and practices of the Church are preserved. Bishops are equal in authority and cannot interfere in the jurisdiction of another Bishop. Administratively, these Bishops and their territories are organized into various groups or *synods* of Bishops who gather together at least twice a year to discuss the state of affairs within their respective Sees. While Bishops and their synods have the ability to administer guidance in individual cases, their actions do not usually set precedents that affect the entire Church.

Diakonoi

Originally, Deacons – male and female - were chosen from among the faithful to assist in the work of the Church and as co-workers with the Bishops. Originally, seven Deacons were chosen by the Apostles and their duties were twofold: first they had the responsibility of gathering the food and other goods which were brought to the Church as offerings, and of distributing these donations to the needy whom the Church supported; it was also their duty to prepare for the Eucharistic gatherings and the common meals in which the whole Church participated. Consequently, the Deacon's role was both to extend the Church's charity to those who required it and to lead the people in the liturgical gatherings.

This idea of serving at tables very early influenced the comparison of Deacons to angels, for just as the angels serve God, Deacons serve the heavenly banquet of the Holy Church.

Because of this, the Deacon's stole (*orarion*), with which he binds himself before approaching the Holy Table at the *Anaphora*, is often compared to the wings of the angels and his stole and cuffs are often stamped with the words *Holy, Holy, Holy*, the hymn which the angels sing as they surround the Throne of God. Moreover, the Deacon's *sticharion* (robe) is a longer version of the Bishop's *sakkos*, signifying his relationship as the Servant of the Bishop.

Historically, the Deacon's duties were visiting the sick and the imprisoned, caring for the demoniacs, responsibility for the widows and orphans, instructing the *catechumens* and preparing them for Holy Baptism, and taking Communion to those who were absent from the Eucharistic gatherings. Eventually the Deacons also taught and preached the Holy Gospel, a role later given to the Priests. In all these actions they acted on behalf of the Bishop and the whole Church and were directly responsible to the Bishop in all things. The Deacon is not an independent agent; but is often described as the eyes and ears of the Bishop. Deacons include *hierodeacons* (deacon-monks), *archdeacons* and *protodeacons*. The ancient office of Deaconess was subsumed by the office of Abbess.

Presbyteroi

As the Church became larger, it became necessary to create a further level in its hierarchy. The *presbyteros* (elder), which became *prester* and then *Priest* in English, was a holy man who takes an officiating role in worship with the distinguishing characteristic of offering sacrifices.

Priests can be *archpriests, hieromonks* (Priestmonks), *archimandrites* (senior Priestmonks) or *protopresbyters*. They are vested with the authority to lead worship and officiate at all Sacraments except that of Ordination, which only a Bishop can affect. The Priest is usually assigned a *Parish* in which he ministers both the Word of God and the Sacraments.

Progression of Ordination

The typical progression of ordination became: Reader, Subdeacon, Deacon, Priest, Bishop. Each ordination must take place in order, although it is possible to ordain a layman to all five offices in the course of a weekend. The organization of the Orthodox Church is both hierarchical and *conciliar* (or synodal). It is hierarchical in that Priests, Deacons, and laymen are expected to follow their Bishop and to do nothing without their Bishop; and in that Jesus Christ is the head of every Bishop. It is conciliar or synodal in that there is no single Pope whom all the Bishops follow (the Pope of Alexandria functions as a Patriarch), but rather the Bishops meet together in synods or councils and reach binding agreements through consensus. A Bishop, even the Patriarch, is bound to obey the decisions of his synod. A council with representatives from all the Churches is an *Ecumenical Council.*

Although Orthodox clergy are given considerable honour by the Orthodox Church, each ordination is also viewed as a kind of martyrdom. The Orthodox cleric agrees to be a servant of both Jesus Christ and of the people of the Church: many of the vestments are intended to remind him of this. Much is expected of the clergy, both practically and spiritually; consequently, they also have a special place in the *litanies* that are prayed, asking God to have mercy on them.

The expansion of the early Christian movement was not without problems; nor was it spontaneous. Persecution and actual martyrdom awaited most of its initial members. The aggressive new missionary community, nevertheless, was destined to survive and grow in numbers.

Christian Persecution

Persecution of Christians in the Roman Empire began with the Crucifixion of Jesus. Judas having killed himself, of the eleven remaining Apostles, only one—John the Apostle, the son of Zebedee and the younger brother of the Apostle James—died of natural causes in exile. The other ten were reportedly martyred by various means including beheading, by sword and spear and, in the case of Peter and Andrew, crucifixion.

It is generally agreed however, that from Nero's reign until 250 AD, the persecution of Christians by Romans was limited to isolated, local incidents. Although it is often claimed that Christians were persecuted for their refusal to worship the emperor, general dislike for Christians likely arose from their refusal to worship the gods or take part in sacrifice, which was expected of those living in the Roman Empire. Jews also did neither of these but instead paid the *Fiscus Iudaicus* - the tax imposed on all persons who practiced Judaism. Christians refused to obey Roman law and did not pay the religious tax either, causing civic resentment. As a result, Christians were persecuted by local authorities on a sporadic and ad-hoc basis, often more according to the whims of the local community than to the opinion of imperial authority.

According to Cambridge Ancient History 'It was pressure from below, rather than imperial initiative, that gave rise to troubles, breaching the generally prevailing but nevertheless fragile, limits of Roman tolerance: the official attitude was passive until activated to confront particular cases and this activation normally was confined to the local and provincial level.'

The first documentable Empire-wide persecution took place under Maximinus Thrax, Roman Emperor from 235-238. He viewed Christians as unsupportive enemies of the state and persecuted the clergy ruthlessly: the Bishop of Rome,

Pontian, as well as his successor, Anterus, are said to have been martyred in his reign. Then Christian sources aver that a decree was issued requiring public sacrifice, a formality equivalent to a testimonial of allegiance to the Emperor and the established order. The Emperor Decius authorized roving commissions visiting the cities and villages to supervise the execution of the sacrifices and to deliver written certificates to all citizens who performed them. Christians were often given opportunities to avoid further punishment by publicly offering sacrifices or burning incense to Roman gods, and were accused by the Romans of impiety when they refused. Refusal was punished by arrest, imprisonment, torture, and executions. Christians fled to safe havens in the countryside and some purchased their certificates, called *libelli*. Several councils held at Carthage debated the extent to which the community should accept these lapsed Christians.

The persecutions culminated with Diocletian and Galerius at the end of the third and beginning of the fourth century. Their persecution, considered the largest, was to be the last major Roman Pagan persecution and was the cause of many martyrdoms and the making of many saints. But the process also heavily influenced the development of Christianity, shaping the selection of the Canonical Gospels, Christian theology and the structure of the Church. Among other things, persecution sparked the cult of the saints, facilitated the rapid growth and spread of Christianity, prompted defenses and explanations of Christianity, and raised fundamental questions about the nature of the Christian Church.

The first four centuries of the Christian era were among the most creative: it was then that the Church achieved a certain self-identity, even self-awareness, which has since remained normative for Orthodoxy itself. Two developments affected its self-understanding: the first was the establishment of the New Testament. These writings were received and acknowledged by the community of the Church because they coincided with its own Tradition and the witness of the Holy Spirit since Pentecost. Strictly speaking, Christians lived solely by this Tradition decades before the content of the New Testament was determined. In the circumstances, Scripture in the Orthodox Church is therefore routinely interpreted within the context of the Church's living memory – now given the name Tradition.

Equally crucial for the life of the Church was the formation of its administrative structure; the hierarchy of Bishop, Priest and Deacon. By the early second century, this settled system with its threefold pattern was already in place in many areas. The Last Supper -- the first liturgy -- could not have taken place without the presiding presence of the Lord. Thus, from the beginning, the existence of a presiding head was taken for granted by the Church. This establishment of a local 'monarchical' episcopate is still at the very centre of Orthodoxy.

Galerius, who had previously been one of the leading figures in persecution, in 311 issued an edict which ended the Diocletian persecution of Christianity. Galerius reigned for another 2 years and was then succeeded by an emperor with distinctively pro Christian leanings, Constantine the Great.

Constantine was exposed to Christianity by his mother, Helena. At the Battle of Milvian Bridge in 312, Constantine commanded his troops to adorn their shields with the Christian symbol in accordance with a vision that he had had the night before. After winning the battle, Constantine was able to claim the emperorship in the West. He legalized Christianity in 313, but it was not until Theodosius I in the latter 4th century, however, that Christianity would become the official religion of the Roman Empire.

The Byzantine Church

The Emperor Constantine

The early fourth century marks the end of the period of persecutions and the Church's formative age: it also marks the dawn of the medieval period. With the fourth century we are standing on the threshold of a new civilization -- the Christian Empire of medieval Byzantium. The accession of Constantine was a turning point for the Christian Church. After his victory, Constantine supported the Church financially, built various *basilicas*, granted privileges (e.g., exemption from certain taxes) to clergy, promoted Christians to some high ranking offices, and returned property confiscated during the Great Persecution of Diocletian.

Between 324 and 330, he built a new city that came to be named for him: Constantinople. It had overtly Christian architecture, contained Churches within the city walls, and had no pagan temples. In 330 the city became the capital of the Byzantine or Eastern Roman Empire. It also soon became the focus of the new emerging Orthodox civilization.

The Emperor played an active role in the leadership of the Church and was instrumental in summoning the Council of Nicaea, the first Ecumenical Council, in 325 which issued the Nicene Creed, which among other things professed a belief in 'One Holy Catholic Apostolic Church.' Constantine thus established a precedent for the emperor as responsible to God for the spiritual health of their subjects, and thus with a duty to maintain orthodoxy. The Emperor was to enforce doctrine, root out heresy, and uphold ecclesiastical unity. In accordance with a prevailing custom, Constantine was baptised on his deathbed.

The Byzantine Empire

Historical opinion remains divided on the question of Byzantium's contribution to civilization. Still, its lasting legacy lies arguably in the area of religion and art; it is these which give Byzantine culture much of its unity and cohesion. The new cultural synthesis that developed was clearly Christian, dominated by the Christian vision of life, rather than the pagan.

When the Eastern Roman Empire was succeeded by the Byzantine Empire in the 4th century, Greece and the Sporades Islands came under Byzantine rule and became Orthodox in religion: in 347 AD, Rhiginos is mentioned as the Bishop of Skopelos and subsequently its patron saint. Byzantine evidence can be seen all over the Sporades Islands in the legacy of hundreds of Churches and a wealth of religious art.

On February 27, 380, with the Edict of Thessaloniki put forth under Theodosius I, the Roman Empire officially adopted *Trinitarian Christianity* as expounded in the Nicene Creed as its state religion. After its establishment, the Church adopted the same organisational boundaries as the Empire: geographical provinces, called *dioceses*, corresponding to imperial governmental territorial division. The Bishops, who were located in major urban centres as per pre-legalisation tradition, thus oversaw each diocese.

The Roman Empire in the west finally collapsed in 476. At that time the Western Roman Empire was reduced solely to Italy: Britain had fallen to the Angles and Saxons, Spain to the Visigoths, Africa to the Vandals and Gaul to the Franks. In 532 the Emperor Justinian secured peace for the Empire on the Eastern frontier by signing an 'eternal peace' treaty with the Sassanid Persian king. This required in exchange the payment of a huge annual tribute in gold and did not last much beyond Justinian's reign. However, Justinian also constructed the Church of *Hagia Sofia* (Holy Wisdom) in the 530s. This Church would become the centre of Byzantine religious life and the unrivalled centre of Orthodox Christianity.

The Pentarchy

Within the Roman Empire, five major Episcopal Sees were established: usually called the *Pentarchy*, they consisted of Rome, Constantinople, Alexandria, Antioch, and Jerusalem. Justinian was the first (in 531) to use the title of *'Patriarch'* to designate exclusively the Bishops of the *Pentarchy*, setting the Bishops of these five sees on a level superior to that of other Metropolitans or Bishops. The prestige of these sees depended in part on their Apostolic founders, from whom the Bishops were therefore the spiritual successors. Though the Bishop of Rome was still held to be the First among equals, Constantinople was second in precedence as the new capital of the empire.

The Bishops acted in concert at *Ecumenical Councils* especially called to formulate the dogma of the early Christian Church, but there were often disagreements at philosophical, liturgical, doctrinal and political levels.

The Patriarch of Constantinople

In Orthodoxy, no one Bishop is the Head of the Church: instead, in the sixth century, after the collapse of the Western Roman Empire and during this pivotal period in the history of the Church, the official title of the leader of the Church of Constantinople became *'Archbishop of Constantinople, New Rome, and Ecumenical Patriarch.'* The Ecumenical Patriarch has always been ranked as *primus inter pares* (first among equals) in the Eastern Orthodox communion, which is seen by followers as the *One, Holy, Catholic, and Apostolic Church.* As well as being head of the Patriarchate of Constantinople and of the Holy Synod, he is the Archbishop of Constantinople, and co-head of the independent religious State of Mount Athos.

Heresies and Ecumenical Councils

The Byzantine Empire survived for over a millennium: the single longest chapter in the history of the Church. Among the events and developments which exercised the greatest influence on the life of the Church, the seven Ecumenical Councils with their doctrinal formulations were of particular importance. Specifically, these assemblies were responsible for the formulation of Christian doctrine. As such, they constitute a permanent standard for an Orthodox understanding of the Trinity, the persons of Christ, and the Incarnation. The Councils constituted an authoritative norm against which all subsequent speculative theology was and is measured. Their decisions remain binding for the whole Church: non-acceptance constitutes exclusion from the communion of the Church. This explains the separation from the body of the Church of such groups as the Jacobites, Armenians, Copts, and Nestorians. Ultimately, acceptance of these councils by the entire community of the Church is what gave them validity and authority. By and large, however, their reception was also due to the great theologians of the age; their literary defence of the theology of these Councils was decisive. The writings of such Church Fathers and saints as Basil, Athanasius, Chrysostom, Gregory of Nazianzus, Cyril, and Gregory of Nyssa still constitute an inexhaustible theological source for the contemporary Orthodox Christian.

The Growth of Greek Orthodoxy

Heraclius Augustus, Byzantine Emperor from 610 to 641 AD was responsible for introducing Greek as the Eastern Empire's official language, thus ending the last remnants of Latin and ancient Roman tradition; and for returning the True Cross, one of the holiest Christian relics, to Jerusalem after its capture by the Persians in 614.

Religious rites and expression within the Eastern Empire now became noticeably different from the practices upheld in the former imperial lands of western Europe; and within the former, the southern Byzantine provinces differed significantly in culture and practice from those in the north; while the loss of the southern territories to the Arabs further strengthened Orthodox practices.

The Iconclastic Crisis

We will see that the visual arts play a prominent part in Orthodox piety and liturgical life: Byzantine religious art is among the empire's most enduring legacies. The fundamental objection to images is that depicting or representing the divinity of Christ will invariably lead to idolatry, which is expressly forbidden by Scripture to the Christian. The Seventh Ecumenical Council drew a clear distinction between veneration (*proskynesis timetike*) by which an icon should be honoured, and worship (*latreia*) which belongs alone to God. In sum, it is altogether unlawful to worship icons, for God alone is worshipped and adored; they could and should be venerated, however. The Fathers went on to say that the Son of God, the image of the Father, can be depicted pictorially precisely because he became visible and describable by assuming human nature and by becoming man. Any repudiation of the Lord's image is tantamount to a denial of the mystery of the incarnation. The defeat of iconoclasm is celebrated annually by the Orthodox Church on the first Sunday of Lent. This 'Feast of Orthodoxy' commemorates the final restoration of images on 11th March 843.

The Byzantine Rite

Before its rise to political prominence in the fourth century, Constantinople had been only a minor Bishopric without any liturgical tradition of its own. Its liturgical life was gradually formed from other local liturgical elements and traditions: older centres such as Antioch and Jerusalem made major contributions to this process. Also involved in the building up of this 'Byzantine rite' was the city's resident imperial court with its own elaborate ceremonial. By the ninth century, given Constantinople's growing importance in the Church, this new liturgical synthesis became the standard and eventually replaced all other local rites within the Church. The liturgy and the whole cycle of services used today in the Orthodox world is substantially identical with the original Byzantine rite of Constantinople.

The Orthodox Commonwealth

The Byzantine Church was never confined or isolated, as was the Byzantine Empire. Instead, under the Patriarch Photius, it vigorously sent out missionaries to Eastern Europe and the Slavic world. The choice of the brothers Cyril and Methodius for the mission was a stroke of genius and missionary insight, for both spoke the Slavic dialect then in use among the Slavic settlers near their native city of Thessaloniki. Having received their commission, they immediately set about creating an alphabet, the so-called Cyrillic; they then translated the Scripture and the liturgy. Hence the origins of Church Slavonic, the common liturgical language still used by the Russian Orthodox Church and other Slavic Orthodox Christians. Although their first mission to Moravia was unsuccessful (they were forced to flee by German missionaries and the changing political situation), their work was not in vain. Before long Byzantine missionaries, including the exiled disciples of the two brothers, turned to other areas. By the beginning of the eleventh century most of the pagan Slavic world, including Russia, Bulgaria and Serbia, had been won for Byzantine Christianity. Bulgaria was officially recognized as a Patriarchate by Constantinople in 945, Serbia in 1346, and Russia in 1589. All these nations, however, had been converted long before these dates. The conversion of Russia actually began with the baptism of Vladimir of Kiev in 989, on which occasion he was also married to the Byzantine princess Anna, the sister of the Byzantine Emperor Basil II.

This expansion into the Slavic world also created an Orthodox 'Commonwealth'. Byzantine art, literature, and culture were no longer confined within Byzantium's own political frontiers, but extended far beyond into the Balkans and the north of Russia. The Slavic nations were not only Christianized, but civilized by the Byzantines: a major factor in the formation and future development of Slavic culture. But if the conversion of the Slavs was pivotal in the destiny of the young Slavic nations it was equally decisive for the future of the Orthodox Church. It was in the main this missionary vigour which preserved Byzantine Christianity's universality. The inclusion of Slavic Orthodoxy into the Orthodox fold permanently enlarged the Church's area of geographic distribution; equally, the Slavic element brought immense riches into the Church's midst.

East and West

Byzantine Christianity employed the vernacular language of the people and went on to create native-speaking Churches in the Balkans and elsewhere. Orthodox Christianity, in brief, insisted on preaching the Gospel in the ordinary language of the people so as to be directly and immediately understood by the new converts. At the same time, Western Christianity was zealously imposing a uniform Latin liturgical language on its own converts. The result was yet another strain on relationships between the two halves of the Christian Church. German invasions in the west and the rise of Islam with its conquest of most of the Mediterranean coastline further intensified this separation by driving a physical wedge between the two worlds. Communication between the Greek East and the Latin West actually became physically dangerous and practically ceased.

The coronation of Charlemagne as Emperor by the Pope and the revival in 800 of a western Holy 'Roman' Empire illustrated how far the gulf had widened. For the East, the West was acting as if the Roman Empire, with its legitimate emperor in Constantinople, had ceased to exist. Such a declaration of independence and emancipation from Byzantium was a threat to the unity of Christendom and, indirectly, the shared faith of the One Church.

The Great Schism

The East-West Schism of 1054, sometimes known as the *Great Schism*, formally divided the State Church of the Roman Empire into Eastern (Greek) and Western (Latin) branches, which later became known as the **Eastern Orthodox Church** and the **Roman Catholic Church**, respectively.

Relations between East and West had long been embittered by political and ecclesiastical differences and theological disputes. Prominent among these were the issues of *filioque*, (the relationships between the Trinity); whether leavened or unleavened bread should be used in the Eucharist; the place of Constantinople in relation to the *Pentarchy*; and the Pope's claim to universal jurisdiction.

For Roman Catholicism, the Church is founded upon Peter, and upon his sole representative on earth, the Pope of Rome. Catholics defend the '*Petrine Principle*' of Apostolic Succession, thus the locus of the Church is the Bishop of Rome. Roman Catholicism believes that the Church on Earth is substantially different from that in heaven and thus Christ rules directly the Church in Heaven, but not on earth. He utilizes a *'vicar'*, the Pope of Rome, who is *supreme leader* of the Church on Earth.

For Greek Orthodox believers, the Church is founded on St Andrew, 'the first called' of the Apostles, whose ministry was Greece. The Church is founded upon Christ in the fullness of the Christian Faith that was handed down once and for all from the beginning: the locus of the Church is the Faith. For Orthodox, Christ needs no Vicar on Earth for He rules from the Altar of every Church in the Eucharist.

17

Orthodoxy believes that the Church in Heaven and Earth are one and that Christ rules them both as the sole head.

The Crusades

The Crusades were a series of military conflicts conducted by Christian knights for the defence of Christians and for the expansion of Christian domains. Generally, the word crusades refer to the campaigns in the Holy Land against Muslim forces sponsored by the Papacy. There were other crusades against Islamic forces in southern Spain, southern Italy, and Sicily, as well as the campaigns of Teutonic knights against pagan strongholds in North-eastern Europe.

The final breach between the Churches of East and West is often considered to have arisen after the capture and sacking of Constantinople by the Fourth Crusade in 1204. Although Crusades against Christians in the East by Roman Catholic crusaders was not exclusive to the Mediterranean, the sacking of Constantinople and the Church of Holy Wisdom and the establishment of the Latin Empire as a seeming attempt to supplant the Orthodox Byzantine Empire in 1204 is viewed with some rancour to the present day. Many in the East saw the actions of the West as a prime determining factor in the weakening of Byzantium. This led to the Empire's eventual conquest and fall to Islam. In 2004, Pope John Paul II extended a formal apology for the sacking of Constantinople in 1204; the apology was formally accepted by Patriarch Bartholomew of Constantinople. Many things that were stolen during this time, such as holy relics, riches, and many other items, are still held in various Western European cities, particularly Venice.

The Church During The Tourkokratia (1453-1850)

In 1453, Constantinople fell to the Ottoman Empire, as western Christianity stood by and did nothing. By this time Egypt had been under Muslim control for some seven centuries, but Orthodoxy was very strong in Russia which had recently acquired an autocephalous status. The Russian Orthodox Church was the only part of the Orthodox communion which remained outside the control of the Ottoman Empire; and thus Moscow called itself the *Third Rome*, as the cultural heir of Constantinople.

Eastern Christians fleeing Constantinople, and the Greek manuscripts they carried with them, became one of the factors that prompted the literary renaissance in the West at about this time. Those that remained, the entire Orthodox communion of the Balkans and the Near East, became suddenly isolated from the West. For the next four hundred years, they would be confined within a hostile Islamic world, with which they had little in common religiously or culturally. It is, in part, due to this geographical and intellectual confinement that the voice of Eastern Orthodoxy was not heard during the Reformation in 16th century Europe. As a result, this important theological debate often seems strange and distorted to the Orthodox. They never took part in it and thus neither Reformation nor Counter-Reformation is part of their theological framework.

The new Ottoman government that arose from the ashes of Byzantine civilisation was neither primitive nor barbaric. Islam not only recognised Jesus as a great prophet, but tolerated Christians as another *People of the Book*. As such, the Church was not extinguished nor was its canonical and hierarchical organisation significantly disrupted. Its administration continued to function. One of the first things that Mehmet the Conqueror did was to allow the Church to elect a new Patriarch, Gennadius Scholarius. The Hagia Sophia and the Parthenon, which had been Christian Churches for nearly a millennium were, admittedly, converted into mosques, yet countless other Churches, both in Constantinople and elsewhere, remained in Christian hands. Moreover, it is striking that the Patriarch's and the hierarchy's position was considerably strengthened and their power increased. They were endowed with civil as well as ecclesiastical power over all Christians in Ottoman territories.

Islamic Law makes no distinction between nationality and religion, therefore all Christians, regardless of their language or nationality, were considered a single *millet*, or nation. The Patriarch, as the highest ranking hierarch, was thus invested with civil and religious authority and made *ethnarch*, political and religious head of the entire Christian Orthodox population. Practically, this meant that all Orthodox Churches within Ottoman territory were under the control of Constantinople. Thus, the authority and jurisdictional frontiers of the Patriarch were enormously enlarged.

Religious Rights Under Islam

However, these rights and privileges, including freedom of worship and religious organisation, were often established in principle but seldom corresponded to reality. The legal privileges of the Patriarch and the Church depended, in fact, on the whim and mercy of the Sultan and the Sublime Porte, while all Christians were viewed as little more than second-class citizens. Moreover, Turkish corruption and brutality were not a myth: that it was the 'infidel' Christian who experienced this more than anyone else is not in doubt; nor were *pogroms* of Christians in these centuries unknown. Frustrating, too, for the Church was the fact that it could not bear witness to Christ. Missionary work among Moslems was dangerous and indeed impossible, whereas conversion to Islam was entirely legal and permissible. Converts to Islam who returned to Orthodoxy were put to death as *apostates*. No new Churches could be built and even the ringing of Church bells was prohibited. Education of the clergy and the Christian population either ceased altogether or was reduced to the most rudimentary elements.

Corruption

The Orthodox Church found itself subject to the Turkish system of corruption. The Patriarchal Throne was frequently sold to the highest bidder, while new patriarchal investiture was accompanied by heavy payment to the government. In order to recoup their losses, Patriarchs and Bishops taxed the local parishes and their clergy. Nor was the Patriarchal Throne ever secure. Few Patriarchs between the 15th and the 19th centuries died a natural death while in office. The forced abdications, exiles, hangings, drownings, and poisonings of patriarchs are well documented. But if the patriarch's position was precarious so was the hierarchy's. The hanging of Patriarch Gregory V from the gate of the Patriarchate on Easter Sunday 1821 was accompanied by the execution of two Metropolitans and twelve Bishops. (The gate still remains closed in St. Gregory's memory.)

The above summary - stark and short as it is - is sufficient to convey the persecution, decay, and humiliation that Eastern Christendom suffered under Ottoman rule. The grave problems that western Christians had to face as a result of the French Revolution and the secularization of western society in general might be said to pale against these facts.

Independence and the Modern Church

One of the earliest nations to be influenced by the French Revolution's explosive ideas was Greece; it was the first to break the Turkish yoke, winning its independence early in the century. Although the Patriarchate's primatial status has never been in question - it is, and remains, the first see of Orthodoxy - its geographical frontiers were considerably reduced as a result of the struggle for freedom undertaken by the various Orthodox nationalities under Ottoman rule. The new independent nation states could not remain ecclesiastically under the jurisdiction of a Patriarch who was still within the orbit of the foreign and hostile Ottoman state. The new Greek nation, in short, could not be headed by the Patriarch.

Before long, a Synod of Bishops declared the Church of the new Kingdom of Greece *autocephalous,* meaning that it could elect its own head or *kephale* and this status was recognized by Constantinople in 1850.

The Church of Greece is today governed by a Holy Synod presided over by the Archbishop of Athens. Mt. Athos and the semiautonomous Church of Crete alone remain under the Patriarch's jurisdiction. The island of Cyprus, however, is independent of both Constantinople and the Church of Greece. Its autonomous status dates from the Third Ecumenical Council (431) which accorded it this unique position. Up to that time, it had been subject to the Patriarchate of Antioch. Like Greece, this ancient Church is governed by a synod of Bishops and a presiding Archbishop.

As we have seen, the *ethnarchic system* introduced by the Ottomans brought most of the autocephalous and patriarchal Slavic Churches under the jurisdiction of Constantinople. This subjection, with its loss of Patriarchal status, was never popular. As a result, several independent national Churches came into being once political freedom was achieved. The Church of Serbia, which had lost its Patriarchate in the Turkish period, became autocephalous in 1879, and its Primate was recognized as Patriarch by Constantinople in 1922. Romania, today the largest self-governing Church after Russia, was declared autocephalous in 1885 and became a Patriarchate in 1925. Finally, the Church of Bulgaria declared itself autocephalous in 1860, but it was not until 1945 that Constantinople recognized it; its Metropolitan in Sofia assumed the title of Patriarch in 1953. Russia, which was outside the Turkish fold, was recognized a Patriarchate by Constantinople in 1589. Nevertheless, this too, was eventually abolished, but not by Constantinople. Peter the Great replaced it by a governing Synod in 1721. The *Synodal Period* that followed lasted until the Bolshevik Revolution, when the Patriarchate was once again restored (1917). Today, Russia ranks fifth after the four ancient Patriarchates of Constantinople, Alexandria, Antioch, and Jerusalem.

It is plain from what has been said that the authority enjoyed by Constantinople today is no longer based on any vast ecclesiastical jurisdiction. In the last century and a half it has been stripped both of its former territories and most of its flock. Greece and the Balkans are no longer under its jurisdiction. Inside Turkey itself, moreover, the Orthodox Christian communities of Asia Minor have disappeared. The Patriarch's immediate flock today is, in the main, composed of those Orthodox still living in Constantinople. The Patriarchate's position, therefore, rests on its primatial status, rather than on any wide territorial jurisdiction. World Orthodoxy, like the ancient Church, is essentially a decentralized body consisting of four ancient Patriarchates and numerous local or national Churches, most of which enjoy full self-governing status. Despite the lack of a centralized authority, however, all members of this body are bound together by a common canonical and liturgical tradition, by a single doctrinal and Sacramental unity, and by a common faith stretching back to the original Christian nucleus of Apostolic times. For Orthodox, behind historical reality lies the true Catholic and Universal Church.

Confrontation with Atheistic Regimes

For much of the twentieth century a good portion of the Orthodox Church has had to live under the new political framework of *atheistic totalitarianism*. The dislocation of Communism is the latest in a long series of misfortunes - Arabic, Seljuk, Crusader, Mongol, Ottoman - with which it has had to cope in the last millennium and a half.

There is, however, one significant difference between this latest crisis and those of the past: the previous non-Christian political regimes under which the Church had to live were rarely deliberately anti-Christian. In plain English, there has never been an exact precedent for the Communist catastrophe. None of the past regimes were ever as insistent as Communism in its belief that religion must not be tolerated. According to Lenin, a Communist regime cannot remain neutral on the question of religion but must show itself to be merciless towards it. There was no place for the Church in Lenin's classless society.

The result of this militant atheism has been to transform the Church once more into a persecuted and martyred Church. Thousands of Bishops, monks, clergy, and faithful have died as martyrs for Christ, both in Russia and in the other Communist nations. Their numbers may well exceed the Christians who perished under the Roman Empire. Equally frightening for the Church was Communism's indirect, but systematic, strangulation policy. In the Soviet Union, in addition to the methodical closing, desecration and destruction of Churches, ecclesiastical authorities were not allowed to carry on any charitable or social work. Nor for that matter, could the Church own property. The few places of worship left to the Church were legally viewed as state property which the government permitted the Church to use. More devastating still was the fact that the Church was not permitted to carry on educational or instructional activity of any kind. Outside of sermons during the celebration of the divine liturgy it could not instruct the faithful or its youth. Catechism classes, religious schools, study groups, Sunday schools and religious publications were all illegal.

The result was the dispersion of Orthodox Christians to the West. Emigration from Greece and the Near East in the last hundred years has, in fact, created a sizable Orthodox *diaspora* in Western Europe, North and South America, and Australia. As a result, Orthodoxy's traditional frontiers have been profoundly modified. Millions of Orthodox are no longer 'eastern' since they live permanently in their newly adopted countries in the West.

...of Bells

The Greek Orthodox Church Today

The Panagiotatos (Patriarch)

The proper title for the Ecumenical Patriarch of Constantinople is *Panagiotate (Your All Holiness)*. The current Patriarch (since 1991) is Bartholomew I. In addition to being the spiritual leader of 300 million Orthodox Christians worldwide, he is the direct administrative superior of dioceses and archdioceses serving millions of Greek, Ukrainian, Russian and Albanian believers in North and South America, Western Europe, Australia and New Zealand, Hong Kong, Korea, Southeast Asia and parts of modern Greece which, for historical reasons, fall under his jurisdiction.

Bartholomew has become better-known than any of his predecessors in modern times as a result of his numerous pastoral and other visits to numerous countries in five continents: he has set up a permanent bureau of the Orthodox Church at the EU headquarters, in addition to enhancing the long-established Patriarchal Centre in Pregny-Chambésy, Switzerland; his ecological pursuits have won him the epithet of the *Green Patriarch*.

Ekklisia tis Ellados: the Church of Athens and All Greece

The Church of Greece was formerly a part of the Ecumenical Patriarchate of Constantinople, but was declared *autocephalous* (having its own head) in 1833 in a political decision of the Bavarian Regents acting for Otto, the first King of Greece after the War of Independence, who was a minor. The newly freed people could not accept the command of a Head of Church that was still at the mercy of the Ottoman Empire. The new Church was only recognized as such by the Patriarchate in 1850 with the issue of a special '*Tomos*' decree which brought it back to a normal status, under certain conditions. As a result, it retains precise special links with the Mother Church.

Its canonical territory is confined to the borders of Greece prior to the Balkan Wars of 1912-1913, with the rest of Greece, mostly in the north, being subject to the jurisdiction of the Ecumenical Patriarchate of Constantinople. However, most of the dioceses of the latter are *de facto* administered as part of the Church of Greece for practical reasons, under an agreement between the Churches of Athens and Constantinople. The head of the Church of Greece and of the Holy Synod is *Makariotatos* (Archbishop) Ieronymos II (Ioannis Liapis), Archbishop of Athens and All Greece (2008-). His title is *Makariotatev* (Your Eminence).

The Eastern Orthodox Church of Christ is established by the Greek Constitution as the 'prevailing' religion of Greece and as such the mainstream Orthodox clergy's salaries and pensions are paid for by the State at rates comparable to those of teachers.

The Metropolis

A *metropolis* is a see or city whose Bishop is the *Metropolitan* of the surrounding province. For administrative reasons these Bishops have a title that equates to extra responsibilities, also called *Makariotatos* (Archbishop) or *Metropolitos.* Since the seventh century, Orthodox Canon Law has not allowed married men into the Episcopacy. Skopelos, Skiathos and Alonissos are part of the *Metropolis of Chalcis, Istiaia and Sporades Islands.* The Bishop is Chrysostomos (Konstantinos) Triantafyllou (appointed 2001).

The Ordained Ministry

There are three orders within the ordained ministry of the Orthodox Church: the Bishop, the Priest and the Deacon. Although all other mysteries may be performed by a *presbyter* (a Priest), ordination may only be conferred by a Bishop, and ordination of a Bishop may only be performed by several Bishops together. *Cheirotonia* always takes place during the **Divine Liturgy**.

Church Hierarchy

The Episkopos and his duties

The highest level of Ordination is that of the Bishop. His proper title is the *Theophilesttos* and he is addressed as *Theophilestate* (Your Grace). Ultimately he carries most responsibility before God for the community. In Greek he is called *Episkopos* which literally translated means *Overseer*. All Bishops are equal in the Orthodox Church, and there is no office anything like the Pope as *Supreme Pontiff*. Bishops are almost always chosen from the monastic ranks and must remain unmarried. While Orthodox Bishops are all equal, within the Church they may have different administrative duties, honours and rank. Depending on his jurisdiction and rank, he may be called *Episkopos* (Bishop); *Metropolitan* (head of a large city or a Diocese); *Makariotatos* (Archbishop - head of an Orthodox country or capital city); or *Patriarch* (head of an ancient or ethnic Church).

The duties of a Bishop

The Orthodox Church is *episcopocentric*, because everything depends upon the Bishop and nothing can be done without him. Today, every Priest is but an extension of his Bishop: every local parish Priest performs his duties and receives his authority only from his Bishop.

An Orthodox Bishop is the Teacher of the Faith, the Carrier of Sacred Tradition, and the living Vessel of Grace through whom the *energeia* (divine grace) of the Holy Spirit flows into the rest of the Church. He is the living icon of Christ, the most perfect celebrant of the Holy Mysteries and is empowered with the authority of Apostolic Succession.

The Bishop can bless with both the right and left hands. He forms his fingers to represent the traditional *Christogram* 'ICXC', which is the first and last letter abbreviation of the Greek words for Jesus Christ, 'IHCOYC XRICTOC'. By this response to a request for a blessing, the Bishop emphasizes that he is blessing '*In the Name of Jesus Christ.*'

Ordination

The Clergy in the Orthodox Church are the ordained leaders of the Community: St. Paul says in the Bible that they will answer before God for the people in their care. Therefore, to become a Priest in the Orthodox Church, it is necessary first to be ordained by an Orthodox Bishop. Usually, after a period of serving as a Deacon, the Bishop decides when a candidate is ready to be ordained into the order of Priesthood. The candidate must be an Orthodox Christian who is in good standing with his Bishop. In Orthodoxy, the normal minimum age for ordination is thirty, but a Bishop may dispense with this if needed. Nowadays, the candidate must also complete four years in a traditional college with an under- graduate degree (usually in philosophy or religious studies or something similar); and then complete three to four years at an Orthodox seminary. During the ordination of the Priest, the people must give their approval by calling out '*Axios!*' '*Worthy!*' during the Sacrament of Ordination.

The Presbyteros

A *presbyteros* (elder), which became *prester* and then *Priest* in English, is the second level in the ministry. He is vested with the authority to lead worship and officiate at all Sacraments except that of Ordination, which only a Bishop can affect. The Priest is usually assigned a Parish in which he ministers both the Word of God and the Sacraments. Priests can be *archpriests, archimandrites or protopresbyters.* A Priest is allowed to marry so long as he does so before ordination.

The Deacon

The Deacon, addressed as *Evlavestatos* in writing, or *Evlavestate* when speaking, is now the first level of the

Priesthood, and the office has fallen out of use to a great extent in the Western Orthodox world. After being vested as a Deacon, he is given a liturgical fan (*ripidion* or *hexapterygion,* the heavily embroidered squares of material carried by the clergy), and he is led to the side of the Holy Table where he uses the *ripidion* to gently fan the Holy Gifts (consecrated Body and Blood of Christ). The Deacon helps at services, in parishes, or may be attached as an assistant to a Bishop. He is not given authority to lead services on his own and thus he cannot officiate at the Eucharist or other Sacraments on his own. Deacons can also be *Archdeacons* or *Protodeacons* (a rank of respect given after many years of service) The position of Deacon is often occupied for life.

Other officers of the Church

The Eastern Orthodox Church has two minor orders, those of reader and sub-deacon. Candidates for ordination receive the clerical tonsure prior to being ordained by the laying on of hands to these minor orders. There is a distinction between the laying on of hands for minor orders (*chirothesis*) and that for major orders (*chirotony).* Those in these lesser orders are not considered clergy in the same sense as those in major orders. In times past there have been other minor orders depending on need. The latter are older men performing various tasks such as tending the offering candles, tolling the bell, or taking the position of chanters during services.

Hypodeacon – Sub-deacon

This is the highest of the minor orders of clergy in the Orthodox Church. This order is higher than the reader and lower than the Deacon. It later became the practice to ordain as many sub-deacons as were necessary to meet the needs of the people in the areas of philanthropy, social work, teaching and administrative needs of that community. Nowadays, the office is more often used in the West as a 'fast track' to the Priesthood proper. Today *sub-deacons* are not of the Deaconate of the major clergy, but comprise a separate office of members of the laity.

The sub-deacon has practical responsibilities in the care of the altar, in cleaning it, looking after the clergy vestments and the cloths of the Holy Table, cleaning and mending them, and changing them according to the feasts, fasts and seasons. For this reason, he has a general blessing to touch the Holy Table and the Table of Oblation, which Readers and other servers may not do. He is also responsible for the training of new servers and takes responsibility for the altar boys when they are carrying the *Exapteryga* (angels) accompanying the cross in processions out of Church.

The wife of a Deacon is called *Diakonissa* in Greek. Like the wife of a Priest, she should normally be addressed with both her title and her name in informal situations: ie *Diakonissa Sophia*.

Anagnostis – The Reader

This is the second highest of the minor orders of clergy. This order is higher than the Doorkeeper (now largely obsolete) and lower than the sub-deacon. The Reader's essential role is to read the Old Testament lessons (parables) and the Epistle lessons during the Divine Liturgy, *Esperion* (Vespers) and other services, as well as to chant the Psalms and the verses of the Prokimen, Alleluia and certain antiphons and other hymns during the Divine Services. Due to this fact, it often falls to the Reader within a parish to construct the variable parts of the Divine Services according to the often very complicated rules. This can lead to a very intimate knowledge of the structure of and rules pertaining to the services. There is a special service for the ordination of a Reader, although in contemporary practice a layman may receive the Priest's blessing to read on a particular occasion.

Protopsaltis – Chief Cantor

A Cantor (*protopsaltis*) is the chief singer in a Church with responsibilities for the Ecclesiastical choir; he is also called the *precentor*. The Cantor or Chanters sing the many hymns called for during the Divine Services. A Chanter must be knowledgeable about the ecclesiastical modes as well as the complex structure of the services; he must be Orthodox and properly ordained to service a parish by the Bishop. He or they are stationed at a *psalterion*, a chanting podium positioned to the south and sometimes also to the north side of the Sanctuary.

The Cantors were first established in the Greek Orthodox Church during the *Tourkokrateia*, the Turkish Occupation. During this period, Christian communion was forbidden or by necessity often became infrequently celebrated, and the tradition of having a few 'stand ins', the Cantors, came into existence to say the responses for all.

The congregation is usually made up of four different groups: the *clergy* and minor clergy; the *faithful* (people who have taken communion - all children should be in this category, and most adults) stand closest to the altar and sing and do all the responses to the Priest; the *co-standers* (people who are regular communicants but have special permission from the Priest for that Sunday not to partake of Communion for a particular reason – perhaps as a short penance), who may also sing and respond to the Priest but only at certain parts; the *Penitents* (people who do not take communion because they have excommunicated themselves by perpetual sin or sin unto death, or by not coming to Church for 3 weeks in a row -there are several classes of penitents, including mourners), who are not allowed to respond.

Technically a penitent is the only one who can kneel on a Sunday since they do not partake of the resurrection through communion; this is where the need for kneeling stalls first originated in the Western Church.

Altar Servers

In the Eastern Orthodox Church, altar servers assist the higher clergy during services. They might carry the cross, candles or liturgical fans in processions and entrances; maintain the censer, ensuring it has enough live charcoal, loading it with incense and handing it to the Priest or Deacon when required; preparing the *zeon* (hot water) in time for it to be added to the chalice at the Divine Liturgy; preparing the *antidoron* (bread) for the people to receive after Holy Communion; and any other necessary tasks so that the celebrant need not be distracted during the service. An altar server is vested in the *sticharion* only.

The minimum age varies by local circumstance, but boys must be mature enough to carry out their duties without disrupting the sanctity of the altar.

Altar servers, regardless of age, are subject to all the normal restrictions for those not of higher clerical position. Anyone who is bleeding, or has an open sore, is not permitted to enter the altar. They may not touch the altar table or anything on it under any circumstances, nor the *prosthesis* without a blessing. They may not touch the sacred vessels, the *chalice* and *diskos* (paten) at any time. They may not stand directly in front of the altar table or pass between the front of it and the iconostasis, but must cross between the altar and the High Place if they need to move to the opposite side.

The Pappas

The *Pappas* (Priest) is the spiritual father of his parish, and every parishioner ought to respect him as such. Depending on the situation the Priest may be addressed as *Aidesimotatos (Reverend Father* in writing), or *Aidesimotate – (Father* in person) - or in Greek Orthodoxy, when speaking of him, his first name is used (eg. *Pappas Dimitris* / Father James). The title of *Father* is to remind him that he is to treat his parishioners, his parochial family, as a father treats his children, that is with love, kindness, patience, and understanding. Being edified by his example, the parishioners will respect him as their spiritual father and as their true guide along the path of salvation.

In the Eastern traditions, only men may become Priests; canonically the minimum age is 30 years of age, although exceptions are made from time to time at the Bishop's discretion.

In general it is considered preferable for parish Priests to be married as they often act as counsel to married couples and thus can draw on their own experience. Unmarried Priests usually are monks and live in monasteries, though there are occasions when, because of a lack of married Priests, a monk-Priest is temporarily assigned to a parish.

Widowed Priests and Deacons may not remarry and it is common for such members of the clergy to retire to a monastery. This is also true of widowed wives of clergy, who do not remarry and become nuns when their children are grown.

In the case of married clergy, the wife of a Priest is also informally addressed with a title. Since the *Sacrament of Marriage* binds a Priest and his wife together as '*one flesh*,' the wife in a sense shares her husband's Priesthood: this does not, of course, mean that she has the grace of the Priesthood or its office, but the dignity of her husband's service certainly accrues to her; the Priest's wife becomes an extension of him. Women who may have thought this would be a symbol of status and honour are often mistaken. Frequently, it only makes them a target for upset and the wife of a Priest can often suffer more stress than her husband. The Priest's wife, because of her special role as *Mother* in the community is called *Presbytera*, the feminine form of the word *Presbyter* and should be addressed with both her name and her title: ie *Presbytera Maria*.

The duties of the Pappas

The most significant liturgical acts reserved to Priests are the administration of the Sacraments, including the celebration of the Eucharist, Holy Baptism and the Sacrament of Reconciliation, a rite of Repentance, also called 'Confession'. The presence and ministry of a Priest is required for a parish to function fully.

Priests are heavily involved with the people of their community: a Greek Orthodox Priest works to handle all of the spiritual needs of his parishioners; he carries out weddings, baptisms, funerals, or any other types of special events that happen within the Church. A primary responsibility of the parish Priest is to continue the ongoing education of the faithful in matters of dogma, tradition, precepts, and sacred rites of the Church. He supervises the Church School, gives direction to its instructors, and decides on appropriate resources and texts in conformity to diocesan directives. By the virtue of his office, the Priest has supervision over every organization in the parish; directing its life, activities, and administration.

The Priest must also include in his ministry personal contact with all parishioners, including visiting the homes of all parishioners during the days of the celebration of the *Feast of the Theophany* (Epiphany). For an Orthodox Christian, the home is a house-Church, the place of their spiritual struggle and so a place where there are often temptations and trials in their everyday life. This annual blessing dedicates it again to the Lord and brings refreshment for those who live there. A small table, covered with a clean white cloth, is set up before the icon corner, with a lighted candle and a bowl of water which has been blessed. The Priest commemorates all the house occupants, who then lead him around the house from room to room to sprinkle it with the holy water. If the number of homes to be visited is too great, or if winter weather makes it impractical, these visits may be done at another appropriate time of year.

Because the Priest is the spiritual father, he must not delay visiting each parishioner who has fallen ill. He is to make no distinction as to whom he visits, for all need the healing power of his prayer. However, the Priest does not have the pastoral role of a Catholic Priest or a Protestant clergyman: he must instead be most diligent in preparing homilies for his flock, giving this priority over administrative duties; these are taken over by the Deacon.

The protopresbyter (head Priest) on Skopelos is Pappas Nicholas, based at the former cathedral Church of *Chora*, Sto Christo. The twenty four Churches and chapels of the oldest part of town come under his primary jurisdiction, but he oversees all religious affairs on the island as a whole.

Priestly attire

Eastern Orthodox Priests mostly retain the traditional dress worn for the past thousand years. This includes a black *under-cassock* (the *rasson*), an ankle length garment worn by all major and minor clergy and monastics, which is gathered at the waist with a narrow cloth belt, and has a high collar buttoned in the front. The inner cassock is usually worn by all clergy members under their *liturgical vestments* (robes which are worn during Church services).

Over this is worn a black *over-cassock* (the *riassa* or *exorason*) with very wide sleeves, a voluminous garment worn over the inner cassock by Bishops, Priests, Deacons, and monastics as their regular outer wear. In Greece, Chanters may wear it in Church, usually with no inner cassock beneath but directly over secular clothing. A *cassock vest* ('kontorasson', 'amaniko' or 'gileko') is sometimes worn over the inner cassock. This is a closely fitted collarless vest, usually falling slightly below the waist.

Many also wear a large cross, called a *pectoral cross*. The cross is more often worn by Priests in western countries to distinguish them as Christian. As a general rule, the Slavic Churches tend to give pectoral crosses to all Priests, whereas those in the Churches of Greek and Arabic descent (i.e., those from the Byzantine Empire) receive pectoral crosses only as an honorific token. Some Eastern Orthodox Priests wear a collar similar to that of Western clergy, although this is falling out of favour since this leads to their being confused with Roman Catholic or Protestant clergy. The Priest also sports a 'chimney-pot' style hat, called a *kamelaukion*, over his tied-back hair.

When celebrating services, Orthodox Priests always wear special liturgical vestments. In this category you may find *epitrachelions* (literally 'about the neck'; the *Stole*). This is one of the most important vestments, hanging from the neck down to the feet. An Orthodox Priest must wear this particular vestment to perform a Sacrament. The *epitrachelion* signifies the double portion of grace bestowed on a Priest, for the celebration of the Mysteries.

The black- coloured vestments indicate mourning for the events memorized during Holy Week. There is no actual rule about colouration for non-monastic clergy, but black is the most common. Blue or grey are also seen especially if the Priests are on unofficial business, while white is sometimes worn for *Pascha* (Easter).

One of the pious practices of the Orthodox Church is to reach out and touch the Priest's vestments as he passes by in the *Great Entrance of the Divine Liturgy*. This practice is in imitation of the woman who was healed by touching the hem of Christ's robe. It has become a pious custom by which prayers are attached and thus carried into the altar at the *Entrance of the Holy Gifts*. Special care should be given not to tug on the vestments or trip the Priest when reaching out. It is never appropriate to touch the sacred vessels (*chalice* and *discos*) in this procession. It is an unwritten rule that women who are menstruating should not touch either the Priest himself or his clothing.

Many Priests and all monks of the Orthodox Church follow the law of the Nazarene as written in the *Book of*

Numbers, as a symbol of their complete devotion to serving the Lord: '..a razor shall not come upon his head, until the days be fulfilled which he vowed to the Lord: he shall be holy, cherishing the long hair of the head all the days of his vow to the Lord... (Numbers 6:5-6)'. The significance of the Nazarene vow was a sign of God's power resting on the person who made it. To cut off the hair meant to cut off God's power – this is the point of the story of Samson. Greek Monastic tonsure – the growing, rather than the cutting off of hair - is a version of the Nazarene vow and is the reason Priests in Greece have long hair and untrimmed beards.

Showing respect for the Priesthood

It is a strong Orthodox custom to show respect toward the Priest as one responsible before God for leading the community. One physical expression of this is to kiss his hand. This is an ancient custom signifying respect and love to his office, but also, since the Priest holds the Holy Mysteries in his hands during the Divine Liturgy, shows respect to the Holy Eucharist: the Church believes there is a blessing for the person who does this. When the Priest or Bishop blesses the faithful, he forms his fingers to represent the Christogram ICXC, a traditional abbreviation of the Greek words for *Jesus Christ*.

The etiquette is as follows: when one approaches an Orthodox Presbyter or Bishop (but not a Deacon), one makes a bow by reaching down and touching the floor with the right hand, then places the right hand over the left (palms upward), and says: '**Eulouisoume pateras**' or '**Evlogites Pateras'** *'Bless, Father'*. The Priest or Bishop then answers, '*Borei o lordos eulouisoume sas*' '*May the Lord bless you,*' blessing with the Sign of the Cross, and places his right hand in the hands of the supplicant, who can then kiss it. On taking leave of the Priest or Bishop, a blessing should be asked for again, just as when he was first greeted.

When speaking to Orthodox clergy of Priestly rank on the telephone, the conversation should always begin by the asking of a blessing: '*O Pateros Evlogites*', '*Father, bless.*' The conversation should be ended by asking for a blessing again.

It is not appropriate to invoke a blessing on a clergyman by saying: '*May God bless you.*' This shows a certain spiritual arrogance before the image of the cleric, as laymen do not have the Grace of the Priesthood and the prerogative to bless in their stead.

The duties of the Deacon

The Deacon prepares the elements necessary for Holy Communion. All of the offerings were originally collected in the *Diaconicon*, a separate room outside the Church where vestments, holy vessels and food are kept, and where the bread and wine are prepared for the Holy Liturgy. (This is why many of the older Churches, such as that of Aghios Ioannis Kastri, now known as the 'Mamma Mia!' Church, are actually two separate buildings.)

Having completed the preparation of bread and wine for communion, the Deacon leaves the *Diaconicon* at the proper time and, entering the Church, proceeds to the altar where he presents these gifts to the celebrant as an offering of the people. This is the origin of the *Great Entrance* in the Divine Liturgy.

Within the service, it is the Deacon's function to bring the people together and unite them both in corporate prayer and in their function of fulfilling their role as members of the Body of Christ, the Church. He may not give a blessing, however, since this right belongs solely to the Priests and Bishops. Rather he leads them in their offerings to the altar-- through their material offerings (*prosphora)* and in their prayers—so that the celebrant may offer up *(anaphora*) their sacrifice unto God. His function consists primarily in making sure that the corporate action of the Eucharist is fulfilled through the participation of all the members of the congregation in their several functions at their proper time and in their proper order.

At the Altar, all the Deacon's actions are performed in behalf of the faithful and it is his role as servant to the celebrant and the people that makes him the bond of unity between the two. In this way there is not a single act of the Divine Liturgy where the faithful and clergy are not united in a common action and prayer, for the faithful are present at all times at the Altar; through their offerings and the Deacon's presence as their servant.

The Deacon also leads the people in prayer, expressing what the immediate, changing needs of the people are and thereby bringing these needs to the Church. His '*social worker*' function among the congregation, working closely with the faithful and dispensing the charity of the Church – he knows who is sick, who has died, who is travelling, who is out of work or whose crops have failed – means that he is able to include these needs in his *litany*. In this way, by announcing the '*daily news and needs*' of the faithful during the litanies, the Deacon informs the faithful who needs help and for whom prayers are needed: the faithful respond either '*Lord have mercy*' or '*Grant this O Lord*' to each petition.

The Orthodox Faith

The difference between Orthodox Christianity and the various other Christian religions is that other religions promise a certain blissful state, even after death. Orthodoxy however perceives itself to be not a quest for bliss, but a cure from the illness of religion. Orthodox believers must overcome the assumption that moral, spiritual, and survival knowledge can be derived only from scripted traditions and pre-formulated rule. Adopting the *preceptive dogmas* (meaning those taken beforehand; to be instructed or forewarned) written into historical and religious texts, is not sufficient.

When the term *precept* came into use in the fourteenth century, early in the development of the English language, it connoted a command of divine origin: the Ten Commandments of the Old Testament were precepts believed to originate from God, a superhuman agency. The *pre-* in precept implies that the command imparted, or the belief inculcated, comes before experience rather than arises out of experience: rules are a crutch for those who can only blindly follow, without understanding.

Orthodoxy sees itself as a spiritual infirmary, offering the healing *(catharsis)* of the heart, achieved by man through his own experiences. Thus he will finally attain **theosis** — the only desired destination of man, which is the healing of mankind. **Theosis** was experienced by all the Saints, who have set an example of the way to reach it. However, man was created with free will, and each must choose his way through life by himself. Man's orientation toward his fellow man is indicative of his inner state, and that is why this will be the criterion of *Judgement Day*, during *Christ's Second Coming*. This does not imply that faith, or man's faithfulness to Christ is disregarded. Faith is naturally a prerequisite, because men's stance toward each other will show whether or not they have God within them.

Followers of the Greek Orthodox religion believe in eternal life: thus the Church strongly emphasises a positive outcome in death — the deceased falls into sleep, but is alive with God. Whilst death is the separation of the soul (the spiritual dimension of each person) from the body (the physical dimension); the physical body will be reunited with the soul at the *Last-Judgement*.

Orthodox Christians hold that man was originally created at one with God, but he disrupted that communion, by refusing to fulfil the 'image and likeness of God' within him. Thus corruption and sin, whose consequence is death, entered his mode of existence. Jesus, the Perfect Man and Perfect God united together, restored human existence, enabling human beings to incorporate into Himself and therefore to participate in divinity once more. The understanding of the process by which this is achieved is the perception of Meta-history. The Meta-historical attitude demonstrates a critical distancing from materials whose content may be uncritically compounded with folk lore and metaphysical speculations, a factor that initially appeared in the era and setting of Greek rationalism and may be said to have properly begun with the Greek historian Herodotus, who questioned sources in order to arrive at a semblance of truth.

Meta-history and Redemption

Meta-history does not automatically assume a *cause and effect* dynamic operating from past to present, such that we can derive every event that happens later from something that happened earlier. Instead, Meta-history realizes how past and present are related, without assuming strict causal continuity: it states that the full formula of historical continuity must include the *future*.

The future is not a passive experience where Man ends up because he is driven there, or that he just drifts into, sliding unawares through the present on the momentum of the past. The future is dynamically operative in the interplay of past and present. It is as powerful a determinant of the present as the past. The panorama of the past may not contain the causes of all that happens in the present, but it does show the background of human experience as it unfolds in the here and now. Remember the old adage: those that do not learn from the past are bound to repeat it – in the future.

Meta-history always questions assumptions about social order, and takes a critical view of the fashionable ideology inherent to any such assumptions, while at the same time it seeks to discover the inherent patterns that might insure sanity and stability for human society over the long term; themes taken up by the Orthodox Church.

The Sunday services of the **Triodion** preceding Lent revolve around Man's relationships with his fellow men. On the first of these Sundays (the **Sunday of the Publican and the Pharisee**), the theme is how the outwardly pious Pharisee justifies himself and denigrates the Tax Collector. On the second Sunday (the **Sunday of the Prodigal Son**), the older brother (a repetition of the seemingly pious Pharisee) is sorrowed by the salvation of his brother. Likewise, seemingly pious, he too had false piety, which did not produce love. On the third Sunday, the **Sunday of the Last Judgement** or *Meatfare Sunday,* this condition reaches Christ's seat of judgement, and is evidenced as the criterion for man's eternal life. In all these circumstances, pious hypocrisy, Church going, religious formulas and paying lip-service to the conventions of faith are shown to be not enough for man to be regarded as a true believer: more will be demanded at the Final Judgement.

At the beginning of Great Lent, on the *Κυριακή της Απόκρεω* (or in common parlance *η Πρώτη Σήκωσης* or the First Lifting, as in food from the diet in the Lenten Fast), also called Meatfare Sunday, the Orthodox Priest calls on the congregation 'to commemorate the Second and Incorruptible Coming of our Lord Jesus Christ'. The use of the expression 'commemorate' confirms that the Orthodox Church re-enacts in its worship the Second Coming of Christ as an achieved event and not just something that is historically expected.

Church Teaching

In addition, the Church teaches that one must also be God's sons by following Christ, his only-begotten divine Son, and by seeing Christ in everyone and by serving Christ through them. Salvation and final judgement will depend upon deeds, not merely on intentions or even on the mercies of God apart from personal cooperation and obedience. All piety and prayer is ultimately directed towards the goal of serving Christ through his people.

From the reading, the faithful hear:

... for I was hungry and you gave me food, I was thirsty and you gave me drink, I was a stranger and you took me in, I was naked and you clothed me, I was sick and in prison and you visited me. .... For truly I say to you, if you did it to one of the least of these my brothers, you did it to me (Matthew 25).

Meta -history answers the need to develop the innate wisdom of Man, who must overcome the assumption that moral, spiritual and survival knowledge can be derived only from scripted traditions and pre-formulated rules. He will realize what it takes to be human only in the process of discovering what humanity knows; and by understanding, acting upon it. This discovery arises only through exploring in life the poetic-visionary resources of humanity, such as the *Parables of Jesus* or the *Book of Revelation*.

Paradise and Hell in the Orthodox Tradition

The **Gospels of the New Testament** mention paradise and hell frequently. Paradise, eternal life, and the kingdom of God, are all related. References to hell include everlasting torment, everlasting fire, the outermost darkness and the place of fire. The Kingdom is the divine destination of mankind, prepared for those who remain faithful to the will of God. Eternal fire is hell, prepared for the devil and his angels (demons), not because God desired it, but because they are without repentance, (that is they are unwilling to turn, to re-think, and participate in redemption). At the beginning of history, God invited man into paradise, into the Garden of Eden. At the end of history, man has to face both paradise and hell in the *Judgement Day of the Second Coming*: this is one of the central subjects of the faith of Orthodox Christianity.

However, in Orthodoxy, paradise and hell are not two different places. Rather, they signify two different conditions originating from the same source, that are perceived by man as two differing experiences. More precisely, they are the same experience, except that they are perceived differently by man, depending on his own individual internal state. Paradise and hell are therefore the same reality: depicted in the portrayal of the *Second Coming* on the walls of every Orthodox Church.

Stand before the frescoes and you will find the one described as follows, usually on the western wall on the side of death (hence the old expression 'Gone West' for someone who has died, which originated in Ancient Egypt at Thebes; the living exist on the east bank of the Nile; the dead on the west). From Christ, the central figure, a river of fire flows forth. It is like a golden light at the upper end, where the saints are. At its lower end, the same river is fiery, and it is in that part of the river that the demons and the unrepentant are depicted. The painting shows Christ becoming the resurrection into eternal life for those who accepted and followed Him: to those who rejected Him, He becomes their separation and their hell.

In Orthodoxy, paradise and hell are not a reward or a punishment, but the way that each person individually experiences Christ, depending on the condition of their own heart. God doesn't punish in essence, although, for educative purposes, the Scripture does mention punishment. The more spiritual that Man becomes, the better he can comprehend the language of Scripture and Sacred Tradition. The goal in Orthodoxy is to provide the means by which man will be able to eternally look upon Christ as paradise and not as hell; and partake of His heavenly and eternal kingdom.

Sin and Salvation

Salvation refers to this process of 'being saved' from death and corruption and the fate of hell. The Orthodox Church believes that its teachings and practices represent the true path to salvation and God. Yet, it should be understood that you do not have to be Orthodox to participate in salvation: God is merciful to all.

Orthodox believe that salvation (whether for Orthodox or non-Orthodox) cannot be earned: it is rather a gift from God, which Man is free to reject if he chooses. Salvation – the reunification with God - is continually offered by God and has to be accepted by the believer, since God will not force the gift on humanity: to be saved, therefore, man must work together with God in a process whereby his entire being, including his will, effort and actions, are perfectly conformed with, and united to, the divine.

The discovery of what humanity knows is possible because each member of the species is endowed with ancestral wisdom that must be orally and creatively revived. The preservation of this wisdom, expounded by Jesus and the early Apostles, is the sole purpose of the Orthodox Church, which expects each member of the faith to freely choose his own fate, so that he can face the *Judgement of the Second Coming* without fear.

The Orthodox approach to sin is that it is not about breaking some set of rules; rather, it is the name for any behaviour which fails to live up to the higher goal of being like God. Thus, in the Orthodox tradition sin is not viewed as a stain on the soul that needs to be wiped out, but rather as a pervading sickness or a failure to achieve a goal. Sin, therefore, does not carry with it the guilt for breaking a rule, but rather the impetus to become something more than what we are. Because each person's experience is unique, dealing with one's sinful habits needs individual attention and correction. The ultimate goal for this process is to become more Christ-like in one's actions, by following the *Sacraments, or Sacred Mysteries.*

The Mysteria – the Sacred Mysteries

The *Sacred Mysteries* not only lie at the heart of the faith of the Skopolites – as of all Greeks everywhere- but also actually govern the lives of the islanders through their involvement in the *Liturgical Year* of the Church. This is the arrangement of the Church's celebrations of the various events in the life of Christ and the mysteries of its faith throughout the year. From the time of the Apostles, not just Orthodox, but all Christians have gathered together on the first day of the week (the day of the Resurrection, the Lord's Day), to celebrate the *Lord's Supper.* In the course of time, these weeks were organized into two 'seasons': Lent/ Easter; and Advent/Christmas; the death and the birth of Christ. Between these seasons a sequence of Sundays and other seasons are punctuated by celebrations of various feasts of the Lord, the Virgin Mary and the saints.

The people who direct this activity are the Bishops, Priests and Deacons, helped by the laity – the men who take an active part in the services and in pastoral duties within the Church Community; and the women who clean the Church; cook everything from the bread of the *Divine Eucharist* to the celebratory meals of the *Agape Service*; and carry the responsibility for family and traditions in ways that have remained virtually unchanged for more than two thousand years.

Called in Greek *Rozo* or *mysterion* (the mystery), the *Sacraments* state that the inner core of life is the spirit of sharing; which is opposite to the spirit of exploitation and selfish hoarding of resources. The Church as the Community of the Kingdom of God imparts to its members the values of the *shared life* in and through the *Sacraments,* which can only take place within the context of a believing community, involving the entire Church. They are composed of prayers, hymns, scripture lessons, gestures and Processions: many parts of the services date back to the time of the Apostles.

The Orthodox Church has avoided reducing the *Sacraments* to a particular formula or action. Often, a whole series of sacred acts make up a *Sacrament.* Water, oil, bread and wine are but a few of the many elements which the Orthodox Church employs in worship. All these things remind the believer that *matter* is good and can become a medium of the Spirit, underlining the central truth of the Orthodox Christian faith: that God became flesh in Jesus Christ. One of the Church's most important functions is to make these *Sacraments* and the *Liturgy* (the customary public worship) available to her people as divine help in the battle for the soul taking place in the living body.

The Sacred Mysteries

The Sacraments are considered the visible ways through which the Holy Spirit is imparted to believers. The Greek Orthodox Church has seven Sacraments, or *Mystiria*, of which four are obligatory: Baptism, Chrysmation (anointment with holy oil), Confession and Holy Communion. The optional Sacraments are Matrimony, Ordination and Unction (anointment of the sick). Of these, the most relevant in the lives of elderly Greeks are Communion, Confession and Holy Unction. Many Greek elders consider receiving Holy Communion as imperative. As they age, Confession increases in significance. Importantly, Holy Unction is specifically administered to the physically and mentally ill.

Baptism and Chrismation

The first two Sacraments are *Baptism* and *Chrismation, which take place in the same service.* Baptism of infants (and adults) is by immersion in water three times in the name of the *Trinity* and is both initiation into the Church and a sign of forgiveness of sins. The Priest, with the participation of the godparent, immerses the naked infant in the baptismal font and anoints the child with holy oil. Chosen by the child's parents, godparents must themselves have been baptised as Orthodox Christians. They are expected to have a serious life-long interest in the child's spiritual upbringing.

Chrismation follows immediately after *Baptism* and is by anointing with holy oil called *Chrism. Chrismation* is followed by *Holy Communion.* This means that in the Orthodox Church babies and children are fully communicant members of the Church. *Chrism* can only be consecrated by the Patriarch, or chief Bishop, of the local Church. Some of the old *Chrism* is mixed with the new, thus linking the newly baptised to their forbears in the faith. The *Chrism* is used to anoint different parts of the body with a sign of the cross. The forehead, eyes, nostrils, mouth and ears, the chest, the hands and the feet are all anointed. The Priest says the words, *'The seal of the gift of the Holy Spirit'* as he makes the sign of the cross at each point. The newly baptised Christian is now a layperson, a full member of the people of God (the *'Royal Priesthood'*). All Christians present are called to be witnesses to the Truth. Chrismation is linked to *Pentecost* in that the same Holy Spirit which descended on the Apostles descends on the newly baptised.

The 'renewal' of the child and the new relationship that is formed with the godparent is celebrated by family and friends with feasting and dancing after the Church service. Godparents and parents address each other as *koumbare* (male) or *koumbara* (female) and the child addresses the godparent as *noune* (male) or *nouna* (female). To the Greek family, the relationship of the godparent to family is of special importance and godparents are included in other family celebrations and festivities. If a baby is being baptised you should say to the parents *Na sas zisi* (may the child have a long life).

Exomologisi (Confession or Penance)

All Orthodox Churches use the *Mystery of Penance*, or *Confession*, but in Greek speaking Churches only Priests who have been blessed by the Bishop as *'Spiritual Fathers'* are allowed to hear confession. Children may be admitted to the Sacrament of Confession as soon as they are old enough to know the difference between right and wrong. Through this Sacrament, sinners may receive forgiveness. They enter into confession with a Priest often in an open area in the Church (not in a confessional as in the Roman Catholic tradition, nor separated by a grille). Both Priest and penitent stand and a cross and Book of the Gospels or an icon is placed in front of the penitent, with the Priest standing slightly apart. This stresses that the Priest is simply a witness and that forgiveness comes from God not the Priest. The Priest will then hear the confession and perhaps give advice. After confession the penitent kneels before the Priest, who places his stole on the penitent's head whilst saying a *Prayer of Absolution.*

The frequency of confession varies as it is the individual's decision when to make it. The most devout typically arrange to make confession once a year, often during Lent, leading up to Easter. Individuals may prepare for confession some days before with prayer and fasting, though during Lent, and for major feast days, such preparation may take longer.

The Eucharist

The *Eucharist,* usually called the **Divine Liturgy,** fulfils the command of Jesus Christ at the Last Supper: *'Do this in remembrance of me'.* As in many Western Churches the Eucharist is a service consisting in the first part, of hymns, prayers, and readings from the New Testament, and in the second of the solemn offering and consecration of leavened bread and wine mixed with water, followed by the reception of **Holy Communion.**

Communion is given at every Sunday service and on saints' days and special feast days. The Church welcomes contributions of bread and wine for Communion from the community. Women usually bake the bread (*prosforo*), which is taken to Church early Sunday morning to be blessed by the Priest.

Both parts of the Liturgy contain a procession. At the **Little Entrance,** the *Book of the Gospels* is solemnly carried into the sanctuary and at the **Great Entrance** the bread and wine are carried to the altar. There follows the proclamation of the *Nicene Creed,* frequently by the whole congregation; and the *Prayer of Consecration and Holy Communion.*

The Orthodox Church lays particular emphasis on the role of the *Holy Spirit* in the **Eucharist,** and in the *Prayer of Consecration* calls on the Father to send down his Holy Spirit to effect the change of the bread and wine into the Body and

Blood of Christ. Orthodox believe that by the consecration, the bread and wine are truly changed into the Body and Blood of Christ. Communion is given in a spoon containing both the bread and the wine and is received standing. A sermon is usually preached either after the reading of the Gospel or at the end of the service. At the end of the *Liturgy* blessed, but not consecrated, bread is distributed to the congregation, and non-Orthodox are often invited to share in this as a gesture of fellowship.

Marriage

In the marriage ceremony, the couple commits to each other and to raising a Christian family. The service is conducted around a small table, with several essential items: wedding crowns (*stefana*), two wedding rings, the book of Gospels, a cup of wine and two candles. During the service the rings are blessed and the wedding crowns are exchanged three times.

The Sacrament of Marriage is celebrated through the rite of *crowning*, showing the importance of the eternal union of the couple. Designated scriptures are read and the bride and groom share a common cup of wine. Finally, led by the Priest, the couple circles the small table in the *'Dance of Isaiah'* before they are proclaimed husband and wife. Although marriage is seen as a permanent commitment in life and in death, remarriage and divorce are permitted in certain circumstances.

If a family member is getting married you could wish them *Na zisoun* (may the couple live a long life).

Ordination

Although the Church is a self-governing community the Church recognises the *diaconate*, (Deacons) the *presbyterate* or Priesthood and the *episcopate* (Bishops). Through ordination the Church confers power on certain of its members to undertake the ceremonies and services associated with the various Sacraments. Only men can be ordained in the Orthodox Church. Importantly, Priests and Deacons may be married, but must marry *before* being ordained.

Efheleon - Holy Unction - Anointing of the sick

The Church anoints the sick with oil, following the teaching of St James in his Epistle. This Sacrament has two faces: one turns towards healing, the other towards the liberation from illness by death.' (*Timothy Ware, The Orthodox Church*)

In Greek-speaking Churches this is performed annually for the whole congregation during Holy Week on the eve of Holy Wednesday. Everyone is encouraged to come forward for anointing with the special oil whether they are physically ill or not. This is because it is generally held that all are in need of *spiritual* healing even if they are physically well. Anointing of the sick can also be performed on individuals. People sometimes keep the blessed oil of the sick in their homes.

The Giving of Alms

Almsgiving is not a Sacrament, but is considered a pillar of the personal spiritual practices of the Orthodox Christian tradition. It refers to any charitable giving of material resources to those in need. Along with *prayer* and *fasting*, it is particularly important during periods of fasting, when the Orthodox believer is expected to share the monetary savings from his or her decreased consumption with those in need. Boasting about the amounts given for charity is considered anywhere from extremely rude to sinful.

Prohibited Dates for Sacraments

Within the Orthodox Year, certain Sacraments are not permitted on certain dates.

Baptisms may not be performed from Christmas Day to the Feast of Theophany (December 25-January 6), during Holy Week, or on any of the Great Feast days of the Lord.

Marriages are not performed on fast days or during fasting seasons or on September 14 (Exaltation of the Holy Cross), December 13-25 (Nativity), January 5 and 6 (Theophany), Great Lent and Holy Week, Pascha (Easter), Pentecost, August 1-15 (Dormition Fast and Feast), and August 29 (Beheading of St. John the Baptist). Any exceptions are made only with the permission of the respective hierarch.

Memorial services may not be chanted from the Saturday of Lazarus upto and including the Sunday of St. Thomas, on any Feast day of the Lord or any Feast day of the Theotokos.

The Liturgical Year

Eastern Christianity stresses a way of life and belief that is expressed particularly through worship: Eastern Orthodox Christians worship daily, weekly, and at special times throughout the year. Eastern Orthodoxy is therefore a *liturgical faith*, meaning that Orthodox services use carefully structured and prescribed rituals, called *liturgy*.

Eastern Orthodoxy places great emphasis on tradition, and regards its traditions as holy. Holy Tradition includes scripture, the Nicene Creed, the decrees of the Ecumenical Councils, the writings of the Church Fathers, the icons, and the books of liturgical service, which extend to twenty volumes. Although the liturgy has developed and changed, it is characterized by a sense of faithfulness to practices rooted in ancient traditions. At the heart of Eastern Orthodox Tradition is the commitment to maintaining the beliefs and practices of the Apostles, so that the experience of contemporary Orthodox Christians will conform to the experience of the very first Christians, in an uninterrupted stream of worship and Sacrament. Romanian theologian Dumitru Staniloae famously described the spirit of Orthodox tradition as 'lived experience . . . the uninterrupted life of the Church.'

Though the word '*orthodox*' means '*correct belief,*' its connection with '*correct practice*' is intrinsic to Orthodox faith. By maintaining the correct form of worshipping God, passed on from the very beginnings of Christianity, Eastern Christians believe that they confess the true doctrine of God in the right (orthodox) way.

This is part of the explanation for the differing calendars used by Orthodox Christians and Western Churches. In order to fully understand and appreciate how Eastern Orthodox fasts and feasts within the ecclesiastical year are calculated, you need to understand a few basics. **Fixed feasts** use the Orthodox calendar year, which begins on

September 1, and uses the same days and dates as the Gregorian Calendar used in Western Christianity. **Moveable Feasts** are dependent on the celebration of *Pascha* (Easter) which changes from year to year. Briefly speaking, the date for **Pascha** is calculated as the first Sunday after the first full moon following the *Vernal Equinox*. The Vernal Equinox falls on March 20 most years, and occasionally on March 21.

Both Eastern and Western Christianity use the same calculation. However, they use different calendars! Western Christianity uses the **Gregorian Calendar** (circa 1582). All of Eastern Christianity continues to use the older **Julian Calendar** for the determination of the Paschal date even though some Orthodox jurisdictions use the newer calendar for the celebration of their fixed feasts (e.g., Greece and the Greek Orthodox Archdiocese of America use the *new* calendar for fixed feasts, but the *old* calendar for the determination of **Pascha**). The difference between March 20/21 on the Julian Calendar and the Gregorian Calendar is around 13 days.

Besides the difference between the Julian and Gregorian calendars, the other difference in the determination of Easter between the Orthodox and other Christian Churches concerns the date of **Passover**. After the destruction of Jerusalem in 70 AD and the other tragic events which gave rise to the dispersal of the Jews, **Passover** sometimes preceded the Vernal Equinox.

As an alternative to calculating Easter by the Passover, **Paschal (Easter) cycles** were devised. The Orthodox Church eventually adopted a 19-year cycle, the Western Church an 84-year cycle. The use of two different Paschal Cycles inevitably led to differences between the Eastern and Western Churches regarding the observance of Easter. Varying dates for the Vernal Equinox increased these differences. Consequently, it is the combination of these variables which accounts for the different date of Orthodox Easter, whenever it varies from the rest of Christendom.

In essence, Orthodox Easter (**Pascha**) will always occur on the first Sunday after the first full moon following the Vernal Equinox after Passover. This can lead to a divergence of celebration that may see both East and West celebrating the Lord's Resurrection on the same date, to as many as five weeks difference.

The Orthodox Church will often chart important dates many years in advance. Since baptisms and weddings are prohibited on certain dates and during certain moveable fasts, this is a necessity.

Worship Cycles

The Orthodox Church divides its worship into different cycles of the year, each commemorating separate series of events. They are:

The Fixed Cycle

Commemorations on the Fixed Cycle depend upon the day of the calendar year, and also, occasionally, specific days of the week that fall near specific calendar dates, e.g., the Sunday before the *Exaltation of the Cross*. The texts for this cycle are found in the *Menaion*, the *Book of Months*.

The Paschal Cycle

The commemorations on the *Paschal Cycle* depend upon the date of *Pascha* (Easter), which is the central celebration of the liturgical year. The Easter season extends from the *Easter Vigil* through *Pentecost Sunday*, commemorating the resurrection of Jesus, forty-nine days later. Easter is the *Feast of Feasts*.

8 Week Cycle of the Octoechos

The cycle of the Eight Tones is found in the *Octoechos* and is dependent on the date of Easter. It commences with the Sunday after (eighth day of) Easter, that week using the first tone, the next week using the second tone, and so, repeating through the week preceding the subsequent Palm Sunday.

11 Week Cycle of the Orthros' Gospels

The portions of each of the Gospels from the narration of the Resurrection through the end are divided into eleven readings which are read on successive Sundays at **Orthros** (Matins); there are hymns sung at this service that correspond with that day's *Orthros' Gospel*.

The Twelve Great Feasts

It is important to note that the observance of feast days usually begins at sundown *the day before*. The Orthodox liturgical year (which traditionally begins on September 1, not New Year's Day), is highlighted by the *Twelve Great Feasts*, eight of which honour Jesus, and four of which honour his mother. On the eves of these Feasts, a special aggregate service, known as the **All-Night Vigil**, may be served. Services including vigils, such as on Great Thursday and Great Friday, can last for up to 24 hours. The Twelve Great Feasts are, in chronological order:

- ◆ September 8: *To nao tis Theotokos* The Nativity of the Mother of God
- ◆ September 14: *Ypsosis tou timiou kai zoopoiou staurou* The Exaltation of the Cross
- ◆ November 21: *Hparousiasi tis Theotokos* The Presentation of the Mother of God
- ◆ December 25: *Christougenna* The Nativity of Christ
- ◆ January 6: *Agia Theofania* The Baptism of Christ
- ◆ February 2: *Hparousisi tou Xristou sto Nao* The Presentation of Jesus at the Temple
- ◆ March 25: *O Euangelismos* The Annunciation

- The Sunday before Easter: *Kuriaki ton vaion* Palm Sunday, Jesus' entry in Jerusalem

- Forty Days after Easter: *Kuries Metafraseis* The Ascension of Christ

- Fifty Days after Easter: *Agiou Pnevma* Pentecost

- August 6: *Metamorfosis* The Transfiguration

- August 15: *Apokimisis tis Panagias* The Dormition (Falling Asleep) of the Mother of God

Three of the feasts, *Palm Sunday, the Ascension, and the Pentecost*, are dated in relation to the *Feast of Easter*. The date of Easter is determined by the lunar calendar, which means the date changes each year. Easter and the three feasts are therefore called 'movable' feasts, while the others are 'fixed.' There is a host of other festivals or feasts, generally fixed, throughout the liturgical year, some of which commemorate significant events in the Gospels, and others that commemorate significant individuals from the Bible, along with angels, saints, and martyrs.

Fasting

Many liturgical Christians such as Roman Catholics and Anglicans fast in penitence during Advent and Lent. Eastern Orthodox Christians also fast in penitential preparation for significant holy days, but fasting in the East tends to be more rigorous than fasting in the West. Fasting is seen as an important aspect of Christian discipline, purifying the body as well as the soul, and self-control is regarded as a virtue.

There are **Four Great Fasts** during the Christian year:

- The **Lenten Fast** begins seven weeks before Easter and lasts 40 days.

- The **Christmas Fast**, which occurs during Advent, also lasts 40 days, from November 15 to Christmas Eve.

- The **Fast of the Apostles** begins on Monday, eight days after Pentecost, and lasts until June 28, the eve of the

Feast of Saints Peter and Paul. The length of this fast varies significantly, from one to six weeks, depending on the date of Easter.

- Lastly, the **Dormition Fast** lasts from August 1 to August 14, which is the eve of the Feast of the *Dormition of the Theotokos*. This commemorates the 'falling asleep' or death of Mary, the mother of Jesus.

Orthodox Christians may also fast every Wednesday, the day of Judas' betrayal of Jesus; and every Friday, the day of the Crucifixion.

Fasting is strict by Western standards. Devout Orthodox Christians abstain from meat, fish, dairy, wine, and oil, while others might practice different kinds of fasts, less severe, throughout the year. Married couples will abstain from sex, instead devoting themselves to prayer. Dispensation is granted to those who are physically unable to withstand the deprivations of fasting, such as pregnant and nursing mothers, the very young and the very old, the sick, and those who don't control their diets, such as prisoners and soldiers. Orthodoxy normally relaxes the fast on feast days that occur during the Great Fasts, such as on the *Feast of the Transfiguration*, which falls during the *Dormition Fast*.

The repetitive rhythms of feast and fast throughout the calendar year is thought to conspire to create a sense of timelessness, connecting the believer to the *Communion of Saints* and enfolding the believer in the love of the eternal God.

The Weekly Cycle

Alongside the fixed Cycle of the Months, each day of the week has its own commemoration:

- Sunday—The Resurrection of Christ
- Monday—The Holy Angels

- Tuesday—St. John the Forerunner
- Wednesday—The Cross and the Theotokos
- Thursday—The Holy Apostles and St. Nicholas
- Friday—The Cross
- Saturday—All Saints and the departed

The Akolouthies: the Daily Cycle of Orthodox Services

The *Daily Cycle of Divine Services* is the recurring pattern of prayer and worship that punctuates each liturgical day in the life of the Orthodox Church. Monasteries generally serve the entire *Cycle of Services.* Some cathedrals do, as well. Most parishes do not. The services of the Daily Cycle are usually contained in a bound collection called the **Horologion,** the *Book of Hours.* It provides the fixed portions of the Daily Cycle of services as used by the Eastern Orthodox and Eastern Catholic Churches. Various cycles of the liturgical year influence the manner in which the materials from the liturgical books are inserted into the daily services.

The *Daily Cycle* begins the evening of the night before and proceeds throughout the night and day: hence the custom of celebrating *panagiria* (festivals) the evening *before* the festal date.

- **Esperinos - Vespers** is an evening prayer service usually held at sunset. Its theme is the Glorification of God, the Creator of the World and its Providence.

- **Apodepnon – Compline** is held at bedtime and refers to sleep as the image of Death, illuminated by Christ after His own Death.

- **Mesonyktikon – Midnight Office** refers to Christ's Midnight prayer at Gethsemane and to the coming of the Last Judgement. It is seldom served in parish Churches except at the *Paschal Vigil* of which it is an essential part since during it the burial shroud is removed from the tomb and carried to the altar.

- **Orthros - Matins** is a morning prayer service usually held before the Divine Liturgy on Sunday and other Feast Days.

- **Prote Ora** - First Hour **(Prime)** at 7 am recalls Christ's being brought before Pilate.

- **Trite Ora** -Third Hour **(Terce)** at 9 am recalls Pilate's judgement of Christ and the descent of the Holy Spirit at Pentecost, which happened at this hour.

- **Ekte Ora** - Sixth Hour **(Sext)** at noon recalls Christ's crucifixion, which happened at this hour.

- **Ennate Ora** -Ninth Hour **(None)** at 3 pm recalls Christ's death.

- **Typica** or **Pro-Liturgy** follows the sixth or ninth hour.

Divine Liturgy is not itself a part of the *Daily Cycle* but is inserted into the Cycle, usually after **Orthros** or the Sixth Hour; in some cases it is combined with **Esperinos** (Vespers). The Divine Liturgy is the most frequently attended service and is held every Sunday and major feast day throughout the year. It is sometimes also referred to as the **Divine Eucharist** and is the Service in which the congregation have Holy Communion.

During each service the Priest stands at the Altar. He is human, a member of God's people, but vested with the authority to offer the Eucharist and lead the worship.

The service of **Typika** is related to the Divine Liturgy and is often celebrated on days the Divine Liturgy is not appointed.

The Divine Eucharist - Holy Communion

Those of the Orthodox faith today do not generally take Communion every Sunday: they must fast beforehand – to the point that they must not even have coffee or a cigarette – and receive absolution of sin through Confession before they are deemed completely prepared to receive the host. The fast should last at least 3 days, and is usually one week, in order to purify the body so that it is ready to receive the Body and Blood of Christ. Thus most Orthodox find communion daunting in itself; it is not a habit, nor a right.

Divine Eucharist is celebrated on the day of the sun (the Lord's Day, the day of *Kyrios*, that is *Kiriaki*, Sunday, the first day of the week, in memory of the Resurrection of the Lord.) On this day the Early Christians gathered together to participate in hymns and prayers in the officiating of a certain framework of faith. The Divine Liturgy as such was therefore the centre of the inspiration of the first Christians in their communion with God and with one another. In upper rooms and catacombs the Apostles and later the Presbyters and Bishops of the primitive Christian Church offered the Divine Liturgy for its Sacred Mysteries. They appointed certain days and places, selected the Species to be used, formulated meaningful prayers and hymns, and determined the order as to the service, the celebrants and the communicants. Relics and reminiscences of that time were preserved in the Divine Liturgies of the second century and especially of the fourth century when the Liturgies took their final form.

The Host

Following the oldest traditions of the Church, the *host* is ordinary leavened bread, leaven signifying the Risen Christ. The bread is impressed in the centre with the stamp '*IC-XC, NI -KA*'; on its left it has nine small *elevations* (portions) for the Saints; and on its right a portion for the Virgin Mary. During the consecration, all these portions are cut with a spear and placed on the *Paten* with prayers and commemoration. Portions are also added in the name of the faithful, both the departed and the living.

Both the *Paten* and *Chalice* are then shielded with two small covers and over all is placed the *aer* (literally *aeras*, the air), a veil. The Priest shakes the *aer* over the chalice when the Creed is read; this symbolizes the descent of the Holy Spirit. The *aer* also represents the shroud of Christ. (In the *Liturgy of the Presanctified Gifts*, the *aer* covers the head of the Priest during the Great Entrance.) The Priest censes the *Paten* and *Chalice* and reads the *Prayer of Preparation*, before placing the bread in the chalice with the wine.

Communion

The Priest then offers a piece of bread and a little wine on the liturgical spoon to the communicant, who says his/her name and receives it. Afterwards, the base of the chalice may be kissed.

All who receive Holy Communion from the same cup have to confess the same faith, the common faith: therefore non-Orthodox cannot receive Holy Communion in the Orthodox Church. Neither can a member of the Orthodox faithful receive Holy Communion from another Christian Church: if the Orthodox person does this, he is denying orthodox teachings and becomes a heretic. Special prayers explaining the greatness and holiness of the action are said before and after receiving Holy Communion.

To receive Communion every week is not necessary, but it is a grave sin not to receive it for a period of two years, the maximum time under Canon Law, which is in itself only acceptable in extreme circumstances. Children are allowed to receive Holy Communion once they are Baptised and the fasting regulations do not apply to children up to 8 years old. After that, they fast (not strictly) for two or three days before they receive the host, until they become adults.

The Dismissal

Leaving Church before dismissal deprives the worshipper of a blessing. Worship has a beginning '*Blessed is the Kingdom...*' and an end '*Let us depart in peace...*' To leave immediately after Communion is disrespectful: it shows more respect to wait for at least a few more minutes, and then go.

Handling the Holy Bread (antidoron)

After receiving Holy Communion and at the end of the Divine Liturgy, it is customary to receive a piece of Holy Bread or *antidoron* - the bread that was left over after Holy Communion was prepared. While *antidoron* is not Holy Communion, it is blessed bread, and as such should be eaten carefully so that crumbs do not fall. Non-Orthodox present at the service are encouraged to share this bread as an expression of Christian fellowship. Both adults and children should always remember to treat and consume the *antidoron* with respect.

Bread should never be thrown away: it should always be shared with another living creature – for example feeding it to the birds or to the fish.

Monks and Monasteries

The word 'monk' comes from the Greek *monos*, which means 'alone': A monk is someone who lives alone, who has taken religious vows of poverty and celibacy in order to dedicate himself to a life of disciplined religious practice. The central and unifying feature of Orthodox monasticism is *Hesychasm*, the practice of silence, and the concentrated saying of the *Jesus Prayer*. All ascetic practices and monastic humility is guided towards preparing the heart for *theorea* or the divine vision that comes from the union of the soul with God. In Orthodoxy, God himself chooses the monk, who is then consecrated to the service of God. A monk cannot be 'defrocked': he is bound by his vows until death.

When a man becomes a monk, he is then dead to the outside world, but has been re-born into the holy world of the Monastery. He has given up his past life, his name, his status and property and has taken up the name of one of the saints with the same initial as his original name. Instead of a surname he uses the name of the monastery where he lives. He is given a room and habits to wear. He is also appointed to a particular job, when he is not in Church. From now on, to exit the monastery he needs the permission of the *Igoumenos* (Abbot). Following their ordination many monks never again visit the secular outside world.

Female monks live identical ascetic lives to their male counterparts and are therefore also called *monachoi*, and their common living space is a monastery, not a convent. They are not however, allowed to become ordained.

Monasticism as a permanent institution did not exist before the fourth century. Its institutional origins will not be found in any single specific directive of Jesus or in any particular passage of the New Testament. Its foundations, all the same, are rooted in the totality of the Gospel message the source of both its creativity and strength. Behind the physical withdrawal into the desert or a monastery lies the renunciation of the world and of Satan to which every Christian commits himself at baptism. This renunciation is a basic condition to being a Christian. The monastic vocation, in sum, is intimately bound to the baptismal vow. Entering a monastery is simply another means by which some have chosen to live the absolute ideal of the Gospel: the personal search for holiness is not the monk's special preserve, but monkhood may be seen to be an extreme condition of this quest.

Asceticism

It is because of its essentially Christian goals that *asceticism* spread and influenced Orthodox spirituality, prayer, piety, and general Church life. Besides, the Church itself sponsored and promoted it, having intuitively recognized its unique charismatic ministry, usefulness, and potential for holiness. The *episcopate* of the Church was often recruited from the countless monastic communities dotting the Byzantine countryside. One monastery on Mt. Athos, in addition to producing 144 Bishops, provided the Church with 26 patriarchs: virtually two thirds of the Patriarchs of Constantinople between the ninth and the thirteenth centuries were monastics.

Monasticism was crucial to the Church. As the established faith of the Byzantine Empire, it was often in danger of identifying itself with the state, of becoming worldly and thus losing its eschatological dimension: that is, the belief or doctrine concerning the ultimate or final things, such as death, the destiny of humanity, the Second Coming, or the Last Judgement. The monastic presence has always been there to remind the Church of its true nature and identity with another Kingdom. Its fierce opposition to any compromise of the Christian vision was crucial in the Church's survival and independence. Thus the impact of monasticism on Orthodox Christianity has been all encompassing and far-reaching.

Mount Athos

Mount Athos is the foremost centre of monasticism in Greece. An Orthodox spiritual centre since 1054, Mount Athos has enjoyed an autonomous statute since Byzantine times. It is situated on the northernmost of the three peninsulas jutting into the Aegean Sea from Chalkidi, a narrow rocky strip approximately 50 km long and 10 km wide, rising to 2,033 m. In ancient Greek mythology the peninsula was said to be the stone thrown at Poseidon by the giant Athos. For Christians it was the Garden of the Virgin, the gift that Christ gave his mother.

The precise date of the first Christian establishments on Mount Athos is unknown. However, the monastic movement began to intensify in 963, when the future St Athanasius the Athonite founded *Great Lavra* on the tip of the peninsula. In 972 the first *Typikon* (agreement) was concluded at Karyes between the Emperor Jean Tsimitzes and the monks of Mount Athos. It provided the basis of the exceptional status still enjoyed by the 'Holy Mount' today. The *Typikon* granted by the Emperor Constantine IX Monomachus in 1046 and signed by more than 100 heads of religious communities, banned women, children and more generally all 'smooth-faced persons' from entering the mountainous region.

In 1926, the Greek Government ratified a charter based on the long tradition of the *Typika*. In 1977, when Greece became a member of the European Common Market, the signatory states recognized the specificity of the self-governing region of Athos and its special status. Power in this monastic republic is strictly divided between three assemblies: the *Synaxe,* or the *Holy Assembly*, which meets twice a year, holds the legislative power; the *Holy Community* holds the administrative power, and the *Holy Epistasie* holds the executive power. At Karyes, a civil governor of Athos, under the Greek Foreign Affairs Ministry, ensures that the Charter of 1926 is respected.

Today Athos includes 20 monasteries, 12 skites, and about 700 houses, cells, or hermitages. Over 1,000 monks live there in communities or alone, as well as in the 'desert' of Karoulia where cells cling to the cliff face rising steeply above the sea. The layout of the monasteries has had an influence as far afield as Russia, and its school of painting influenced the history of Orthodox art.

Monastics

The strict life of a male or female monk (they are not called nuns in Orthodoxy) is seen as an important expression of faith: therefore, monasticism is a central part of the Orthodox religion. Eastern Orthodox monks (except novices) are always called *pappas* (Father) even if they are not Priests. Monks who have been ordained to the Priesthood are called *hieromonk* (Priest-monk); monks who have been ordained to the Deaconate are called *hierodeacon* (deacon-monk). Old monks are often called *Gheronda* or *Elder* out of respect for their dedication.

Monastics are sometimes addressed according to their monastic rank: for example, 'Rasophore—monk (name),' 'Stavrophore—monk (name), or 'Schemamonk (name).' For the Orthodox, *Rasophore* female monks and novices are addressed as *aderfi* (Sister). *Mitera* or *Mother* is the correct term for all female monks except novices. Under no circumstances whatsoever is an Orthodox monk addressed by laymen as 'Brother.' This is a Latin custom. The term 'Brother' is used in Orthodox monasteries in two instances only: first, to designate beginners in the monastic life (novices or, in Greek, *dokimoi* (those being tested), who are given a blessing, in the strictest tradition, to wear only the inner cassock and a monastic cap; and second, as an occasional, informal form of address between monastics themselves (including Bishops).

Since married men can become monks, 'virginity' means chastity, not formal virginity. The word translated as 'chastity' (*sophrosyne*) also means 'prudence'. 'Piety' does not mean sentimental piety, but being religious: having a fundamentally religious orientation.

There are very few monks living on Skopelos today – there are only three (a man and two women) in the entire monastery of Evangelistria. However, the monasteries, although they do not host large group retreats, do have several guest rooms available for monks to come during the summer on private retreat, or to study. The male monks come from Mount Athos and stay only a limited amount of time.

Orthodox Symbolism

The visitor to an Orthodox Church is usually impressed by the unique features and the external differences between this place of worship and those of the various traditions of Western Christianity. The rich colour, distinctive iconography and beauty of the interior of an Orthodox Church generally are in sharp contrast to the simplicity which one finds in many Roman Catholic and Protestant Churches. When one enters the interior of the Orthodox Church, it is like stepping into a whole new world of colour and light. The art and design of the Church not only create a distinctive atmosphere of worship, but also they reflect and embody many of the fundamental insights of Orthodoxy.

The Orthodox Church believes that God is the Creator of heaven and earth: the Creator is present through the creative energies of His handiwork. This means that the material world, being valuable and good, is an important means through which God expresses Himself. The Orthodox Church affirms this conviction through its extensive use of material creation not only for the embellishment of its places of worship, but also in its Sacramental mysteries and services. For example, when the bread and wine – *'the first fruits of creation'* - are offered in the Eucharist, they are also a symbolic offering of all Creation to God its Creator.

Since there is no hesitation in using the gifts of creation, the interior of an Orthodox Church is frequently very beautiful. Designed to create an atmosphere which is special, the building is filled with a feeling of joy and an appreciation of God's bounty. Orthodoxy recognizes that beauty is an important dimension of human life: Through iconography, *agiographia* (hagiography - visual images of the saints) and Church appointments, the beauty of creation becomes a very important means of praising God. The divine gifts of the material world are shaped and fashioned by human hands into an expression of beauty which glorifies the Creator.

Most importantly, the interior of the Church is both the background and the setting for Orthodox worship. The art and architecture are designed to contribute to the total experience of worship, which involves one's intellect, feelings, and senses. For this reason, all Orthodox Churches are blessed, consecrated and set aside as sacred space.

Everything about Eastern Orthodoxy is about union with God. The Church building, religious artefacts and the way they are arranged, and all that goes on during worship services – all are filled with powerful spiritual teachings and symbolism, designed to teach the Gospel, put the Gospel into practice, to worship Christ in soul and body, and to focus one's attention on Christ during worship times. Thus, Orthodox worship involves the whole person: spirit, mind, and body, recognising that God became man because he is a physical creature and requires a total (including physical) salvation. Therefore, it involves not only the mind and heart, but also the ears (hymns, the bells of the censer), the eyes (Icons, processions), the nose (the smell of the candles, incense, and rose water, etc.), and touch (making the sign of the cross, and other gestures).

The Church Building

The Early Church

Orthodox Churches mirror the basic elements of the floor plan of a house from the first-century, because the earliest Christian Churches were house Churches. The ancient institution of the household included the functions of modern families and businesses; you could say that the household was a family business. When visitors came to the house to do business with the household, they would come through the front door into a very large room with little furniture. At the opposite end of the room was the family dining room on a raised floor. It had a chopping block front and centre where sacrifices could be made to the gods. (The private rooms for members of the household were behind the dining room.) The father sat against the back wall of the dining room behind the chopping block, and his sons sat against the wall on either side. The sons conducted the actual business under the father's supervision.

Ancient Christians found a glorified version of their Church's floor plan in Revelation 4:2-4: in this passage, the Throne in the middle is the altar, the 24 elders sit in a circle around the Throne instead of in a semicircle behind it, and Jesus, in the role of the Bishop, sits on the altar instead of behind it, because He is also the sacrifice. When the building became a Church, the atrium became the *nave*, the dining room became the *chancel,* and the chopping block became the *altar.* The Bishop sat in the father's place and the Priests sat in the sons' places.

Later, the design of the early Church was basically adopted with little adaptation from a Roman secular building type, the *basilica*, used variously for such purposes as a law court, a council chamber, a covered market and a gymnasium. The word *basilica* means royal, and so by extension the building was a city building. This fitted in with the Church's sense of itself as being the City of God. In any case, the *basilica* was the only building of the pagan Roman Empire which was suitable for large Christian assemblies, since the interiors of pagan temples were designed only for the Priests and the sacrifices, not for the worshipping public.

The Christian Basilica

The Christian Church building itself has many symbolic meanings: perhaps the oldest and most prominent is the concept that the Church is the Ark, the ship in which Noah and his family – true believers- were saved from the wrath of God in the flood of temptations: therefore, many Orthodox Churches are rectangular in design. The *basilica* design further evolved and usually has a curved *apse* in the eastern end.

The symbolic reading of the *basilica* as a ship emphasises the transitory nature of our present life, of our movement towards the heavenly city to come. The *basilica* is primarily, therefore, a Church plan which emphasises action and motion, intended to give a sense of pilgrimage from the fallen world (the West) towards the age to come (the East).

Another element in the Orthodox Church building is the cross-in- square: the transition from square to cross to circle (or cube to cross to dome) as we move up the Church. This affirms the union of earth (symbolised by the square) with heaven (the circle) through the cross of Christ. The symbolic meaning is to create a sense of being present now in paradise: of God being present among the congregation. Pilgrimage and immanence are thus combined.

The oldest Churches on Skopelos, with its early Christian roots, adhere to the earlier design; but later Churches, such as those built in the eighteenth century like the Church of Ag. Rhiginos at the monastery of the same name, are of the cross-in-square design. Architectural patterns vary in shape and complexity, with chapels sometimes added around the main Church, or triple altars; but in general, the symbolic layout of the Church remains the same. Whenever possible, Greek Orthodox Churches face eastward where Christ was born and from where the sun, the source of light, rises.

The Atrium

The *atrium* is the space outside the Church, considered as part of the whole Church plan, and not just an adjunct to it. Originally a courtyard at the entrance to the Church, It had generally fallen into disuse, at least in its full colonnaded form, by around the eighth century. However, all Churches, even those opening directly onto a busy street, have some kind of an interruption - whether it be a small patio, or a set of steps - between the 'world' and the Church itself: In Skopelos *Chora*, Christou Church retains its courtyard; Fanermerini Church has a portico and imposing steps; the tiny Mercurios Church has a simple door step between the street and the Church's interior.

The *atrium* serves various functions. First, it provides a mediatory role between the outside world and the inner sanctuary. Being open to the sky it is outside, while being walled or colonnaded it is also partakes, to a limited degree, of the main Church building and its interior. Second, the courtyard reinforces the transitional nature of the spiritual life. The *atrium* can be seen as the place where the first stage, purification, is emphasised and there was usually a basin for ablutions placed in its centre, or a fountain, representing the Fountain of Life or Pparadise. This is a large, usually stone basin of blessed water, surrounded by columns and surmounted by a roof, normally domed. The fountain tradition continues on Skopelos in a modified form in the Athonite *fiali* (an ornate marble washstand containing holy water) in the courtyard. On Athos it is filled with blessed water which is drunk after a Liturgy. In old *atria* the water was for ablutions before the Liturgy and other services. Otherwise today the duty is served by a prosaic tap.

Third, as part of the mediatory role mentioned above, the forecourt gives a place to pause so that one does not pass directly from the outside to the inside. From the courtyard one can get a glimpse of the inner Church, with its candles and oil lamps and perhaps hear a little of the chanting before entering.

Fourth, the courtyard offers a place for large gatherings and certain liturgical acts, such as the opening of the *Paschal* service. In this way it greatly increases the liturgical floor area of a community without the high cost of a completely enclosed building. In a modified way this idea was exploited in northern Greece during the four centuries of Turkish occupation. Since Christians were not allowed to have outdoor gatherings, they extended the roof line over the west courtyard so that, technically at least, gatherings there were still inside.

Finally, the *atrium* is a statement that the Church (and therefore the Church building) does not exist to reject the world as such, to close its doors to the world which God has made, but rather exists in order to flow out to the world and transfigure it. The atrium acts as a kind of sieve which helps the faithful to leave behind the fallen world as they enter the temple, but it also acts as a river mouth, spreading the life-giving waters of the Liturgy out into the world. Or to reverse the image, the forecourt is the hands of the Church, receiving material creation so as to offer it on the altar.

The Holy Church

One meaning of the word *'holy'* is 'set apart'. Orthodox Churches are holy places in that they are set apart for God. Rules about not entering certain areas, or touching certain objects, are not so much bans or prohibitions but rather safeguards of that holiness. Everything in the Orthodox Church is done with a blessing: in every situation it is proper to ask a blessing. This is why seeming prohibitions against entering or touching things are not seen as prohibitions but as worshippers not having a blessing to enter there or to touch that.

An Orthodox Church is designed to promote and enhance prayer and allow the worshipper to leave behind the outside world. The use of this 'worship space' for other purposes is foreign to the tradition of Orthodoxy, and thus even national flags and other things that do not have a direct function in worship are prohibited.

The Christian life is a three-stage progress from dissipation and fragmentation towards a healing and union of all human faculties, and eventually of union as whole people with Christ. This progress has been classically described by the Church fathers as a movement through the three stages of repentance or purification, then of illumination or perception of the mysteries of God within creation, and finally of union with God.

The Church building itself is thus divided into three main parts: the *narthex* (vestibule), the *nave* (from the word *navis* meaning ship) and the *sanctuary* (also called the *altar* or *holy place*). The narthex is where non-Orthodox visitors were traditionally asked to stand during services. It is separated from the nave by '*The Royal Gate*'. On each side of this gate are candle stands (**menalia**) representing the pillars of fire that went before the Hebrew people escaping from Egypt.

The Narthex

The *narthex* is the first part of the building, where members of the congregation enter and generally prepare themselves for entrance into the Nave for worship. The *narthex* is usually a long narrow space, oriented on the south-north axis. This is probably whence it got its name, from the Greek word *narthica* or reed, with its long narrow and hollow stem. Centuries ago this area was the place where *catechumens* (unbaptized learners) and penitents remained during parts of the services. Today, the beginning of the Baptismal service and in some parishes, the Marriage Service, begins in the *narthex* and proceeds into the *nave:* this procession symbolically represents a gradual movement into the Kingdom of God, as marriage is one of the holy Mysteries (Sacraments) of the Church. In many Orthodox parishes, the *narthex* is the area where the faithful do the sign of the Cross, make an offering, receive a candle, light it before an icon, (which symbolises their acceptance of Christ as the light of the World), and kiss the icons (first the Icon of Christ and then the others). It is in the *narthex* that they slow down their thoughts and begin their prayer: the narthex is a place of preparation for entrance into another reality, namely the Heavenly worship of the Church. If they arrive during the reading of the Bible or during any processions, they should stand still until they are finished before lighting a candle or doing anything else in the *narthex.* Visitors to Churches should stay in this area if there is a service being conducted.

The Nave

The *nave* is the large centre area of the Church. Here the faithful gather for worship in the eternal place of the assembled Church, which includes both the living and the departed. Large full-length icons of Christ, Mary, and other saints immediately engage those entering the *nave.* The saints serve as examples to the ordinary faithful that they too can attain the destiny of heaven if they live according to the teachings of the Church. Other icons may depict important events in the life of Christ. The icons at the entrance to the *nave* remind the Orthodox Christian that Christ and the Saints are his invisible hosts when he comes to Church. His first act upon entering Church is to salute them by making the sign of the cross. Often the worshipper also lights a candle upon entering as a reminder that he is to reflect the light of Christ in the world.

Most Orthodox Churches in Skopelos follow the old custom of having an open *nave* with no seats, except a few by the walls for the old and the infirm called the *Stadia,* although there are chairs in *Faneremini*. (In ancient days, when the people sat they would sit on the floor.) The *nave* is associated with illumination, particularly through the word (Scripture readings, sermons and singing are done here).

The distinctive features of this area include on the left, the **baptistery,** symbolic of a womb emphasizing that the Sacrament of Holy Baptism is a rebirth, a resurrection of the infant into the life and faith of the Church; and the **pulpit,** symbolizing the stone which was used to seal the tomb of Christ, the tomb from which the angel proclaimed the good tidings of the Resurrection to the women who had come to anoint His body. Often the pulpit is decorated with icons of the Lord and the four Gospel writers, as it is from here that the Gospel is proclaimed and the sermon preached.

The **Chanter Stand** is on the right, as is the **Throne of the Bishop**, a historic remnant of the Byzantine Empire where it was used by the royalty of the land. It has remained in the modern Orthodox Church as the Throne of the visiting royalty of the Church, the Bishop, the Archbishop or Patriarch, from which he presides as a living icon of Christ among his people. Even in the Bishop's absence, the Throne reminds all that the parish is not an isolated entity but is part of a diocese which the Bishop heads. An icon of Christ sits on the Throne when no person does so.

The wooden structure in the southeast corner is called the **kouvouklion,** which is used once a year on Holy Friday and represents the Tomb of Christ. The choir and the Cantors frequently occupy areas on the far sides of the nave. Most of the congregation stand here during services. Traditionally, men stand on the right and women on the left. This is for a number of reasons: in a patriarchal society, men and women stand at the same distance from the altar, so that their equality before God is emphasized. The idea of separating the sexes was inherited from the Jewish tradition of doing so within synagogues; separation of sexes also followed the practice of choirs in which different levels of voice are placed in groups to facilitate harmony. Orthodox children are considered full members of the Church and should stand attentive and quiet during services. There may be a choir area at the side or upstairs in a loft at the back.

It should be noted that not all services take place within the *sanctuary*. Many are celebrated in the centre of the nave, in the midst of the congregation. In so doing, Orthodoxy emphasizes the fact that the worship of the Church is offered by, and for *all* the people. The nave represents *Heaven on Earth*.

The Dome

Several Churches on Skopelos are basilicas, but also incorporate a dome, designed to inspire meditation on heaven and the mysteries of the Almighty. Unlike the pointed steeples of Western Churches, which point to God far away in the Heavens, the dome is intended to be an all-embracing ceiling, upheld by walls firmly embedded on the earth. The *basilica's* forward movement, with its sense of pilgrimage from the fallen world (the west) towards the age to come (the east), contrasts with the circular dome which emphasises contemplation or vision; creating a sense of being present now in paradise, of God being present among the congregation. Together this symbolizes that the physical Church and the heavenly Church are visibly and invisibly unified: there is no distinction between the two, not even in death. It reveals that in the Kingdom of God and in the Church, Christ unites all things in himself, in Heaven and on Earth.

The dome usually carries an icon of Christ depicted as Ruler of the Universe (*Pantocrator*); the one who 'holds' (*crator* in Greek) all things in his hands. Whenever the dome is supported by four columns, one finds on them icons portraying the four Gospel writers John, Luke, Matthew, and Mark. Below the icon of Christ are frequently painted the Old Testament prophets of Israel, who wrote about the coming of

Christ on Earth. A Cross—the instrument of salvation— surmounts the dome on the exterior.

Many of the most important events in an Orthodox Christian's life - baptism, the reception of the Eucharist, marriage, and the funeral take place at the intersection of these two planes - under the dome and just in front of the *Royal Doors* of the altar.

The Solea

The area between the nave and the Sanctuary is known as the *Solea*: it is here where all the Sacraments of the Church are administered. The *Solea*, that elevated portion of the *nave* just in front of the *iconostasis* stretching from the pulpit to the Bishop's Throne, is where the clergymen and chanters stand at various times to perform weddings, baptisms, funeral, memorial services, and doxologies.

In the *nave* before the altar area and the icon screen, there are usually two large candelabras standing before what are called the **Great or Royal Doors** in the centre. This speaks of the Church's ancestry in Judaism, where similar stands were seen in the Jewish temple. They represent the column of light by which God guided the Jews at night to the Promised Land and remind believers that they too, have a promised land, the Kingdom of Heaven. Just as God guided the Jews to their promised land, so today He guides Christians through the teachings of the Gospel and the grace of the Sacraments to their own.

The Iconastasion

At the Eastern end of the Church is a raised dais with an icon-covered screen or wall (*iconostasis* or *templon*) separating the *nave* from the *sanctuary*. The origin of this very distinctive part of an Orthodox Church is the ancient custom of placing icons on a low wall before the *sanctuary*. In time, the icons became fixed on a standing wall, hence the term *iconostasion.* In contemporary practice, the *Iconostasion* may be very elaborate and conceal most of the *sanctuary*, or it may be very simple and open. Many of the Churches on Skopelos have a very old and very beautiful *iconastasion,* dating back hundreds of years.

This division serves to remind worshippers that God's reign is not complete and that they can often find themselves 'separated' from God, through sin. However, during the *Divine Liturgy*, when they have access to the Holy Gifts, believers are also reminded that, through Christ, Heaven and Earth are united and that through Him, they have access to the Father.

The *Iconostasion* has three entrances which are used during services: there is a **Deacon Door** on either side, usually with icons of the archangels Michael and Gabriel, who minister unto God and serve as guards of the Sanctuary, and the centre entrance which is called the **Royal Door** or the *'Beautiful Gate'*, through which of men, only the clergy may pass. It is through this door, also, that Christ passes every Sunday during the Liturgy in the form of the Gospel, the Eucharist and in the person of the Priest, serving as a constant reminder that the only way into the altar, the only way into Heaven, is through the doors which were opened by Christ. A curtain or door usually conceals the Altar when services are not being celebrated. Non-believers should not go or look through the door without being invited.

On the right-hand side of the **Iconostasion** are always the icons of *Christ* and *St. John the Baptist.* On the left-hand side are always the icons of the *Theotokos* (Mother of the Lord) and the patron saint or event to which the Church is dedicated. In addition to these icons, others may be added, depending upon custom and space.

The Sanctuary

The **Agion Vema** *(the Sanctuary)* or **Agia Agion** *(Holy of Holies)* is considered the most sacred part of the Church, and is the area reserved for the clergy and their assistants: it is always located toward the East because Christ, the Light of the World, is symbolised by the rising sun. Orthodox Priests, when standing at the altar, face East, away from the congregation. When they are within the *Sanctuary*, and when they bring the Sacramental host to the congregation, the Priest removes his hat, as he is in the presence of God.

In addition, the *Sanctuary* is elevated from the floor of the nave by a set of steps. The floor of the Church symbolizes the *Earth*, the ceiling the *Universe* with the stars and planets represented by the chandeliers. The altar symbolizes *Heaven* which lies somewhere between the earth and the universe and is thus elevated by steps as a reminder of this relationship.

In the *Sanctuary* are the square Altar Table, the *Proskomide* (where the Gifts for Holy Communion are prepared), and the *Large Crucifix* reminding worshippers of Jesus' sacrifice on the Cross for their salvation. The *Sanctuary* contains all the necessary implements for conducting the various services. As the *Sanctuary* is the place wherein special Liturgical actions are performed (prayers and blessings), it is reserved only for those authorised and/or ordained to perform or assist in those functions.

The work of the clergy and their attendants is to stand at the Holy Table and offer up special prayers. The work of the people is to pray and worship God, and this is done in the *Nave*. In some services, the clergy never enter the *Sanctuary* at all but join the people in the *Nave* for prayer. Thus, it is not a question of the *Sanctuary* being prohibited, but of the worship space of the Church being arranged for specific purposes and each area being used by those assigned to perform those functions.

The Altar

The *Altar* or *Holy Table* is the heart and focal point of the Orthodox Church, associated with union, particularly through participation in the Eucharist. It is here that the gifts of bread and wine are offered to the Father, as Christ commanded Christians to do. A gold **Artophorion** *(tabernacle)* rests on the altar table in the middle of the sanctuary together with candles: it contains the Holy Gifts, the Body and Blood of Christ, which are consecrated each year on Great Holy Thursday and placed in the *artophorion*. The Holy Gifts contained in the *tabernacle* are reserved for use in emergencies or visits to the sick and the infirm who cannot attend the liturgy, but they are not used during the liturgy itself. A votive light, known as the *eternal light,* burns constantly in front of the *tabernacle* as a reminder of the presence of Christ.

When the Divine Liturgy is not being celebrated, the **Book of Gospels**, ornamented with a gold or silver covering, rests on the Altar. On one side is depicted the Crucifixion of Christ and on the other side, His Resurrection. The gospel book contains excerpts from the four Evangelists whose icons are depicted individually on each of the four outside corners.

The altar table symbolizes the *tomb of Christ* and is usually made of marble. Entombed within the altar itself is a relic of a Saint or Martyr which was installed during the Church's consecration. Behind it is a large cross with the painted figure of Christ, which is detachable so that it can be used during the *Great Friday* (Good Friday) service. Situated on either side of the cross are two **Hexapteryga** (gilded, six-winged seraph discs on standards for use in processions).

The **Antimension,** a silk cloth containing relics of a saint that is consecrated by a Bishop, also rests here: it can be folded, transported, and used, if necessary, as an altar itself. Liturgy may only be performed once a day on any particular *Antimins.* Thus a second Liturgy on the same Altar Table that same day would require the use of a second *Antimins,* typically from another Orthodox Church.

The Proskomide
A small alcove can be usually partially seen to the left of the altar table, which houses the *Table of Preparation*

where the preparatory service of the liturgy is held. This is the *Proskomide*, where the elements of bread and wine for the Sacrament of Holy Eucharist are prepared before the Divine Liturgy. The alcove represents the *Manger of Bethlehem* and usually holds an icon of the Nativity. The service of preparation is purposely hidden in the alcove as a reminder that Christ was also hidden from the world for most of His young life, while He prepared Himself for His ministry.

The Apse

There appears in the apse of the Church the icon depicting the Virgin Mary with the Christ Child. This is the icon of the *Platytera*, from the Greek *platytera ton ouranon*, meaning *'She who is wider than the heavens'*- so called because she gave birth to Christ who as God is the Creator of all things. This icon unites the roof of the Church with the floor, symbolically uniting the heavens and the earth. The Mother of God, hovering between the heavens and the earth serves as *'the heavenly ladder, whereby God has descended'* and as *'the Bridge leading those on earth to heaven'*. As such Orthodox pray *'Through the prayers of the Theotokos, Saviour save us'* in the Divine Liturgy.

The Diakonikon

The *Diakonikon* is the place where other liturgical items are stored by the Priest; specifically he keeps the book of the Gospels and liturgical texts on this shelf (relics of the saints would be kept on this shelf as well). It is here that the icons, which are brought by the faithful to be blessed, are placed for 40 days. The icon traditionally placed here is either that of the Resurrection or that of the Extreme Humility of Christ.

Early on in Orthodox Church history, these shelves were not found in the altar area. Instead the Holy Gifts were prepared and the liturgical items of the Church were kept in a separate building, the **skevophylakion** (*the place for guarding the vessels*); and it was from this place that the Gospel and the

Offerings were brought into the Church at the appropriate time in the service by the clergy. This practice, as we have seen, still continues in some of the oldest Churches of Skopelos, and is the reason that Churches have a small building next door.

The Sacristy and Vestry

In addition to the areas noted above, a Church might have rooms at either side of the *Sanctuary* to store books and vessels for liturgical use (often called a **Sacristy**) and/or to store the vestments of the clergy and attendants (**a Vestry**). Near the **narthex,** some Churches may also have vestibules, or cloak rooms.

A Generic Plan of an Orthodox Church

The following presents a simplified plan of any Orthodox Church, intended to generally orientate the visitor.

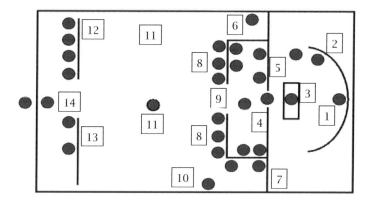

1 The Agia Prothesis

This is where the Priest prepares the bread and wine before Communion. It is a symbol of the stable where Jesus was born in Bethlehem.

2 Themiatos (Incense)

This is an incense censor used in worship. The sweet smelling incense rises up as a symbol of prayers rising up to God.

3 Altar

The altar in an Orthodox Church is usually square. In its centre is a Bible and the *Minsio*, showing Jesus in the tomb. This is the Church's authority from the Archbishop to be an Orthodox Church. The *Antophilagio* is a symbol of the Church. In it is a small box that holds communion bread which has been blessed and set aside by the Priest on the Thursday of Holy Week. Throughout the year, this bread is taken by the Priest by people who are too ill to come to Church to share in communion. There is also a stand holding a book of liturgy, and an icon of Jesus. Two oil lamps and beeswax candles are lit during the Church services.

4 Stavros (Cross)

Over the centre of the *Iconostasi* is the *Stavros*. Usually, it shows Jesus on the cross, with His mother Mary, and Ag. John, who wrote the Gospel of John in the Bible. It remembers the moment when Jesus asks John to care for His widowed mother.

5 Iconostasi

This is a screen of icons showing different saints. Christ is on the right of the door, with John the Baptist beside him. On the left of the door is Mary the mother of Jesus, with the patron saint of the Church beside her. A lamp hangs over every icon, symbolising Christ as the light of the world.

6 Chanters

This is a lectern used by a Chanter. The Chanters stand on either side of the Church to lead the worship.

7 The Amvonas

This is where the Deacon stands to read the Gospel.

8 Saints' Days

Members of the Orthodox Church are named after saints. When it is the day of the saint that a member is named after, the person brings five loaves (as used for the *Proskimide*), a bottle of olive oil (for the lamps), a bottle of Communion wine and asks for a *Litia* or an *Artoklasia*. The names of those to be prayed for are listed (all living). At the end of the short service the congregation sing the song of the saint and the bread (and sometimes wine and oil) is distributed to the congregation at Vespers or at the end of the Liturgy.

9 The Soleas

The area inside the rail is called the *Soleas*. The worship is led from here.

10 The Cathedra

This is the Chair where the Bishop sits. If the Archbishop is here, the Bishop sits on the smaller chair instead. On the Cathedra is an icon of Christ, to show that it is his Throne.

11 The Nave

This is where the people sit or stand.

12 Collection Box

People give money here to pay for the running of the Church.

13 Table for candles

People light candles in front of the icons when they pray. The candle is:

♦ A sign of love for the person shown in the icon

♦ A sign of a prayer

♦ A sign of the presence of the person shown in the icon through the power of Christ's resurrection.

Each candle symbolizes the individual soul, which, as it were, each person holds in their own hand.

The extinguishing (or giving up) of the candle at the end of the service symbolizes the fact that each person will have to surrender their soul at the end of their life.

14 Entering the Church

When worshippers come into a Church, they first light a candle, and kiss the icon of Jesus. On Sundays the icon is of the Resurrection because this is celebrated every Sunday. If it is a special festival the icon in the centre of the Church will show the saint to be celebrated. Then they light a candle and kiss the nearby icon of Mary the Mother of Jesus. The lighted candle is a symbol of their prayers. Worshippers may light one for each of the people for whom they are praying.

Church Decoration

Everything one sees within an Orthodox Church is there to serve as an aid in Orthodox worship of God, to serve as a constant reminder of Orthodox Christian heritage and tradition, and to help believers understand the message and truth taught by Christ and the Apostles. The paintings and icons of the Orthodox Church serve as constant reminders that it is a Church of the *living*. Believers do not worship alone, but rather all the members of the Church Triumphant in Heaven: in other words, all the saints, martyrs and early Church Fathers are present with them each Sunday, praying and worshipping God together. Orthodox Church decoration reminds them that with *Christ Pantocrator*, there is no death, but only eternal life.

Although the number of subjects has increased with time, the following arrangement of Orthodox Church decoration is the norm, with adjustments for variations in the architectural setting, and to this day new Orthodox Churches use it as a guide. A visitor can see this entire concept in action in the Church of *Aghios Nicholaou*, the state Church of Skopelos, or indeed, to some degree in any of the Churches of the island.

The Garden

The interior of an Orthodox Church as a whole was conceived as an image of the cosmos. There is a theologically and aesthetically coherent scheme worked out in conjunction with the cross-in-square plan, which provides the ideal 'hierarchy' of spaces and surfaces. The cubic nave (representing earth) surmounted by the dome represents earth united to heaven. It is paradise with the tree of life in its midst. It is a walled garden, and so one often finds the soldier martyrs depicted on the lower register, for they guard paradise (the word paradise is a Persian one, meaning a walled and, usually, a royal garden). On the upper registers are depicted scenes in the life of Christ. Below that are various saints. This shows that the whole life of Christ finds its fulfilment in the saints, in the deification of human persons.

The Dome and Christ Pantocrator

Portrayed against a field of gold suggestive of heaven and eternity, *Christ Pantocrator*, the Almighty, looks down upon His world from the central dome. Below Him, extending into the drum of the dome, are *angels* and *prophets*, His attendants and witnesses. 24 Old Testament Patriarchs that figure into the genealogy of Christ are depicted, from the first man, Adam, through Seth, Noah, Cainan, Mahalalel, Jared, Lamech, Shem, Japheth, Arphaxad, Sala, Heber, Saruch, Nachor, Thara, Abraham, Isaac, Jacob, Phalec, Ragau, Methuselah, Enoch, Enos, and Abel. In the four corners of the Church supporting the dome are depicted the *four pillars of the Orthodox Christian faith*: the four *Evangelists*; Mark, Luke, Matthew and John. Often, these evangelists are depicted with the symbols of the four beasts described by St. John, '...and round about the Throne, were four beasts full of eyes before and behind. And the first beast was like a lion (Mark), and the second beast was like a calf (Luke), and the third beast had a face as a man (Matthew), and the fourth beast was like a flying eagle (John)'.

The Apse and Mary Theotokos

In the quarter-sphere of the main apse, midway between the dome and ground level, is Mary the *Theotokos*, Birth-giver of God, placed there as the link between heaven and earth: through Mary, Christ in heaven entered the world as man. Sometimes on the arch leading into the apse we see Gabriel depicted to the left and the Mother of God on the right - that is, the Annunciation. The Archangel's declaration and Mary's agreement therefore pass through the actual space of the Church temple, from one side of the apsidal opening to the other. This shows that the Church's space is itself sacred space, and that the people in it continue to be part of the salvation drama. The apse is towards the East, where the sun rises, and so is doubly fitting as a place to depict the Incarnation.

Below Mary, on the apsidal wall but visible over the altar, figures the *Communion of the Apostles*, exemplar of the Eucharist, with Christ as the Priest and angels as acolytes.

The Feast Cycle

Lower than the dome but on the upper level is the *Feast Cycle*, comprising major scenes from the life of Christ (such as the *Annunciation, Nativity, Presentation in the Temple, Baptism*). These scenes not only recapitulate the Church year but also form a collective image of the Holy Land.

The West, the Koimesis of the Theotokos and the Last Judgement

On the lower wall surfaces are frontal figures of saints, celestial counterparts of the assembled worshippers. The Western end of the Church, towards the setting sun, often has depictions of the Last Judgement. Immediately above the door there is frequently depicted the *Theotokos, her Dormition* (Koimesis).

Icons

Like most religions, Christianity concerns itself primarily with the spiritual world. Christians believe in a God they cannot see, pray for the salvation of non-material souls, and anticipate an afterlife characterized primarily by spiritual pleasures. However, Christianity is also a religion that embraces the material world rather than renouncing it. Christians believe that a good God created the physical world and Christ took on a physical body, and so conclude that matter must be good in itself. And like those of most religions, followers of Christianity rely on material objects to enhance their religious experience.

In Orthodoxy, *icons* (from the Greek *eikon* meaning 'image') a religious work of art are the means by which this is achieved. Icons may be cast in metal, carved in stone, embroidered on cloth, painted on wood, done in mosaic or fresco work, or printed on paper or metal. The iconic pictures of saints painted on the walls of the Churches throughout Greece are called *hagiography* and they were an early form of animation. They were a 'book' explaining the Orthodox faith for those unable to read. The composer Sir John Tavener, one of Britain's most famous followers of Orthodox Christianity, describes icons as 'the most sacred, the most transcendent art that exists'.

Creating free-standing, three-dimensional sculptures of holy figures was resisted by Christians for many centuries, out of the belief that *daimones* inhabited pagan sculptures, and also to make a clear distinction between Christian and pagan art. To this day, in obedience to the commandment not to make 'graven images' Orthodox icons may never be more than three-quarter bas- relief.

Most icons in fact are usually an elaborate, two dimensional painting. They often have a gold leaf background and are usually on wood. They depict Christ, his mother Mary, scenes from the Bible or the lives of the Saints.

Jesus himself is called the *'image of the invisible God'* in Colossians 1:15, and is therefore in one sense an icon. As people are also made in God's image, people are also considered to be living icons, and are therefore 'censed' along with painted icons during Orthodox prayer services.

The Gospel of St Luke and the First Icons

The Apostle and Evangelist Luke is the author of the Gospel of Luke, the companion of the Apostle Paul and is numbered among the Seventy Apostles. A Greek, he was a native of Syrian Antioch and a physician. After St. Paul's martyrdom, St. Luke preached the Gospel throughout Italy, Dalmatia, Macedonia, and other regions.

In his Gospel, Saint Luke wrote with an extraordinary spiritual sensitivity about the Virgin Mother and the Child Christ, of the healing Christ, of Christ in prayer, of the suffering Christ, of the Crucified Christ, and of the mysterious Risen Christ appearing on the road to Emmaus. The Gospel of Saint Luke is intended to be read more deeply, searched on each page for the icon that slowly emerges from between the lines and behind the words, becoming visible to the eyes of faith.

Luke is then reputed to have taken the written word and transformed it into pictures, producing images expressed through colour and form: because they contain hidden meanings, these pictures are not merely paintings. They are written in the same way as words on the page. Each image is received and then turned over in the mind: it can mean focusing on a single detail; the face, the eyes, a hand, a gesture. Meditation before an icon allows one to linger for a long time in the transforming presence of the light of God, in an attempt to 'receive' the message it is giving. Luke wrote (painted) icons of the Apostles Peter and Paul and of the *Theotokos*, Mary. This is mentioned in the Church Service of the *Small Paraklesis to the Theotokos*:

Speechless be the lips of impious ones,
Those who do not reverence
Your great icon, the sacred one
Which is called Directress,
And was depicted for us
By one of the Apostles,
Luke the Evangelist.

It is recounted that Saint Luke depicted the Virgin Mother with the Infant Christ in three icons. He showed them to her. The Theotokos looked at them with joy and then blessed them, saying, 'May the grace of Him to Whom I gave birth be within them.' For this reason, St. Luke is considered the founder of Christian iconography.

Folklore says St Luke painted an icon of the Theotokos whilst he was in Northern Greece organizing the early Christian Church. The Monastery of *Zoodochos Pigi*, one of the many monasteries located in Skopelos Town, now cares for this icon. Whether painted by St Luke or not, the icon is extremely old and the people of Skopelos are under pressure to allow it to be taken to the Icon Museum of Athens. The monastery, to be seen up the steps at the end of the old harbour, was built in the 18th century and belongs to the monastery Xiropotamou of Mountain Athos.

The Iconographer and His Art

The iconographer prepares for the painting of an icon with prayer and fasting. In the icons of Eastern Orthodoxy, and of the Early Medieval West, very little room is made for artistic license. Almost everything within the image has a symbolic aspect: Christ, the saints, and the angels all have halos. Angels (and often John the Baptist) have wings because they are messengers. There is no tradition of naturalistic realism in their execution: the depiction of each personage is governed by strict conventions. Figures have consistent facial appearances, hold attributes personal to them, and use a few conventional poses.

Colour too plays an important role. Gold represents the radiance of Heaven; red, divine life. Blue is the colour of human life, white is the uncreated essence of God, only used for resurrection and transfiguration of Christ. If you look at icons of Jesus and Mary you will see that Jesus wears a red undergarment with a blue outer garment (God become Human) and Mary wears a blue undergarment with a red over-garment (human granted gifts by God), thus the doctrine of deification is conveyed by icons. Letters are symbols too: most icons incorporate some calligraphic text naming the person or event depicted. Even this is often presented in a stylized manner.

St Luke, a physician, is also associated with painters for the following reason: long ago, there were no art supply shops. Artists bought their pigments from apothecaries, the same place physicians got their supplies.

Anthi Balsamaki

Anthi Balsamaki has a house in Skopelos town. She comes here every summer and will eventually move back here full time. She is one of the most respected iconographers at the Benaki Museum in Athens. A graduate of the Athens School of Fine Arts (the icon painting workshop of K. Xynopoulos), she is in charge of the Benaki Museum icon painting workshop.

To date, she has had eight solo shows; she has been responsible for the icon decoration of many Churches in Greece and abroad; and her works are in many private collections. She is one of the few women icon painters permitted to paint the icons on Church walls, having received a special dispensation to this end from the Ecumenical Patriarchate in Constantinople. She is also the author of a series of books discussing the technique and the symbolic nature of images in Orthodox iconography.

Iconoclasm

Iconoclasm, (which means image breaking) divided Byzantine society and politics in the 120 years following 700 AD. Around that year, the Byzantine Empire nearly succumbed to the armies of a new faith, Islam. In striking distinction to Christianity, Islam forbad the use of religious images, yet it was clearly an alarmingly successful faith. Suddenly, the use of images in Church seemed to raise a huge and fundamental political question.

In 726 Emperor Leo III the Isaurian and his advisors concluded that perhaps the reason for these attacks and the near destruction of the empire was that they had somehow managed to anger God. Leo hit upon the idea of destroying religious images to appease God, since in his opinion their veneration came close to breaking the commandment about idolatry. So a great wave of iconoclastic violence swept the Orthodox Church.

Under his son Constantine V, a council forbidding image veneration was held at Hieria near Constantinople in 754. The theological debates went on for well over a century, and were very complex. Image veneration was reinstated by the Empress Regent Irene, under whom another council was held reversing the decisions of the previous iconoclast council and taking its title as *Seventh Ecumenical Council*. The council *anathemized* (consigned to the devil) all who held to iconoclasm, i.e. those who held that veneration of images constitutes idolatry. Then the ban was enforced again by Leo V in 815. The last iconoclast emperor was Theophilos.

Throughout, the ordinary people had remained on the whole very firmly attached to their icons. After Theophilos died in 842, his widow Theodora, acting as regent for their young son, Michael III, restored the veneration of Icons as an acceptable form of worship.

The Triumph of Orthodoxy

This event is known as the *Triumph of Orthodoxy*. It re-established the veneration of icons as the defining touchstone of true Orthodox faith; the central focus of Byzantine devotion; a vital ingredient in the flourishing and the survival of the Empire.

For another five hundred years the Byzantine Empire was able to keep the Islamic threat at bay. When the Muslim threat returned even stronger than before, the leaders of Constantinople encouraged the people to look back to that great moment of 843, when the faith had been reordered and the Empire restored, and to draw comfort from the past as they faced a frightening future. In 1370 the feast of the *Triumph of Orthodoxy* was established in the Church. Every year since, on the first Sunday in Lent, the Orthodox Church throughout the world celebrates it.

Medieval Times

Of the icon painting tradition that developed in Byzantium, with Constantinople as the chief city, only a few icons from the eleventh century remain and none preceding them. In part this was because of the Iconoclastic reforms during which many were destroyed; because of plundering by Venetians in 1204 during the Fourth Crusade; and finally because of the taking of the city by the Islamic Turks in 1453.

When Constantinople was invaded by the Turks, in order to prevent the Church icons from being burnt and destroyed, the monks threw them into the sea. It is believed that they were then carried by the currents and winds to the shores of Greek islands and the mainland over the centuries. Because Skopelos is populated on its north coast facing Constantinople, many of these icons were found here. The monasteries and Churches of *Evangelistra, Ag Ioannis Kastri* and *Panagia Livadiotisa* are all built on the sites where miraculously appearing icons were said to have been discovered.

The Symbolism of Icons

Icons are described as 'windows into the kingdom of God' and are seen as both a form of prayer and a means to prayer. These stylized pictures are not (as is often thought) objects of idolatrous worship: instead, they are the instrument by means of which Holy persons may be venerated; in no instance are they, themselves, an object of worship. Through the material icon, one is directed beyond to a transcendental glory: by worshipping at the Icon the Orthodox Christian enters into a sacred place with God. The icon is venerated and often candles and oil lamps are burnt before them. The worshipper kisses the icon, making the sign of the Cross and may kneel or prostrate before it.

Icons are not only used in worship in the decoration of the Church, but also in private homes: and in most Orthodox businesses, shops and restaurants, some of these Holy figures may be found. Virtually every house in Skopelos has an *iconostasis* (icon stand) containing various icons deemed to have an importance to the family. They represent certain saints for whom family members are named. In times of need a person may beseech these saints for help. Perhaps the single most revered icon in Greece is that of the Virgin Mary.

Saints

The concept of sainthood is common to all branches of Christianity: *The Apostle's Creed*, affirmed by all Christian denominations, states belief in the *'communion of saints'*. The Orthodox Church believes death and the separation of body and soul to be unnatural; a result of the Fall of Man. They also hold that the congregation of the Church comprises both the living and the dead. All persons currently in heaven are considered to be saints, whether their names are known or not. By this definition, Adam and Eve, Moses, the various prophets, martyrs for the faith, the angels and archangels are all given the title of Saint. However, in Orthodoxy, the only true 'saint' or holy one (*Hagios*) is God Himself. Holiness or sainthood is a gift *(charisma)* given by God to man, through the Holy Spirit. Man's effort to become a participant in the life of divine holiness is indispensable, but *sanctification* itself is the work of the Holy Trinity, especially through the power of Jesus Christ and through communion with the Holy Spirit.

Saints play a prominent role in the rituals of Eastern Orthodox Christianity. Orthodoxy canonizes saints, recognizes saints' feast days, names Churches after saints, displays icons and statues of saints, and prays to saints to intercede for them before God. This set of practices is sometimes called the *'cult of the saints'* (not in the sense of a sect, but in the sense of the Latin word *cultus*, worship). In Orthodoxy, the Virgin Mary is the pre-eminent saint.

Children born into Greek families are often given the name of a Greek Orthodox saint. Traditionally, the first-born son is named after his grandfather, while the first-born daughter is named after her grandmother. As a result cousins often share the same names.

Theosis

The ultimate goal of the saint is to imitate God and live the life of deification (**theosis**). Aghios Maximos the Confessor wrote in the seventh century that the saints are men who have reached *theosis*: they have avoided unnatural development of the soul, that is, sin, and tried to live the natural way of life (i.e., living according to created nature), turning and looking always towards God, thus achieving total unity with God through the Holy Spirit. Saints have several special characteristics:

♦ They are first of all *'friends'* of God.

♦ Secondly, through their genuine piety and absolute obedience to God, they pleased Him and have therefore been *'sanctified'* both in soul and body, and subsequently glorified in this world.

♦ Thirdly, they have been accepted in God's bosom after their passing from the world into eternal life.

♦ Fourth, many of them have been given special grace or favour to perform miracles either before their departure from this world or after.

♦ Fifth, saints have been granted the special gift to pray and intercede for those still living in this world and fighting the 'good fight' for the glory of God and their own perfection in Christ. This intercession springs from the fact that they also are part of the *'Communion of Saints'*. They share prayers and good works with Christians on Earth and there is a constant interaction and unity between the glorified saints in Heaven and Christians who still live in the world.

Categories of Saints

Through the work of the Holy Trinity all Christians could be called saints: in the early Church as long as they were baptized in the name of the Holy Trinity, they received the *Seal of the Spirit* in *chrismation* and frequently participated in the Eucharist.

Nowadays, many Orthodox theologians classify the saints in six categories:

- ♦ **The Apostles,** who were the first ones to spread the message of the Incarnation of the Word of God and of salvation through Christ.

- ♦ **The Prophets,** because they predicted and prophesied the coming of the Messiah.

- ♦ **The Martyrs,** for sacrificing their lives and fearlessly confessing Jesus Christ as the Son of God and the Saviour of mankind.

- ♦ **The Fathers and Hierarchs of the Church,** who excelled in explaining and in defending, by word and deed, the Christian faith.

- ♦ **The Monastics,** who lived in the desert and dedicated themselves to spiritual exercise (*askesis*), reaching, as far as possible, perfection in Christ.

- ♦ **The Just,** those who lived in the world, leading exemplary lives as clergy or laity with their families, becoming examples for imitation in society.

Veneration of Saints

The saints are honoured and venerated in a variety of ways in Orthodox Churches in order to express their love and gratitude to God, who has 'perfected' the saints. One well-known form of devotion is the use of icons. Icons of saints are often found in Churches, homes, and sometimes even on car dashboards. Pictures of saints are also placed in Churches and homes, as well as on holy cards, religious medals, and various other objects.

Icons and images of saints are used in various ways. Common rituals include kneeling in prayer before them, touching or kissing them, gazing at them in contemplation, or simply using them as teaching tools. Before modern times, icons and images (such as stained glass windows) were an important source of knowledge for illiterate Churchgoers, and they still act as a supplement to hearing sermons and reading.

Special prayers are also said for the saints, commonly as part of Church services. One such prayer is the *Contemporary Litany of the Saints*. A litany is a long prayer said *antiphonally* (responsively). Following is an excerpt from the *Contemporary Litany*, (with the leader's part in regular type and the people's response in italics):

Lord, have mercy. *Lord, have mercy.*
Christ, have mercy. *Christ, have mercy.*
Lord, have mercy. *Lord, have mercy.*
Holy Mary, Mother of God, *pray for us.*
St. Michael, *pray for us.*
Holy angels of God, *pray for us.*
St. John the Baptist, *pray for us.*
St. Joseph, *pray for us.*
St. Peter and St. Paul, *pray for us.*

The Intercession of the Saints

In every Liturgy, Orthodox Christians ask God the Father to accept, on their behalf, 'the prayers and the intercession' of all the Saints who now live in heaven. The Fathers of the Church also accept as a matter of course the prayers and the intercession of all the saints.

Recognition of Saints

Unlike the Catholic Church, the Orthodox Church does not follow any official procedure for the recognition of saints. Initially, the Church accepted as saints all those who had suffered martyrdom for Christ. The saints are saints thanks to the Grace of God, and they do not need official ecclesiastical recognition. The Christian people, reading their lives and witnessing their performance of miracles, accept and honour them as saints. Saints are usually canonized by the *Synod of Bishops* within a particular autocephalous Church, but sometimes saints come to be popularly venerated without official canonization.

The Significance of Canonization

The primary purpose of canonization is to *officially authorize* veneration and intercession of a particular saint. The investigation process that precedes canonization seeks primarily to ensure that the person is in heaven and God is working through him or her.

Being canonized as a saint means that:

- The saint's name is added to the catalogue of saints (meaning that veneration is authorized)
- The saint is invoked in public prayers
- Churches may be dedicated in the saint's memory
- The Mass can be offered in the saint's honour
- Feast days are celebrated in the saint's memory
- Images of the saint are made in which his or her head is surrounded by a halo
- The saint's relics (remains) are enclosed in vessels and publicly honoured.

The Importance of Miracles

In the Roman Catholic Church, for those who have died naturally, at least one miracle is necessary to be declared *Blessed (beatified)* and at least two miracles are necessary to be declared a saint (*canonized*). These miracles must have occurred after the person's death (to demonstrate that the person is in heaven and able to assist the living), but miracles during his or her lifetime are also taken into account as evidence of God's favour. In all cases of canonisation, the official recognition of saints grows from the consensus of the Church.

The glorification of saints in the Orthodox Church differs from Roman Catholic tradition in practice: it is believed that when an individual who has been sanctified by the grace of the Holy Spirit *'falls asleep in the Lord'*, God may or may not choose to glorify the individual through the manifestation of miracles. If so, the devotion to the saint will normally grow from the *grass roots* level. There is a service in the Orthodox Church in which a saint is formally recognized by the entire Church, called *glorification.* This does not, however, 'make' a saint but simply accords him or her a place on the calendar with regular services in his honour.

The Service of Glorification

A strong element in favour of glorification can be the perceived miraculous condition of physical remains (relics), although that alone is not considered sufficient. In some Orthodox countries such as Greece it is the custom to re-use graves after three to five years due to limited space. Bones are respectfully washed and placed in an ossuary, often with the person's name written on the skull. Occasionally when a body is exhumed something believed to be miraculous occurs to reveal the person's sainthood. There have been numerous occurrences where the exhumed bones are said to suddenly give off a wonderful fragrance, like flowers; or sometimes the body is said to be found incorrupt despite having not been embalmed (traditionally the Orthodox do not embalm the dead) and having been buried for three years.

Eventually, miracles will have grown to such a degree that a formal *Service of Glorification* will be scheduled. A *glorification* may be performed by any Bishop within his diocese. Often there will be a formal investigation to be sure that the individual is Orthodox in their faith, has led a life worthy of emulation, and that the reports of miracles attributed to their intercessions are verifiable. The glorification service does not make the individual a saint; rather, the Church is simply making a formal acknowledgement of what God has already manifested.

Martyrs need no formal glorification; the witness of their self-sacrifice is considered sufficient.

Timothy Ware (Bishop Kallistos of Diokleia) has written about canonization in Orthodoxy: 'In private an Orthodox Christian is free to ask for the prayers of any member of the Church, whether canonized or not. It would be perfectly normal for an Orthodox child, if orphaned, to end his evening prayers by asking for the intercession not only of the Mother of God and the saints, but of his own mother and father. In its public worship, however, the Church usually asks the prayers only of those whom it has officially proclaimed as saints; but in exceptional circumstances a public cult may become established without any formal act of canonization.'

Rarely, the Orthodox Church adopts a Roman Catholic saint who was canonized after the Great Schism of 1054, as it did Hungary's King Stephen I in 2000, who had been previously canonized by Pope Gregory VII in 1083.

Miracles in Orthodoxy

Phenomena classed as miracles after a saint's death include the following:

♦ *Healings* attributed to intercession of the saint or contact with relics. Example: almost all Orthodox Saints, including Rhiginos, patron saint of Skopelos.

♦ *Incorruptibility* – the saint's body does not decay after a long period in the grave. Example: Gerasimos of Kefalonia, the patron saint of the island of Kefalonia. He died in 1579. After his death, his body was buried twice and exhumed intact, thus leading the Church to ordain him as a saint. His body is guarded and protected in a glass casement at the monastery near Valsamata, as it has never decomposed. Kefalonians throughout the world still revere and pray to him.

♦ *Liquefaction* – the dried blood of the saint liquefies every year on the day of his or her death. Example: St.

Januarius (c.275-305), patron saint of Naples. After his martyrdom, his blood was collected and saved by a woman called Eusebia. Three times a year, the dried blood liquefies in front of thousands of people assembled to witness this event in Naples' Cathedral. Saint Januarius' feast day is celebrated on September 19 in the calendar of the Catholic Church and on April 21 in the Eastern Church.

♦ *Odour of sanctity* – the body exudes a sweet aroma instead of the normal stench of decay. Example: Demetrius of Thessaloniki the Myrrh-streamer, one of the most popular saints in the Orthodox world. He was martyred around the year 306 in Thessaloniki, and his cult rapidly grew during the Middle Ages, when he was regarded as the patron and protector of the city, militarily as well as spiritually. His relics were confirmed through their miraculous outpouring of myrrh - hence the saint's epithet. His feast day is celebrated on October 26.

Miracles during the life of the saint that have been reported:

♦ *Levitation* – the saint floats in the air. Example: St Irene Chrysovalan tou, an abbess, who was seen by one of the female monks of her monastery, motionless, totally absorbed in prayer and in a state of levitation about one metre above the ground. The monk also observed that two nearby cypress trees had bent their heads to the earth in homage before her. When she left her state of prayer, Irene blessed the trees and they returned to their former state.

♦ *Bilocation* – the saint reportedly appeared in two places at once. Example: Nicholas of Myra, an early Christian Bishop, who was in the Middle Ages venerated as patron of sailors and protector of blessed marriages.

Three generals, who had, although innocent, been jailed, were released when the saint appeared to the responsible officials in Constantinople, although he was at the same time seen in his study in Myra.

Unlike in Roman Catholicism, the appearance of *Stigmata* in which the human body exhibits the five wounds of Christ is a phenomenon foreign to the Orthodox experience and, as such, the Church has no official position towards it. The Church believes that the best thing to do is to remain focused on Christ and not give much heed to these phenomena.

Important Orthodox Saints

The Greek word for saint is *Aghios*, meaning 'holy'. The Orthodox Church gives a special place to the honour and veneration of the Virgin Mary, the Mother of God; the Angels; and St. John the Baptist.

Mary Theotokos

The Third Ecumenical Council in Ephesus (431 A.D.) officially adopted the term *Theotokos* (Mother of God) in honour of Mary. There is a period of fasting (the first 14 days of August) and numerous feasts and hymns dedicated to her. Her image is traditionally painted above the Sanctuary and called *'more spacious than the heavens' (Platytera)*. The Virgin Mary, being the mother of God, earnestly intercedes for believers, for she gave her flesh to Christ in all humility and obedience, so that the Word of God could become man.

Mary visited Mount Athos and so loved the beauty of the place that she asked God if she could have it for her garden. Since then, no other woman is allowed to set foot on the holy mountain.

St John the Baptist

St. John the Baptist, whose icon is found on the Iconostasis of all Orthodox Churches, was the prophet who prepared for the coming of Christ on earth and baptized him on the day of the *Theophany* (Epiphany). This was perceived to be John's main role in life and the Church from earliest times dedicated the day following Epiphany to his memory. John was beheaded by Herod Antipas according to the wish and instigation of his wife Herodias and step-daughter Salome. Herodias ordered that John's head not be buried with his body to thwart his resurrection. Therefore, she took his head and buried it deep in the ground in the fortress of

Machaerus. Johanna, Herodias' servant secretly unearthed it, removed it to Jerusalem and buried it on the Mount of Olives.

After a considerable period of time, a monk discovered an earthen vessel and in it a head, which was mysteriously revealed to him to be the head of the Baptist. He reverenced it and reburied it in the same spot. It remained concealed during the Saracen raids and during the period of iconoclastic persecution. When the veneration of icons was restored, Patriarch Ignatius (847-857) saw in a vision the place where the head was hidden. He informed the emperor, who sent the delegation that found the head for the final time.

Eastern Orthodox faithful believe that John was the last of the Old Testament prophets, thus serving as a bridge between that period of revelation and the New Covenant. Following his death, John descended into Hades and there once more preached that Jesus the Messiah was coming, so he was the Forerunner of Christ in death as he had been in life: the Baptist appears at the time of death to those who have not heard of Christ, and preaches the Good News to them, that all may have the opportunity to be saved. As the baptizer of Christ, John is the patron saint of godparents.

Every Tuesday throughout the year is dedicated to the memory of Saint John the Forerunner (*Prodromos*). The Eastern Orthodox Church remembers him on six separate feast days, listed here in order in which they occur during the Church year (which begins on September 1):

> September 23 — Conception of St. John the Forerunner
>
> January 7 — The Synaxis of St. John the Forerunner. This is his main feast day, immediately after *Theophany* on January 6 (January 7 also commemorates the transfer of the relic of the right hand of John the Baptist – the one that baptised Christ - from Antioch to Constantinople in 956)

February 24 — First and Second Finding of the Head of St. John the Forerunner

May 25 — Third Finding of the Head of St. John the Forerunner

June 24 — Nativity of St. John the Forerunner

August 29 — Beheading of St. John the Forerunner

In addition to the above, September 5 is the commemoration of Zechariah and Elisabeth, St. John's parents.

John is depicted as an ascetic wearing camel hair, with a staff and scroll, or bearing a book or dish with a lamb on it. In Orthodox icons, he often has angel's wings, since Mark 1:2 describes him as a messenger.

Archangel Michael

The Orthodox believe the angels to be incorporeal beings, created by God before the actual creation. They are immortal, not by nature but by the grace of God, and are called '*second lights*,' the first light being God Himself. Their nature was originally changeable, but after the Incarnation of Christ, the angels were considered as *saved (sesosmenoi)* and, therefore, unaltered. The Fathers believed that every believer has his own 'guardian angel'; the angels pray for Man, sing, and unceasingly glorify the Holy Trinity. They also serve as examples that people should follow.

The Holy Archangel Michael is one of the most celebrated of the Angels and bodiless powers; he is called the *Archistrategos*, or *chief commander*, of all of them. The name Michael means '*like unto God*' or '*Who is like unto God*' He has interceded for humanity multiple times and continues to serve as the Defender of the Faith. He first appears in the Old Testament in the book of Joshua's account of the fall of Jericho. St Michael is most often invoked for protection from invasion by enemies and from civil war, and for the defeat of adversaries on the field of battle. Countless legends, particularly in Christian, Judaic, Islamic, and Celtic traditions, discuss Archangel Michael's renowned strength and wisdom. He is also recognized in Christianity for being the guardian and protector of God's Church and people; and for miracles of healing.

He is celebrated primarily on November 8th , the *Synaxis of Michael and all the Bodiless Powers of Heaven*; September 6th also marks the miracle of the Archangel at Colossae, when he protected the Church from a flood artificially created by pagans. The site of the miracle became known as Chonae, which means *fissure* or *plunging*.

The Prophet Elijah

Elijah is one of the greatest of the prophets and the first dedicated to virginity in the Old Testament. He was born in Tishba of Gilead into the Levite tribe 900 years before the Incarnation of the Word of God. The name Elijah (the Lord's strength) given to the infant defined his whole life. From the years of his youth he dedicated himself to the One God, settled in the wilderness and spent his whole life in strict fasting, meditation and prayer. Called to prophetic service, which put him in conflict with the Israelite king Ahab, the prophet became a fiery zealot of true faith and piety. According to the Tradition of Holy Church, the Prophet Elijah will be the Forerunner of the Dread Second Coming of Christ. He will proclaim the truth of Christ, urge all to repentance, and will be slain by the Antichrist. This will be a sign of the end of the world.

In iconography the Prophet Elijah is depicted ascending to Heaven in a fiery chariot, surrounded with flames, and harnessed to four winged horses. He is prayed to for deliverance from drought, and to ask for seasonable weather. He is commemorated on July 20th.

Ag. Basileios o Megas (the Great)

Basil was the Greek Bishop of Caesarea Mazaca in Cappadocia, Asia Minor (modern-day Turkey). He was an influential theologian who opposed the heresies of the early Christian Church. In addition to his work as a theologian, Basil was known for his care of the poor and underprivileged. He used all his personal wealth and the income from his Church for the benefit of the destitute; in every centre of his diocese he built a poor-house; and at Caesarea, a home for wanderers and the homeless. Basil established guidelines for monastic life which focus on community life, liturgical prayer, and manual labour. He is one of the fathers of communal monasticism in Eastern Christianity; considered a saint by the traditions of both Eastern and Western Christianity. He is also one of the **Three Great Hierarchs**, recognised as a Doctor of the Church in both Eastern Orthodoxy and in the Roman Catholic Church.

St Basil is also called 'the revealer of heavenly mysteries' (*Ouranophantor*), a 'renowned and bright star,' and 'the glory and beauty of the Church'. Sickly since youth, the toil of teaching, his life of abstinence, and the concerns and sorrows of pastoral service took their toll on him. St Basil died on January 1, 379 at age 49. His head is in the Great Lavra on Mount Athos.

In some countries it is customary to sing special carols (*kalanta*) on January 1st in honour of St Basil: this is the custom on Skopelos. He is believed to visit the homes of the faithful, and a place is set for him at the table. People visit the homes of friends and relatives, and the mistress of the house gives a small gift to the children. A special bread (*Vasilopita*) is blessed and distributed after the Liturgy. A silver coin is baked into the bread, and whoever receives the slice with the coin is said to receive the blessing of St Basil for the coming year.

Ag. Ioannis Xrysostomos

St John Chrysostom, the Archbishop of Constantinople, was an important Early Church Father. He is known for his eloquence in preaching and public speaking, his denunciation of abuse of authority by both ecclesiastical and political leaders, the *Divine Liturgy of St. John Chrysostom*, and his ascetic sensibilities. After his death in 407 he was given the Greek epithet **chrysostomos,** meaning '*golden mouthed'* in English, and Anglicized to *Chrysostom*. The Orthodox and Eastern Catholic Churches honour him as a saint and count him among the **Three Great Hierarchs,** together with Basil the Great and Gregory Nazianzus. He is recognized by the Eastern Orthodox Church and the Catholic Church as a saint and as a Doctor of the Church. Churches of the Western tradition commemorate him on 13 September. Although he died on September 14, St John's celebration was transferred to November 13 in Orthodoxy because of the *Feast of the Elevation of the Holy Cross*. St John Chrysostom is also celebrated on January 27 and January 30. He is known in Christianity chiefly as a preacher, theologian and liturgist. Among his homilies, eight directed against Judaizing Christians remain controversial for their impact on the development of Christian antisemitism.

Ag. Grigorios o Nazianzinos

Saint Gregory the Theologian was a 4th-century Archbishop of Constantinople. As a classically trained (in Athens) orator and philosopher he infused Hellenism into the early Church, establishing the paradigm (distinct concepts or thought patterns) of Byzantine theologians and Church officials. Gregory made a significant impact on the shape of Trinitarian theology among both Greek- and Latin-speaking theologians, and he is remembered as the *'Trinitarian Theologian'*. Much of his theological work continues to influence modern theologians, especially in regard to the relationship among the three Persons of the Trinity. Along with the brothers Basil the Great and Gregory of Nyssa, he is known as one of the Cappadocian Fathers. Gregory is a saint in both Eastern and Western Christianity. In the Roman Catholic Church he is numbered among the Doctors of the Church; in Eastern Orthodoxy and the Eastern Catholic Churches he is revered as one of the *Three Holy Hierarchs*, along with Basil the Great and John Chrysostom. He is commemorated on January 25th.

Ag. Spiridon

Saint Spyridon, Bishop of Trimythous (ca. 270 – 348) is a saint honoured in both the Eastern and Western Christian traditions. He lived his earthly life in righteousness and when the Arabs took Cyprus, his body was disinterred and taken to Constantinople. The relics were found to be incorrupt, and contained a sprig of basil, the 'royal plant,' both of which were taken as a sign of divine confirmation of his sanctity. When, in 1453, Constantinople fell to the Turks, Spyridon's relics were removed again; this time, to the island of Corfu by a Corfiote monk called Kalohairetis, where they remain to this day, except for the relic of his right hand, which is now located in Rome. He is commemorated on December 12th. His memory is also celebrated on *Cheesefare Saturday*, the Saturday before Great Lent.

Ag. Dimitrios tis Thessalonikis

Saint Demetrius of Thessaloniki was a Christian martyr who lived in the early 4th century. Thessaloniki remained a centre of his veneration, and he is the patron saint of the city. A young man of senatorial family, he was run through with spears in around 306 AD in Thessaloniki, during the Christian persecutions of the emperor Diocletian or Galerius. During the Middle Ages, he came to be revered as one of the most important Orthodox military saints, often paired with Saint George. According to believers, his relics started emitting a liquid and strong scented myrrh. This gave the saint the epithet '*Myrovlitis*', the Myrrh-streamer. He is commemorated on October 26th.

Ag. Nektarios

Saint Nectarios of Aegina (1846–1920), Metropolitan of Pentapolis and Wonderworker of Aegina, was officially recognized as a Saint by the Ecumenical Patriarchate of Constantinople in 1961. His Feast Day is celebrated every year on 9 November. Both during his life and after his death, St Nectarius has performed thousands of miracles, especially for those suffering from cancer. There are more Churches dedicated to St Nectarios than to any other modern Orthodox saint.

Ag. Charalambos

St Charalambos was an early Christian Bishop in Magnesia, of Thessaly, in the diocese of the same name. His name means joyful light in Greek. He lived during the reign of Septimius Severus (193-211), when Lucian was Proconsul of Magnesia. It is believed that at the time of his martyrdom in 202, Charalampus was 113 years old. The skull of Saint Charalambos is kept at the Monastery of Saint Stephen at Meteora. Many miracles are traditionally attributed to the fragments of his relics, which are to be found in many places in Greece and elsewhere. The feast day of Saint Charalambos is normally commemorated on February 10, the exception being when this date falls on the Saturday of Souls preceding Great Lent or on Clean Monday (the first day of Lent), in which case the feast is celebrated on February 9. He is remembered during the Divine Liturgy, when *prosphora* breads are consecrated at the beginning of the Greek Orthodox communion. The five breads are: the *prosphoro* for St. Charalambos; the *prosphoro* for the Virgin Mary; the nine-part *prosphora* for the saints; the *prosphoro* for the living; and the *prosphoro* for the dead.

Ag. Pharnourios

Of all the many Saints in Greece, one more deserves special mention. This is St. Pharnourios, the 'finder of lost things' who has become famous for assisting the faithful in revealing lost or hidden spiritual matters of the heart, finding objects, directing or revealing actions that should be taken, restoring health and similar situations. He is then honoured by the faithful through a symbolic bread, called the *Phanouropita* which can be brought to the Church, at any time, for a blessing, in the hope that so doing will prompt the lost item to reappear, or the problem to be resolved. The pita is small and round, like a cake, and should be made using either nine or eleven ingredients: it must be shared with at least seven other people. The basic ingredients include sifted flour, sugar, cinnamon and oil.

The icon of Pharnourios depicts a young soldier holding a sword in one hand and a lit candle in the other. In Skopelos *Chora* this saint is honoured at the Pharnourenimi Church – the one with the clock.

The Feast Days of the Saints

Throughout early Christianity, Christians customarily met in the places where the martyrs had died, to build Churches in their honour, venerate their relics and memory, and present their example for imitation by others. The early Christians met on the name-day of a saint, which in practice usually was the day of his death. These gatherings took place either around the tomb of the saint or in the Church, which kept and preserved his holy relics, or in Churches with great historical and theological significance. Such a gathering, called a feast-day or festival (*Panagyris*), commemorates the memory of the saint.

Small chapels and Churches throughout Greece are visited by a Priest on the feast day of the Church's saint. A feast day is primarily celebrated through the hymnography of the Church's divine services appointed to be celebrated on such day. The faithful participate in the feast, listen to a speech praising the deeds or the martyrdom of the venerated saint, and in general derive spiritual profit from the celebration. Look out for the announcement of a *panagyris* – small Churches are usually decorated outside with flags and banners. The festival takes place on the eve of the saint's day.

The feasts of the Orthodox Church, as with the canonization of saints, always comes from the living devotion of the Christian people. Feast days of the Church are not "institutions" which are legislated by some ecclesiastical authority apart from the interest and consent of the people. If there were no popular interest and veneration of a certain holy person, there would be no official canonization and no liturgical festival established in their honour.

However, if someone is recognized as a saint, the Church hierarchy will set the day of the feast and will compose the proper liturgical service and hymno to be used in the celebration. But the celebration will then depend solely upon the will of the faithful. Once established, the feast could only disappear organically, in a way similar to its appearance. It could not be "disestablished" by the decree of any Church authority, only by lack of practice.

As a whole, the Church celebrates the Twelve Great Feasts Days and a number of other feast days with special liturgical and spiritual solemnity. Some preceded by prescribed fasting periods.

Universally celebrated by all the Orthodox are the feasts of Saint John the Baptist: The Circumcision of Christ January 1; The Three Great Hierarchs January 30; The Protecting Veil of the Mother of God October 1; and All Saints the First Sunday after Pentecost.

The feast days of each of the Apostles are also celebrated by the entire Orthodox Church; above all, the Feast of Saints Peter and Paul, June 29.

Among other feast days of other saints universally celebrated by all the Orthodox are:

♦ Saint Nicholas, December 6
♦ Saint George, April 23
♦ Prophet Elias, July 20
♦ Archangel Michael, November 8
♦ Saint Basil the Great, January 1
♦ Saint John Chrysostom, November 13
♦ Saint Gregory the Theologian, January 25

In the Greek Church:
♦ Saint Spiridon, December 12
♦ Saint Demetrios, October 26
♦ Saint Nektarios, November 9

Patron Saints

Three saints are associated with the patronage of the country of Greece, St George, St Nicholas and St Andrew, one of the original Apostles.

Ag. Giorgios

St George was a Greek who became an officer in the Roman army. In the year AD 302, the Emperor Diocletian (influenced by Galerius) issued an edict that every Christian soldier in the army should be arrested and every other soldier should offer a sacrifice to the Roman gods of the time. George refused. After various torture sessions, including laceration on a wheel of swords during which he was resuscitated three times, he was executed by decapitation before Nicomedia's city wall, on April 23, 303. He is immortalized in the tale of Saint George and the Dragon and is one of the *Fourteen Holy Helpers*.

St. George is most commonly depicted in early icons, mosaics and frescos as wearing armour contemporary with the depiction, executed in gilding and silver colour, intended to identify him as a Roman soldier. After the Fall of Constantinople and the association of St George with the Crusades, he is more often portrayed mounted upon a white horse. The dragon he is defeating is the depiction of the struggle against evil.

St George is very much honoured by the Eastern Orthodox Church, wherein he is referred to as a 'Great Martyr'. His major feast day is on April 23rd. If, however, the feast occurs before Easter, it is celebrated on Easter Monday instead.

Ag. Nikolaos

Saint Nicholas, also called Nikolaos of Myra, was a historic 4th-century saint and Greek Bishop of Myra (Demre, part of modern-day Turkey) in Lycia. Because of the many miracles attributed to his intercession, he is also known as *Nikolaos the Wonderworker* (o *Thaumaturgos*). He had a reputation for secret gift-giving, such as putting coins in the shoes of those who left them out for him, and thus became the model for Santa Claus, whose modern name comes from the Dutch *Sinterklaas*, itself from a series of elisions and corruptions of the transliteration of 'Saint Nikolaos'. St. Nicholas is primarily the protector of sailors and seamen. Revered as the great protector, St. Nicholas' feast is one of great devotion. The Greek Navy pays tribute to him with a special ceremony at the Hellenic Naval Academy on his saint's day of December 6th.

Ag. Andreas

A third patron saint of Greece is *St. Andrew*, called *Protokletos* (the first called) in the Orthodox Church, whose bones were entombed after his death and then 300 years later moved by Emperor Constantine (the Great) to Constantinople. Legend suggests that a Greek Monk (although others describe him as an Irish assistant of St. Columba) called St. Rule (or St. Regulus) was warned in a dream that St. Andrew's remains were to be moved and was directed by an angel to take those of the remains which he could to the 'ends of the earth' for safe-keeping.

St. Rule dutifully followed these directions, removing a tooth, an arm bone, a kneecap and some fingers from St. Andrew's tomb and transporting these as far away as he could. That place was Scotland, where St. Rule was shipwrecked with his precious cargo and it is here the association with the Scots is believed to have begun. St. Rule is said to have come ashore at a Pictish settlement on the East Coast of Scotland which later became St. Andrews.

Other purported remaining relics of the saint are kept at the Basilica of St Andrew in Patras: his feast day is November 30th.

Ag. Rhiginos

Hieromartyr Ag. Rhiginos, monk, Bishop, martyr and saint, is the patron saint of the island of Skopelos. St. Rhiginos was born in Livadeia in central Greece, in the late third century to Christian parents, who instilled in him the love of virtue and zeal for truth. At this point it should be said that it is unclear if this Rhiginos was the saint who joined the army and led an extremely ascetic life, something that his fellow soldiers who were idolaters noticed and complained about. Rhiginos was tortured horribly, put in a sack and thrown into the sea, but the bag was torn and two dolphins carried him on their backs and pulled him ashore. Then he was put in jail, along with another saint, Orestis, but miraculously the prison doors were opened and they escaped. They went to Cyprus, where Rhiginos became a monk and taught Christianity

St Rhiginos, at that time a monk from a monastery on Cyprus, was acclaimed as the first Bishop of Skopelos by all of the people. He participated in the Synod of Sardiki, nowadays Sofia, in 347 AD when the 'coup de grace' was given to the heresy of Arius (the teaching that Christ was not God but merely a unique man). During the rule of the Emperor Julian (361-363 AD) the Governor of Greece visited the island and requested the Bishop to renounce his condemnation of the heresy. Rhiginos refused and was executed along with forty others from the island at the Microrhiginos (Little Saint Rhiginos) or Palio Ghiofiri, the small shrine at the T junction opposite the restaurant 'Nastas.' Having died as a martyr, Bishop Rhiginos was made a saint by the Eastern Church and became the patron saint of Skopelos.

The saint's special prayer, **The Troparion**, is as follows:
'Thy righteous acts have manifested thee to thy flock as a model of faith,
a reflection of humility, and a teacher of abstinence, O Father Bishop Rhiginos.

Therefore, through humility thou hast achieved exaltation, and

through poverty, riches. Intercede thou with Christ God to save our souls.'

Relics of Saints and Martyrs

In religion, a relic is a part of the body of a saint or a venerated person, or else another type of ancient religious object, carefully preserved for purposes of veneration or as a touchable or tangible memorial. Relics are an important aspect of some forms of Buddhism, Christianity, Hinduism, Shamanism, and many other religions. The word relic comes from the Latin *reliquiae,* meaning 'remains' or 'something left behind. A reliquary is a shrine that houses one or more religious relics.

In Christianity, relics are the material remains of a deceased saint or martyr and objects closely associated with those remains. Relics can be entire skeletons, but more usually they consist of a part such as a bone, hair or tooth. Pieces of clothing worn by the deceased saint or even an object that has come in contact with a relic are also considered relics. Since the beginning of Christianity, individuals have seen relics as a way to come closer to the saints and thus form a closer bond with God.

As a natural outgrowth of the concept in Orthodox theology of *theosis,* the physical bodies of the saints were considered to be transformed by divine grace and were able to channel the healing power of God as Jesus did. Not just their bodies, but everything connected with the saints and martyrs was able to work miracles: touching their clothing and even being touched by the shadow of their bodies expelled demons, and healed the sick. According to the Early Church Fathers, some saints and martyrs were so filled with spiritual grace, that even their tombs are filled with a special blessing.

A final joy was given to some saints: their relics had a myrrh-streaming property. This wonder was given to the holy relics in order to indicate that such Christians (unlike sinners who please the devil and present a foul odour before God) through the holy mysteries and holy virtues become sweet-smelling to God and to heaven. For this reason the holy relics of some saints poured forth myrrh. This *Patristic* belief still continues today, and people from all over the world visit Churches that possess the relics of martyrs and saints.

The examination of the relics is an important step in the *glorification* (canonization) of new saints. Sometimes, one of the signs of sanctification is the condition of the relics of the saint. Some saints will be *incorrupt,* meaning that their remains do not decay under conditions when they normally would (natural mummification is not the same as incorruption). Sometimes even when the flesh does decay the bones themselves will manifest signs of sanctity: they may be honey coloured or give off a sweet aroma; some relics will exude myrrh. The absence of such manifestations is not necessarily a sign that the person is not a Saint.

A pious veneration of the holy relics was considered to be a constituent part of salvation and from the very beginning of Christianity Churches were built on the graves and relics of saints. Even today the veneration of relics continues to be of importance in the Eastern Orthodox Church and very often Churches will display the relics of saints prominently. In a number of monasteries, particularly those on the Holy Mountain (Mount Athos in Greece), all of the relics the monastery possesses are displayed and venerated each evening. As with the veneration of icons, the veneration *(dulia)* of relics in the Orthodox Church is clearly distinguished from adoration *(latria)*; i.e., that worship which is due to God alone.

Relics still play a major role in the consecration of a Church. The consecrating Bishop will place the relics on a *diskos* (paten) in a Church near the Church that is to be consecrated; they will then be taken in a cross procession to the new Church; carried three times around the new structure and then placed in the Holy Table (altar) as part of the consecration service.

The relics of saints (traditionally, always those of a martyr) are also sewn into the **antimension** which is given to a Priest by his Bishop as a means of bestowing *faculties* upon him (i.e., granting him permission to celebrate the *Sacred Mysteries*). The *antimens* is kept on the High Place of the Holy Table (altar), and it is forbidden to celebrate the Divine Liturgy (Eucharist) without it.

All Orthodox Christians are considered to be sanctified by living the mystical life of the Church, and especially by receiving the *Sacred Mysteries* (Sacraments). The holy Liturgy is performed only on *antimensia*, and the divine service books, especially the **Menaion,** are replete with prayers and hymns which refer to the pious veneration of holy relics. In the Orthodox service books, the remains of all the departed faithful are referred to as *relics*, and are treated with honour and respect. For this reason, the bodies of Orthodox Christians are not traditionally embalmed.

The Relics of Ag. Rhiginos

After his martyrdom, Rhiginos' body was taken back to the mother monastery on Cyprus and is thought to have been interred at Fasoula in the district of Limassol, at a distance of about 7 kilometres north of the city of Limassol. The chapel of Saints Rhiginos and Orestis stands on the north end of the village. His grave's exact location was revealed to a Priest when the saint appeared to him through a dream.

Hitherto, the resting place was a tomb thought to have belonged to a lord, as it was decorated by paintings, which can be distinguished even today: one of them depicts a hunter in the woods. It has been established that the sarcophagus definitely dates to the 5th century. At present, the tomb is under the auspices of the Department of Antiquities. The Saint's relic is connected to a series of miracles in Cyprus and according to oral tradition, it protected the village when it was in danger. Every year on the 20th August, the celebration of the saint takes place in Fasoula at the chapel's precinct. The rest of the year, the chapel celebrates only baptioms.

After many years a Skopelitian sea captain called Hatzi Konstantinos brought back parts of the holy relic from

Cyprus and they were enshrined in the Monastery of Prodromos (St John the Baptist) in Skopelos, before being transferred to the town's Cathedral *'stou Christou'* (the Birth of Christ), above the harbour. Later still the relics were transferred to a new monastery built in 1728 on the site of older places of worship. The Monastery of Rhiginos is situated 2 km north east of the town, on top of a small hill.

The former Byzantine building, a one room *basilica* with a vaulted nave, was demolished in order to build the existing large cruciform Church. On the west side is the tomb of the former Bishop of Skopelos St Rhiginos, consisting of a small stone sarcophagus housing the sacred relics and dating from the 4th century A.D.

The monastery cells are located in the southwest corner and are now dilapidated. Fragments of columns derived from an ancient Doric temple survive and there is a fountain which supplies water to the monastery.

Every year on the 24th/25th of February thousands of worshippers gather in this monastery from the surrounding islands (Skiathos, Alonnisos) and Volos to honour the saint, who shows his love for his flock by continuing to perform healings and other miracles. Many locals name their children Rhiginos or Regina after him.

The procession begins on the eve of the festival, when the holy relics are taken from the monastery and the congregation processes with litanies to the *Chora*, then through the streets of town to the Church of The Birth of Christ; before returning the next day.

The Enduring Traditions Of Orthodoxy

Rules Within The Orthodox Community

The Orthodox Church is united by its theology: all members of the Church profess the same beliefs regardless of race or nationality. In practice and traditions, however, there are variations in style depending on country of origin and/or local custom. These local customs are referred to as differences in *typica* and are accepted by Church leaders since they are not perceived to conflict theologically with basic Orthodox teachings. Thus many Orthodox Churches adopt a national title (e.g. Albanian Orthodox, Greek Orthodox, Russian Orthodox, etc.) and this title serves to distinguish which language, which Bishops, and which of the *typica* are followed by that particular congregation.

Members of the Church are fully united in faith and the Sacred Mysteries with all Orthodox congregations, regardless of nationality. Differences in *praxis* (practice) tend to be slight; they involve such things as the order in which a particular set of hymns are sung or what time a particular service is performed. In general, an Orthodox Christian could travel the globe and feel familiar with the services even if he or she did not know the language in which they were celebrated.

Thus, the Orthodox Church considers itself to be a community, a body with many parts or members, established and maintained by God for the purpose of the Salvation of Souls. All of this impacts on the personal and communal life of Skopelites. In this section information is offered about the duties undertaken by Orthodox parishioners; it tells of Church etiquette and pious customs; of traditions related to fasting, prayer, shrines and chapels in the home and around the island. The purpose is to describe to outsiders what is said and done, and more importantly, to explain the meaning of the rituals involved.

The Church Parish

The Church is divided into *parishes*, which are territorial units each historically under the pastoral care of one parish Priest: the term parish refers not only to the territorial unit but to the people of its community or congregation as well as to Church property within it. The parish is where most people experience what it means to belong to the Church.

In any parish, the Priest's ministry is to build a community of faith built on the Scriptures, in the Sacraments, in the whole prayer-life of the community, and in fellow parishioners. Parish unity is not meant to be just a cosy fellowship: it is to be a communion of faith and witness. The parish is supposed to be a servant community, a community for others. In other words, it is meant to be a small-scale version of all that the Church is called to be.

Every day the people of the parish are tied together in communities by listening to common readings of the Scriptures in conjunction with the common Orthodox daily prayers. These readings were fixed by the Church some fifteen hundred years ago: Church goers are reading the same Scriptures as other Orthodox, not only in different countries, but also indifferent centuries. The living and the departed are joined together by common bonds.

There are three Priests in Skopelos town and five main Churches: the three Priests rotate between the parishes. It is customary for the congregations to follow their Priest on the days when their own Churches are closed for services. Glossa and Elios, of course, have their own Churches, the most prominent being those to Aghios Nikolaos, the patron saint of sailors; and their own Priests.

The Parish Council

For the Church community to exist and live effectively and efficiently, certain rules over the centuries have been created and enforced. Parishes are run by parish council members, who affirm when they take their oath of office that they '...will fulfil faithfully and sincerely the duties and obligations required of a member of the Parish Council....' No contract is signed, but a promise is made which rests on the shared commitment of all council members to serve the Church, which is regarded as the Body of Christ on earth. To serve on the council is a ministry and a mission: members are called to use the gifts with which they have been blessed to carry out the work of the Church.

Generally speaking, members of the parish council see themselves as caretakers of the Church's money and material possessions: others in the Church take care of other parish needs. Once the parish plan is developed as an outgrowth of the identified needs, it is necessary to advertise it to the congregation. The various phases of the programme require the involvement of people in the parish, and this is where stewardship is practiced: whatever the elements of the particular programme, it will require many special skills and talents. An awareness of the talents possessed by individuals in the congregation is thus very useful. These volunteer skills not only help to accomplish the various tasks, they keep people involved in meaningful aspects of parish life.

Parishes look after the maintenance of the Church and its services, the keeping of the peace, the repression of vagrancy, the relief of destitution, the suppression of nuisances, the destruction of vermin and even to some extent the enforcement of religious and moral discipline.

Below are some of the guidelines and rules that pertain to the lives of Orthodox Christians; all Greek Orthodox Churches and all Greek Orthodox Christians must comply with them.

Parish Membership

To be a member of a Church parish, one must be a *baptized/chrismated* Orthodox Christian who is in good spiritual standing (see Sacraments; and sections below on

Holy Communion, Baptism, Weddings, and Divorce for further explanation on this).

Although those who are not Orthodox will be welcomed in Church, only Orthodox individuals can be members and therefore receive the Sacraments, become sponsors at baptisms and weddings, and vote in parish elections and general assemblies.

Responsibilities in Holy Communion

No person is allowed to receive Holy Communion in any Orthodox Church unless they are of the Orthodox faith: no Orthodox Christian may receive Holy Communion in a non-Orthodox Church (i.e. Roman Catholic, Episcopal, Lutheran, Baptist, etc.)

Couples who are not married in the Orthodox Church cannot participate in the Sacrament unless their Priest, hearing their confession, deems it necessary for them to receive Holy Communion. Those co-habiting out of wedlock may not receive Holy Communion.

The Church does not permit divorce, but tolerates it: in special cases, marriages may be annulled by the Church. Those who have obtained a civil divorce but have not been released from the Church through Spiritual Court, may not receive Holy Communion, nor be a sponsor at a Baptism or a Wedding.

Responsibilities in Baptism

The sponsor (Godparent) of a child being baptized in the Orthodox Church must be an Orthodox Christian in good standing, and must be involved in the life of the Church: if married, must be married in the Church and if divorced, must have release from the Church through the Spiritual Court. The sponsors must be over 12 years of age. If the sponsor is from another diocese, they must have an accompanying letter from their parish Priest stating that they are in good standing and that there are no impediments concerning their spiritual status as Orthodox Christians. Orthodox Christians may not become sponsors at Baptisms and Confirmations in non-Orthodox Churches (i.e. Roman Catholic, Episcopal, Lutheran, Baptist, etc.)

Responsibilities at Weddings

The best man/woman or *koumbaro/koumbara* must be an Orthodox Christian in good standing and be involved in the life of the Church. Non- Orthodox cannot assume this responsibility. If the *koumbaro/koumbara* is from another diocese, they must have an accompanying letter from their parish Priest stating that they are in good standing with the Church. If an Orthodox Christian is asked to participate in a non-Orthodox wedding (i.e. Roman Catholic), he/she may not receive Holy Communion at that service.

Anyone who has been married in a civil ceremony should make arrangements for the marriage to be performed with the blessings of the Church, as civil ceremonies alone are not sufficient to obtain the recognition by the Church of the sanctity of the marriage.

Divorce

The Church does not permit divorce but it is at times tolerated. A Church divorce may be granted after a civil decree has been given, but only after every effort to reconcile the couple has been made. The Church grants divorce through the Spiritual Court that reviews the case after a petition is made.

Divorce is permitted in the Orthodox Church for various reasons. The more usual divorce occurs under the pastoral guidance of the spiritual director of the spouses when all attempts at salvaging a marriage have been exhausted. In such cases, remarriage may be possible but there is a special rite for a second marriage which contains a penitential element for the dissolution of the first: i.e. some of the more joyful aspects are removed.

Marriage is permitted up to three times in Orthodoxy but each divorce necessitates a short period of Excommunication.

Another type of divorce is what is known as an '*ecclesiastical divorce*', which does not signify the breakdown of the relationship but is a step taken for the sake of the *theosis* of the spouses and with the full support and blessing of the Church. This type of divorce may only take place where there is mutual agreement between the two spouses, and is usually carried out in cases where the husband is selected to be consecrated a Bishop (as Orthodox Bishops are monastic) or where one or both spouses wish to otherwise adopt the monastic lifestyle.

Funerals

It is necessary for Orthodox Christians to participate in the entire life of Christ's Holy Church, therefore funerals can only be performed for those who are baptized Orthodox Christians. The funeral service cannot be performed in Church for those who have committed suicide, unless they were under a doctor's care and the doctor certifies that they were not responsible for their action.

Under no normal circumstances is *cremation* allowed. Christ's whole body was placed into the tomb and the Resurrection makes it clear that the whole of the humanity of believers – body as well as soul – has been called to salvation and eternal life. A religious service cannot be performed over cremated remains. An exception may occur when the Church is confronted with the case of some accident or natural disaster where cremation is necessary to guard the health of the living. In these special situations, the Church allows cremation of Orthodox people with prior Episcopal permission and only by '*economia.*'

Baptized Orthodox, who are married outside the Church, are divorced, but have not been released by the Church through Spiritual Court cannot be brought to the Church for the funeral service unless a Priest had previously heard their confession and was aware of their intentions.

Musical Instruments in the Church

No musical instruments are allowed to be played inside the Church: the voice is the most perfect instrument with which to worship God.

Financial Stewardship

The State pays the stipends of Priests and Bishops. In recent years, *tithing* has been revived in Orthodox Churches as a form of stewardship that God requires of Christians: the primary argument is that God has never formally abolished the tithe, and thus Christians should pay the tithe (usually calculated at 10 percent of all gross income from all sources). The Greek Orthodox Church is supported entirely by the tithes and offerings of its members: no income is generated for the operation of the Church through sales, festivals or any other programme. The operational budget of each Church therefore depends directly upon the annual pledges of its Church members.

Most parishes find themselves relying on the generosity of a few, while the rest pay their minimal dues, giving what they can, often '*in kind'*. Generosity to the Church gives many blessings. Special services given by the Priest, such as the blessing of a business, or a boat, or the home, should receive a sum of money in gratitude. It is not payment as such but in a sense, the giving of alms, and the giving of alms covers many sins. All parishioners are expected to satisfy their financial stewardship to the Church, unless in cases of extreme hardship.

Home Visitation by a Priest

Priests will visit homes to bless them at *Theophany,* or to have the *Sacrament of Efheleon (Holy Unction)* performed. The latter is a Sacrament of Divine Sanction by which Divine Grace imparts to the afflicted, through anointing with oil, the healing of both body and soul. *Extreme Unction* is the absolution of sins before death itself.

The pastoral role of the Church is undertaken by Deacons and Elders, not the Priest.

Life and Worship

In the Orthodox Church, there are many customs and traditions that are an important part of worship: some are cultural and some are pious customs; some are essential and some are not. Should you visit a Church, it is useful to know them, so that you do not unintentionally cause offence.

Pious Customs Connected with Church

Bells

Over the entrance of the Church building, or at times next to it, there is usually a bell tower. Bells are used for a variety of purposes in religious life: for example, to express joy on feast days, baptisms and weddings; or to call the faithful to worship at Church. Different patterns of ringing the bells are used to call the faithful to prayer and to the divine services.

Before services, the bells will ring in sequences of three – literally, *come-to -Church*. Those who are not able to attend cross themselves, identifying themselves in spirit with the worshippers: often, nowadays, the service is made available outside the Church through the means of loud speakers, so that those who are working in town can still be part of the worshipping community. If there is to be a funeral or a memorial service, the bells ring in short sequences of two.

Bells are also used at important points during services when their sound reminds the faithful of the higher, Heavenly world: the ringing of the *Sanctus Bell* represents the coming of Christ in Communion; and finally, the *death knell* announces a death and the passing of a person's soul into the next life.

Chanting

Orthodox services are sung nearly in their entirety. Services consist in part of a dialogue between the clergy and the people (often represented by the choir or the *Psaltis Cantor*). In each case the prayers are sung or chanted following a prescribed musical form. Almost nothing is read in a normal speaking voice, with the exception of the homily if one is given. Because the human voice is seen as the most perfect instrument of praise, musical instruments (organs, guitars, etc.) are not generally used to accompany the choir.

The Church has developed eight *Modes* or *Tones*, within which a chant may be set, depending on the time of year, feast days, or other considerations of the *Typikon* (Church Rules). There are numerous versions and styles that are traditional and acceptable.

Incense

As part of the legacy handed down from its Judaic roots, incense is used during all services in the Orthodox Church as an offering of worship to God as it was done in the Jewish First and Second Temples in Jerusalem. Traditionally, the base of the incense used is the resin of *Boswellia thurifera*, also known as frankincense, but the resin of fir trees has been used as well. It is usually mixed with various floral essential oils giving it a sweet smell.

Incense represents the sweetness of the prayers of the saints rising up to God. It is burned in an ornate golden *censer* that hangs at the end of three chains representing the Trinity. Two chains represent the human and Godly nature of the Son, one chain for the Father and one chain for the Holy Spirit. The lower cup represents the earth and the upper cup the heavens. In the Greek and Syrian traditions there are 12 bells hanging along these chains representing the 12 Apostles (usually there are no bells in Slavic tradition). There are also 72 links representing 72 evangelists. The charcoal represents the sinners: fire signifies the Holy Spirit; and frankincense the good deeds. The incense also represents the grace of the Holy Trinity.

The censer is used (swung back and forth) by the Priest/Deacon to venerate all four sides of the altar, the holy gifts, the clergy, the icons, the congregation, and the Church structure itself.

Church Etiquette During a Service

Lighting candles

Lighting candles is an important part of Orthodox worship. Orthodox believers typically light candles when coming into the Church: they light them as they pray, making an offering to accompany the prayers. There are times, though, when candles should not be lit. It is not proper to light candles during the Epistle and Gospel readings, during the *Little* or *Great Entrances*, or the sermon. If in doubt, a Church sub deacon is usually available to give guidance.

Candles are lit among other things: to glorify God, who is Light; to dissolve the darkness of the night and to banish away the fear which is brought on by the darkness; to bestow honour to the saints, by imitating the early Christians of the first centuries who lit candles at the tombs of the martyrs; to have sins forgiven and burned away.

However, lighting a candle also has a simple and practical reason: to make a financial offering for the various services and expenses of the Church. The Church gives the candle as a blessing for the offering and allows believers to light the flame and invoke the symbolism mentioned above.

The importance of punctuality

The time to arrive at Church is before the service starts. Late arrivals – after the Divine Liturgy begins - should try to enter the Church quietly and observe what is happening. If the Epistle or Gospel is being read or the *Little* or *Great Entrance* is taking place, latecomers should wait until it is finished.

141

If the *Pappas* is giving the sermon, they should stay at the back until he has concluded. The Liturgy should not be interrupted: the best way to avoid this situation is to arrive on time.

Venerating icons

When entering the Church, it is traditional to venerate the icons. Usually, there are icons at the entrance to the Church and many Churches have icon stands in the front as well. When venerating (kissing) the icon, please be aware that it is improper to kiss an icon on the face.

Women who wear lipstick to Church should blot their lips well before venerating an icon, receiving Communion, or kissing the cross or the Priest's or Bishop's hand.

'Let us attend'

On Skopelos, most people stand in Church, although seats are provided at the side for the old and infirm and some Churches, such as Fanouremini have seats in the nave. If you do sit, remember that crossing one's arms and especially one's legs is considered to be very disrespectful. Crossing one's legs in Church is not permitted, not because it is 'wrong,' but rather because it is too casual and relaxed for being in Church. It should be remembered that sitting in Church is a concession, not the normative way of prayer. The congregation should sit attentively, with both feet on the floor, ready to stand at attention, which is what the phrase *'let us attend'* means.

The sign of the cross

Eastern Christianity believes in exercising faith through ritual tradition: this is striking for most people in Western Christianity. And what a visitor observes most often is all the faithful making the sign of the cross – crossing themselves –

some repeatedly and nervously, others slowly and contemplatively.

The proper *Orthodox Cross* is made by holding the thumb and first two fingers of the right hand together and resting the remaining two fingers on the palm. The three fingers together represent the Father, Son, and Holy Spirit, and the remaining two on the palm represent the two natures of Christ as God and man. This is a summary of the Christian Faith.

Orthodox Christians 'cross themselves' differently to Roman Catholics. They touch their right shoulder first, then their left, whereas the Roman Catholics first touch their left shoulder. Crossing oneself is only done with the RIGHT hand: The censing of the Holy Table in the Altar is always done from the RIGHT side first; censing of the *Ikonostasis*, the Congregation and of the Church itself always begins with the right side. The Priest always gives communion with his RIGHT hand, even if he is left handed.

Placing the cross on oneself

Touch the forehead, then the stomach, tracing the vertical part of the cross. From the stomach, bring the hand up to the right shoulder, touching it. Finish placing the cross by touching the left shoulder.

The act of 'Placing the cross on oneself' is a request for a blessing from God. It is made from right to left to mirror the actions of the Priest when he gives a blessing. The Priest, looking at the parishioners, blesses from left to right. Therefore, the parishioners, putting on the sign of the cross on themselves, do it from right to left. When a parent makes the sign of the cross over a child, they will cross them from left to right, just as the Priest blesses. When they make the sign of the cross over themselves, they would do it, logically, the other way.

Sometimes a person will make the sign of the Cross in Church and then bow and touch the floor. This is common in traditional Orthodox worship and is known as a **Metania** or Prostration. Touching the ground is a reminder of the earth from whence Man came and to which he will return.

Other Pious Customs in Church

Prosphoro - Offering

Prosphoro is made by members of the Greek Orthodox faith as altar bread for celebrations of the Divine Liturgy. The bread consists of two loaves baked together, one placed on top of the other. Each loaf is stamped with a seal. The double loaf represents the divine and human nature of Jesus Christ. Traditional Greek homes reserve a pan that is used only for making *prosphoro.*

There are five main *prosphora* which are consecrated during the *proscomidia* at the beginning of the Greek Orthodox communion:

- the *prosphoro* for St. Charalambos,
- the *prosphoro* for the Virgin Mary
- the nine-part *prosphora* for the saints
- the *prosphora* for the living and
- the *prosphoro* for the dead.

Often prepared by a parishioner, the bread is round and consists of two separate parts made from leavened wheat bread. The stamped design on the upper part of the loaf is that of a cross with the letters IC, XC, NIKA, which stands for 'Jesus Christ Conquers,' and is cut out by the Priest during the preparation of the Eucharist.

The service of *artoklasia* (breaking of bread) represents a thanksgiving for God's blessings and commemorates Christ's miracle of multiplying five loaves to feed thousands.

Other sacred breads include *antidora* (from *doro*, 'gift'), which is distributed by the Priest to the faithful following the Divine Liturgy, *artos, panagia*, and Easter cake *(tsoureki).*

The Artos

The most common non-Eucharistic bread is the *artos.* This is in two forms: five smaller loaves which are blessed during a portion of the All-Night Vigil known as the *Artoklassia* (literally, 'breaking of bread'); and a single, large loaf which is blessed during the **Paschal Vigil** and then remains in the Church during **Bright Week** (Easter Week). This *Artos,* symbolizing the Resurrected Jesus is venerated by the faithful when they enter or leave the Church during *Bright Week.* Then, on *Bright Saturday,* the Priest says a prayer over the *Artos* and it is broken up and distributed among the faithful as an *evlogia* (blessing).

Tamas - Offerings

When God fulfils people's wishes or saves them from danger, they express their thanks by making a votive offering, or *tama*. Votive offerings in Ancient Greece were made to *Asklepios*, the God of Medicine, and depicted the part of the body that had been cured (such as eyes, ears, breasts etc). Nowadays, the most common votive offerings are small silver or gold plates with an arm, leg, etc cast in relief.

A *tama* is offered for diseases that have been cured, for children whose lives have been saved, for houses that have escaped a fire or earthquake etc. Offerings usually hang on the icon of the Saint whose help was asked for. Among them are all kinds of valuable or not so valuable pieces of jewellery, as well as other objects, such as medals or any other object of emotional value. If you go into any Church on Skopelos, you will see *tamas* hanging in front of icons.

Memorial Wheat - Kollyva

The Greeks honour their dead with memorial services throughout the year, but Easter is a time when all the dead are remembered. Cemeteries are visited and the names of the deceased are read out loud in Church. When a memorial service takes place, *Kollyva* are blessed by the Priest and given out to the congregation in memory of the deceased.

Kollyva is whole-wheat kernels that have been boiled and sweetened. Fruits, nuts, Jordan almonds and spices are added to it and it is mounded onto a silver tray. The sign of the Cross is made with silver *dragees* or *tragemata* (sweets such as whole almonds coated with a sugar shell) in the centre. On one side of the Cross, you will see the letters: *IC XC NIKA* which means, *'Jesus Conquers'*. On the other side of the Cross are the initials of the deceased.

The eating of *Kollyva* at Church is to remember the departed soul and to pray for their forgiveness. Wheat, raisins and pomegranate seeds are usually amongst the ingredients. They symbolize the resurrection and the sweetness and abundance of life.

The Memorial Services are usually performed at the end of the Sunday liturgy and the blessed *Kollyva* is put into small bags and handed out to the parishioners as they leave.

Pious Customs At Any Time

Prayer

At the centre of worship and belief is the Eucharist surrounded by the *Divine Offices* or the *Cycle of Prayer*. These prayers are sung particularly at Sunset and Dawn and at certain other times during the day and night.

However, personal prayer also plays an important part in the life of an Orthodox Christian, such as before and after meals, before and after bible studies and so on. These prayers are also recited according to custom, usually not out loud, but secretly, as the bible says, or quietly inside the head.

In Orthodoxy, prayer is as much about listening to God as it is speaking to Him. In fact, the listening is even more important than the talking. Therefore, believers concentrate in silence, focusing on only a few words.

For many Orthodox Christians an important form of prayer is the *Jesus Prayer*. This is a sentence which is repeated many times; for example: 'Lord Jesus Christ, Son of God, have mercy on me, a sinner.' The aim of this repetition is to enable the person to concentrate solely on God.

Occasionally, you may see a monk or Priest sitting with a *komboskini* (prayer rope) in their hands. This is traditionally a 33 or 100 knotted circular rope and is used in saying the Jesus Prayer.

Nistia - Fasting

Fasting plays an important part of the Orthodox Christian life because it is believed that fasting can be the 'foundation of all good'. The discipline of training the body can enable a believer to concentrate the mind totally on preparation for prayer and things spiritual. As we have seen, there are four main fasting periods:

♦   The *Great Fast* or the period of *Lent*

♦   The *Fast of the Apostles:* Eight days after *Pentecost* until 28th June. This ends with the Feast of Saint Peter and Saint Paul.

♦   The *Dormition Fast* which begins on 1st August and ends on the 14th August

♦   The *Christmas Fast* from 15 November to 24th December.

There are different kinds of fasts for the Greeks. Some are days of no meat while others strictly prohibit eating dairy products as well. There is also some confusion when it comes to fasting: villagers have told me that it's all right to eat olives but you shouldn't eat olive oil; on Clean Monday, you can eat shellfish and molluscs and fish roe, but you can't eat fish.

The Greek Orthodox Church prescribes fasting for the entire duration of Lent. However, most of the newer generation Greeks fast only during the last two weeks before Easter; Holy Week being the most severe. Fridays and Wednesdays are the exceptions. Most devout Greeks will fast - not eat meat or fish - on those days throughout the year.

Even though today the call to fast is not always strictly followed, nevertheless many devout Orthodox Christians do undergo a time of genuine hardship and it has been said that: 'Orthodox Christians in the twentieth century - laity as well as monks – fast with a severity for which there is no parallel in western Christendom...' *(Timothy Ware, The Orthodox Church)*

Pious Customs Outside of Church

Making the sign of the cross

The Cross is the most powerful Symbol in Christianity, because Christ died on it. The sign of the cross addresses the individual spiritual battle, which is fought on many levels of the self. Making the sign of the cross is 'a blessing, a prayer, a proclamation of the Christian identity, a living mystery, and an acceptance of the role that God has given believers'. Greeks make the sign of the cross whenever the name of Christ is mentioned, at appropriate times during Church services, whenever they pass a Church, and on any other occasion that they wish. As they do so, they identify themselves with worshippers of their faith, past and present and make an affirmation of their nationhood.

The Home Iconostasio

In every Greek home, there will be found a corner – most likely in the master bedroom - with an *Iconostasio*. This

148

is a shelf that houses Icons, various holy items and an oil-candle, which is never left to go out.

The Icons are usually of the Saints' whose names are in the family and of Christ and the Virgin Mary. There will be sprigs of dried basil, olive or rosemary, burnt candles, vials of holy water and holy oil as well as '*Stefania*' or *'crown wreaths'* from the owners' wedding. Any item that is considered blessed and holy takes its place here.

The *'Kantili'* or lantern is usually nothing more than a glass filled with water and olive oil with a *'fitili'* or wick floating on it. The *Kantili* is lit with the *'Light of the Resurrection'* from Great Saturday, and is never left to go out: Greek housewives diligently check the oil level and refill it as needed.

In the more modern houses, the Iconostasion as a shelf is non existent, but there is a wall somewhere in the house that is dedicated to this purpose and has the Icons hanging on it. Often, there is a special heirloom frame deep enough to hold the *stephanas* of the married couple behind glass in the same place.

Greek Shrines

Travelling the roads of Skopelos, it won't be long until the metal boxes on skinny metal legs catch your attention. Behind the small glass doors, a candle flickers, a colour picture of a saint stares back, and the top of the box is crowned with a cross or perhaps a row of Greek letters. Farther along, a brightly whitewashed building the size of a children's playhouse stands out against the grey-green leaves of the olive trees.

Outsiders assume, sometimes rightly, that the shrine is built to act as a remembrance for a traffic accident victim. This is true in some cases, but they are often built by a survivor of a potentially tragic accident, or to publicly thank a saint for a benefit, not to commemorate a tragedy.

149

Some of the shrine locations may have endured as long as the roads themselves. Nicholas Gage, author of *'Eleni'*, a tale of his mother's life in Greece during World War II, writes about the ubiquitous shrines. He points out that 'Shrines to pagan gods were built in the same spots and for the same purpose - to provide the traveller with a moment of rest and prayerful reflection'. And they serve a related purpose for the travellers who will stop for a quick photo opportunity and end up gazing at the endless olive groves disappearing into the distance, or find a glowing-red cyclamen or yellow crocus unexpectedly bursting through the grass at their feet. Pausing at these heartfelt roadside shrines immediately connects the visitor with the enduring life of Greece.

Where there is a beautifully built shrine, look at the edges of the groves beyond. There is often an older predecessor, sometimes less carefully tended, but still remaining as a testament of past faith. These are often boundary markers for family land, built to protect and bring prosperity through faith. As family fortunes improve, so do the shrines. In parts of the island, the shrines take on the appearance of miniature chapels, sometimes with interior spaces large enough to hold small ceremonies.

Family chapels

Skopelos is famous for its hundreds of small family chapels which are usually opened on the feast day of the attendant saint, or to commemorate another important day in the family history. Charming ones stand on headlands, waiting for the last-minute prayers of sailors and fishermen before they sail on the often-rough waters of the Aegean; sparkling white-painted tiny ones nestle in country gardens; others are to be found in the heart of the busy, secular streets of the island's towns and villages.

In many ways, they are status symbols, signifying that a family was or is rich enough to build and maintain their own house of God. But there are many reasons for their existence:

the family might want a place outside of town where they can pray privately outside the regular service time. They might want to give thanks to God that a member of the family had been healed or rescued. They might want to bury dead family members and have prayers said every day. They might want to give honour to a particular saint. They might want to avoid taxation by spending a lot of money quickly.

For whatever reason, during a trip to Greece there is evidence for the visitor everywhere of thousands of years of Greek belief: but to feel it, step inside one of the little chapels. Or stand a moment on a wild roadside by a little shrine where someone's hopes, pains, or life is perpetually commemorated, and feel your spirits restored by a moment of quiet in the heart of Greece.

The double headed eagle, found carved on the doors of many churches on Skopelos, is the symbol of the divided Church of Orthodoxy and Rome, looking to East and West. But the double headed eagle carrying a sword and orb and surmounted by a crown is the symbol of Constantinople. It is most commonly associated with the Byzantine Empire and the Holy Roman Empire. In Byzantine heraldry, the heads represent the dual sovereignty of the Emperor (secular and religious) and/or the dominance of the Byzantine Emperors over both East and West. In the Holy Roman Empire's heraldry, it represented the Church and the State. The same symbol on an orange background is the flag of the Greek Orthodox Church.

The **dolphin** was an early Christian symbol denoting a Christian, or used as a representation of Christ -- most often in combination with the anchor symbol (Christ on the Cross). Dolphins swimming alongside boats represent Christ who guides believers to heaven. They are also a symbol of the Resurrection. Dolphin rings and bracelets, often to be found in the jewellery shops of Skopelos, symbolise Christ allied to the circle of eternal life, as it has no beginning or end.

Each Parish Church decorates
the Epitaphion (bier) of Christ
on Maunday Thursday.

The 'angels' are dressed with
ribbons - they will be changed
to black at the time of the
funeral on Good Friday.

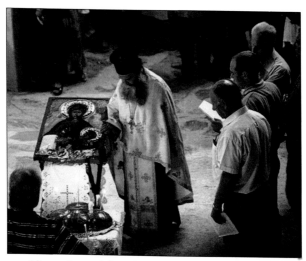

The entire parish gathers around their Church for
Midnight Mass on Easter Saturday.

The Church of Panagitsa tou Pyrgou (the Virgin of the Tower), at the edge of the old port of Chora Skopelos.

Monastery of Ag. Varvara, Mount Palouki, Skopelos, with the Monastery of Ag. Prodromos behind.

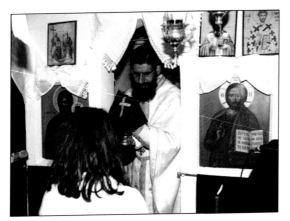

The interior of a family chapel, Skopelos.

An icon at a nameday blessing.

The sacred relics of Ag. Rhiginos in the monastery named after him. Every year, they are carried in solemn procession through the streets of Skopelos *Chora* to the Church of Christos and back again.

An *iconostasion* in a family chapel. Note the embroideries above the Royal Doors.

Pappas Nicholas and Pappas
Kostas at Epiphany; literally,
the appearance of the son of
God on January 6th, when the
imps are driven into the sea.

Ochi Day parade; 28th October.

May Day - a day to gather flowers for the door, in celebration of Spring.

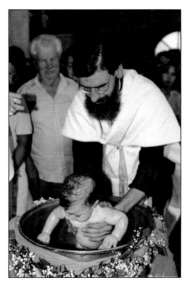

Baptism.

On the left is the engagement
dress of Skopelos. On the right
is the heavily embroidered
wedding dress.

Remembrance is observed by
lighting a candle.

The cemetery at Skopelos *Chora*.

The Vlachi Wedding: the 'bride' - a male - stands beside the Master of Ceremonies at Apocrea.

Traditional costumes.

The entire town takes part in the Vlachi Wedding procession.

and Pomegranates

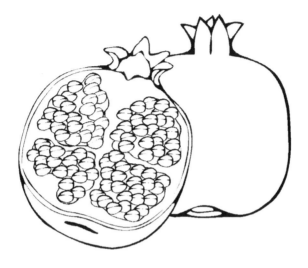

The pomegranate was a pagan symbol associated with Persephone and the annual resurrection of crops in springtime. In Orthodoxy, it is a symbol of the resurrection and the hope of eternal life. Because of its abundance of seeds, it can also symbolize royalty and the church, where the seeds represent the many believers who make up the one Universal Church.

Contemporary Greek Culture

Contemporary Greek culture is extremely rich and diverse, reflecting Greece's location at the crossing point where the West meets the East and the country's great and turbulent history. This deep and tumultuous past greatly influences contemporary lifestyle, the Greek perspective on the world, Greek music, food, customs and traditions, even the way Greeks do business. Greeks as a whole are extremely proud of their history, their cultural heritage and their contribution to literature, art, philosophy and politics. They speak with intense passion of their country as the cradle of European civilization.

A recent study found that Greeks' pride in being Greek surpassed the ethnic satisfaction of every other European nation. Greeks define their natural and ethnic belonging through their culture and tradition. Anyone who has seen the movie *'My Big, Fat, Greek Wedding'* knows this. Traditions, religion, music, language, food and drinks are the pillars of contemporary Greek culture and lifestyle, making the country an attraction point for visitors from all over the world.

The Church

The Greek Orthodox Church, as we have seen, is an integral part of life in Greece where the most important holidays are religious in nature and the national religion is practiced by the majority of the population. Greece and Orthodoxy are closely connected due to the country's historical past. During several occupations, and especially during the 400 years of Ottoman rule, the Orthodox religion played a vital role in maintaining the Greek ethnic and cultural identity. Today the Church is more important in political, civic, and governmental affairs than in many other secular countries.

Officially, and like much of the rest of Europe, the Greek State and the Orthodox Church are separated, but this separation is not written or regulated by the Constitution and the Greek Orthodox Church has a great influence in Greek society. Religion is present in the education sector, both in private and public schools, where children have compulsory religious courses and pray collectively in the morning before the start of classes. The Orthodox Church is also much integrated into the politic matters of the country. The Greek Constitution guarantees freedom of faith, but defines the 'prevailing religion' of Greece as the Eastern Orthodox Church of Christ. Most Greeks, whether deeply religious or not, revere and respect the Orthodox Christian faith, attend Church, observe major religious holiday and are emotionally attached to Orthodox Christianity as their 'national religion'.

Younger people are not as devout Church-goers as their parents and grandparents, yet most will still turn to the Church for holidays or for important rituals such as weddings and funerals. Despite Muslim, Jewish and Roman Catholic religious groups within Greece and the fast moving processes of Europeanization and globalization, Greece remains a profoundly religious country in which Orthodoxy is less an institution than a sentiment, expressed by the population and by the public powers.

National Identity

The republic is seen as the restoration of an independent Greek civilization, and many symbols establish a strong link between past and present, between larger Greek history and the modern nation-state. National holidays stress the struggle to establish and maintain an independent country in the face of conquest and oppression. The national anthem, '*Hymn to Liberty*,' praises those who fought in the War of Independence. The flag displays a cross symbolizing the Greek Orthodox religion on a field of blue and white stripes that depict the sunlit waves of the seas that surround the nation. Statues of war heroes abound, alongside the imagery of the Orthodox Church and antiquity. All this is reflected in a citizenry largely composed of ethnic Greeks: state and ethnic group were seen as the same at the time of the construction of the modern state.

The national identity generally is considered a matter of cultural continuity, with language, religion, democracy, an analytic approach to life, travel, entrepreneurship, cleverness, and personal honour and responsibility as core values that connect contemporary Greeks to the past. An intense relationship to the Mediterranean landscape also plays a role. Alongside this, public consciousness is also characterized by the frustration of unfulfilled hopes, foreign interference, and consignment to marginal status within Europe.

Politics

Greece is a parliamentary republic modelled after the French system. The redrawn constitution of 1975 established a single legislative body with three hundred seats. The President serves as the ceremonial head of state, while the Prime Minister is the head of government. Suffrage is universal for those over eighteen years of age. A large civil service bureaucracy administers a host of national, provincial, and local agencies. Governmental functioning often is described as hierarchical and centralized. A municipal reorganization in 1998 combined smaller communities into larger ones in an effort to strengthen the power of local government.

Two major parties have alternated in power since the end of the military **Junta** in 1974: right wing **New Democracy**, which controlled parliament from 1974 to 1981 and from 1989 to 1993 and the **Panhellenic Socialist Movement (PASOK),** which controlled it from 1981 to 1989 and from 1993 to the present. Other political groups are the **Democratic Left**, the **Communist Party of Greece (KKE)**, and left-wing **SYRIZA**. Greece is presently ruled by a three party coalition, which seems to be becoming increasingly fragile.

Greek citizens maintain a wary scepticism toward politicians and authority figures. When polled about their fears for the near future, Greeks highlighted unemployment (97%), poverty (93%) and the closure of businesses (92%). Despite the awful economic situation, the vast majority of Greeks seem not to be in favour of leaving the Eurozone: default and a Euro exit could endanger Greece's continued membership of the EU. More importantly, though, there is a strong element of national pride. For many Greeks, leaving the Euro would seem like a national humiliation.

Local-level politics on the island operate differently from politics on the national level. Municipalities elect leaders more on the basis of personal qualities than political affiliation, and candidates for local office often do not run on a party ticket, but as independents.

Dealing with the large civil service bureaucracy is seen as a matter for creativity, persistence, and even subtle deception. Individuals often are sent from office to office before their affairs are settled. Those who are most successful operate through networks of personal connections.

The legal system is based on modified Roman law, with strong protection for the rights of the accused. There are criminal, civil, and administrative courts, and since 1984, the police force, which previously was divided into urban and rural units, has operated as a single force. There is little violent crime. Tax evasion often is considered the most serious legal concern.

The Hellenic Armed Forces are divided into an army, an air force, and a navy. There is universal conscription of all males at age twenty for eighteen to twenty-one months of service, with some deferments and exemptions: there are 160,000 soldiers on active duty and over 400,000 reservists. Continuing disputes and past wars are important parts of social memory.

Austerity

Austerity measures focus on cutting pensions. Salaries of better-paid public-sector workers such as central-bank employees, university teachers, judges and hospital doctors, will also be cut. Salaries at public-sector corporations are being reduced by 35% and capped at €5,000 a month, which means take-home pay of just €2,900 for bosses and fewer perks. Some cuts will be backdated: 110,000 civil-service jobs must be cut by 2016. The new cuts in salaries and pensions come on top of the 40% reductions already in place. Greece has experienced a 24% GDP contraction over five years, with unemployment at 25.5 % and youth unemployment at 55%, the highest in Europe. A humanitarian crisis has followed, with homelessness, mental illness and suicide at unprecedented levels. Hospitals cannot work for lack of basic medicines, schools have no textbooks or fuel for heating, people scour rubbish bins for food. The various lists of potential tax evaders, many of them supporters of the mainstream parties, disappear in the drawers of the elites. Politicians and rich tax evaders enjoy permanent immunity, while journalists who reveal them are prosecuted and many ordinary Greek people are afraid: historically, when a power system becomes obsolete radical change follows. The disastrous austerity measures may become the catalyst for changing the 40-year-old power system that has brought the country to its knees.

Civil Society and Corruption

American journalist Michael Lewis noted that modern Greek culture lacks any tradition of volunteerism and altruism and is afflicted by extraordinarily high levels of selfishness and corruption, which to him has culminated in the present Greek government-debt crisis. Commentators both within and without Greece have attributed this critical flaw in Greek culture to the Ottoman Empire's brutal mismanagement of Ottoman Greece, in which individual survival became more important than societal stability, tax resistance became a form of patriotism, and property and commercial tax systems were left in shambles, thereby making it impossible for Greece to create an functional civil society or an efficient modern state.

Despite this, voluntary organizations include hobby clubs, scouts, sports organizations, performance ensembles, environmental groups, craft cooperatives, and political pressure groups. Agricultural cooperatives are widespread, enabling family-based farmers to buy and sell in bulk. Trade unions are less well established.

Medicine and Health Care

The state-run National Health Service, a network of hospitals, clinics, and insurance organizations, was established in 1983. The service provides basic health care even in remote areas, but there is an over concentration of hospital facilities, doctors, and nurses in Athens and other major cities, a situation worsened on the islands by the current economic climate. Private health care facilities are used by those who can afford them. The health status of Greek citizens is roughly equivalent to that of Western Europe. Western concepts of *biomedicine* are well accepted but are supplemented for some individuals by longstanding cultural conceptions concerning the impact that certain foods, the wind, hot and cold temperatures, envy, and anxiety have on health.

Education

Higher education is strongly valued. There is a state run university, technical, and vocational school system whose capacity is short of demand. Entrance is achieved by nationwide examinations, and many secondary school students attend private afternoon schools to prepare for these tests. In the 1990s, 140,000 students annually vied for 20,000 university seats and 20,000 technical college seats. Since the imposition of austerity measures, the number of places is much reduced as institutes of learning have their funding eroded. Many ultimately seek an education abroad.

The Greek Community

Greek culture has evolved over thousands of years and is full of rules of conduct and traditions, many of which stem from the importance of religion in Greek society. The Greek Orthodox Church is a major influence in everyday Greek life. Specific religious festivals and rituals surrounding everything from birth and birthdays to marriage to death keep people's lives firmly rooted in the Church and in Greek culture.

There is an old dictum that *'One Christian is no Christian.'* And this is certainly true in Orthodox Greece. Of course there is the specific calling of the *eremitic* life (that of the hermit or solitary), but this is something which few can aspire to. For the generality of Greeks, they are saved by living in communities: in parishes or monasteries; in families. The necessity for their salvation of living in communities does not simply concern worshipping together, although this is of paramount importance. It means that they must also, as much as circumstances allow, live together, bearing one another's burdens and so fulfilling the law of Christ. Greeks take measures to ensure that there is always some *'community care'* with a host of things to be done to help, support and care for each other.

These are strong and almost unbreakable ties. They create relationships of give and take; Greeks oblige themselves to help the members of their network and can expect the same help back. These ties also create a strong aspect of social control – there are so many people who are entitled to keep an eye on a person and to interfere with what he is doing – not only parents and siblings, but the whole neighbourhood!

Greek culture is thus very group-oriented: building deep and lasting relationships is very important for Greeks. Affection between male adolescents and men is a very warming and refreshing facet of Greek culture, with unabashed signs of physical affection that have nothing to do with sex, but everything to do with friendship. Girls too, can be seen walking hand in hand or arm in arm. Greek men, especially in villages, but in general even in the cities, tend to respect women and to be unaggressive (and often paternal) towards them.

The Greek Family

Greek society consists of close-knit families where important social organizations have gradually evolved from the idea of family. The institution of Marriage also plays an important role in society. Marriage is considered the normal condition of adulthood. The word family in Greece refers to a particular social group whose members are related by blood or marriage at different levels or in different forms or combinations.

The conjugal family includes the husband and wife and their children. The extended family includes the conjugal family as well as ascendants of the husband and/or wife. Interestingly, the National Statistical Service of Greece considers all people who live under the same roof to be members of the family, regardless of whether they are related.

An individual who does not marry or who remains separate from his or her family is quite unusual. Sons and daughters live with their families until they marry, unlike the Northern European tradition of living independently between those two stages of life. However, in Greece as elsewhere, family life has changed with the evolution of the traditional rural life into an urban/industrial system: in contemporary Greek society individuals have an increasing influence on the way in which they wish to organize their private lives and many aspects of social behaviour, relationships, and roles have changed, especially in the cities.

Frequent communication and assistance between the two adult generations and children and youth are also very common for Greek families. The family offers both financial and emotional support to its members. As a result social difficulties like unemployment usually do not spawn problems like homelessness or a high criminality rate as seen elsewhere. Caring for the personal needs of the elderly, infirm, and orphaned is considered a family responsibility.

Family relationships carry over into business with nepotism largely seen as acceptable. It is very common for relatives to work for the same company because Greeks prefer to do business with those they know and trust. Companies are also hierarchical over the traditional respect for age and position.

Greek Family Values

In Greece, it is important to remember that the family, whether rural or urban, is also at the core of many Greek cultural traditions. For those of Greek heritage, immediate kin are often the most important people in their lives: this is the basis of the social structure, such as the wrongdoing of one family member bringing dishonour to the entire family. Through their families Greeks learn about patriotism, religion, traditions and customs and the importance of socialization.

Traditionally, Greek men are expected to provide the majority of financial support for the family while women are expected to provide the majority of the family's household support; although this is another tradition that has relaxed over the years due to modernization and cross-cultural living.

The very traditional view, expressing a conservative attitude toward the social role of women in general and respecting the position of the *oikokyrosyne* (woman of the house) is still strong on Skopelos, where older Greek women have always been required to care for their families, and to remain submissive to their husbands or whoever heads the family. The husband may act as the family's outside representative, but it is the wife who is the organizer of the household, the mediator in family disputes, and the guardian of the family's cohesiveness. Within the private sphere of the family, the opinions of the wife and mother receive great respect as she evaluates the behaviour of her husband and children and protects the family's honour.

Skopelos is a *matrilineal* society: wealth is passed on via the female line. By custom, the parents of each Skopelitan bride provide the new couple with at least a house and some property. The house and property remain in the bride's name.

Older People

The Greek family values their elders immensely. Elders are the cornerstone for each family's individual success and values. Family care of the elderly is still strong in Greece: younger people respect their elders and still accept them in certain roles. The old male is the connecting bond between the younger people who have left the village in search of better circumstances and those who remain. Beyond this psychological role, he acts as supervisor of the family's wealth. Both parents provide help to their children and they in turn help their parents since pensions are usually insufficient. In Greek households, it is normal and expected that a family member will care for an elder relative if he becomes ill or incapacitated. Elders are rarely placed in nursing homes or assisted living facilities. If the family needs additional help to provide care for the family member, it is much more common for the family to hire a private nurse.

Although the parents usually live separately from the young couple, the two pairs retain a close relationship. They visit each other often and both take part in family celebrations and festive lunches. The role of the grandmother is extremely important as care provider for the grandchildren.

Children

Greeks are noted for their strong sense of community. Despite urbanization, village life remains a strong societal influence. Village square-style meetings on topics relevant to the community are common on Skopelos, while the women of the neighbourhood sit on the stepped streets to gossip.

Within the Greek community, children are the centre of concern and of emotional and financial investment, not only for their parents but also for the extended family, whether related or not: the latter forms the basis for family and social relationships and the training of the young. Stories told by grandfathers, grandmothers and the older people of the neighbourhood about their lives and hardships; fairy tales, and nursery rhymes; all refer to and sustain a value system that has little to do with the modern, competitive society.

Greeks love children and will make a fuss of any small child encountered. Babies are treated like kings in Greece, and may be picked up and carried round the restaurant; children may be offered sweets by strangers. This behaviour is natural and normal within Greek society, where young children are still able to play in the street without supervision, in safety.

Social Status

Social status does not relate to economic class but results from a combination of wealth, education, occupation, and what is referred to as honour or love of honour (*philotimo*). While sometimes understood only as a source of posturing and argumentation, this concept refers to one's sense of social responsibility, esteem within the community, and attention to proper behaviour and public decorum. Peer pressure, gossip, belief in forces such as the evil eye, and the strong sense of proper behaviour and social responsibility engendered by *philotimo* operate as informal mechanisms of social control.

Much social life takes place within a close circle of family and friends. Group activities revolve around eating, drinking, playing games, listening to music, dancing, and animated debate and conversation.

Hospitality is seen as both a pleasure and a responsibility. Hosts are generous, and guests are expected to accept what is offered with only token protests. Hospitality is often extended to foreigners, but the deluge of travellers,

171

ambivalence about the impact of tourism, and the improper or condescending behaviour of some tourists complicate the situation.

Kerasma at the Coffeehouse

The coffeehouse is the social space where male social status is egalitarian, compared to the domestic and hierarchical status of women. The coffeehouse offers the male emotional expression of male friendship, 'a sentimental alternative to maternal love and amity of kinship' as it has been described. Regardless of a man's position in the village, he is able to make friendships at the coffeehouse, which may result in the sponsoring of each other as spiritual kin at marriage ceremonies.

Spiritual friendship (**koumbaria**) acts as an antithesis to the socio-economic significance of female wealth through the institution of dowry given by the bride's family. It is constructed between 'friends of the heart' and results in the feeling of **kefi, or 'good mood'.** Unlike kinship relations, there is no structure or function associated with male friendship: the opportunity to be able to choose a friend in the coffeehouse involves the emotional outlet of reciprocity not warranted by more fixed and permanent social arrangements.

The process begins with one friend treating another friend to **kerasma** or a drink. This is a gesture of friendliness that is reciprocated by the other at a later time establishing respect **(sevasmos),** the precursor to friendship. This reciprocity is not a compulsory practice; and it should always be given on another day, or it is implied that the giver cannot afford to buy a drink for a companion.

Friendship can also extend the boundaries of a single coffeehouse where, although a friend may be an outsider **(ksenos)** in the local setting, he will be offered hospitality **(filoksenia)** when coming to meet a friend in his village to drink at his friend's local coffeehouse. Although the friend is an outsider in local terms, hospitality is conceived of as a 'gift' that is symmetrically reciprocated when the friend who has been invited issues a return invitation. The concept of *ksenos* (outsider/foreigner) then changes to *Nos* (insider/ friend) where coffeehouses act to unify the emotional friendships established across village borders.

The gift of drink *(kerasma)* may return a favour *(khari)*. When reciprocal exchange of *kerasma* is established over time, so too is the *parea* - the company or group of friends. The table in the coffeehouse marks this friendship. Groups of friends will always sit at the same table. To the males in the coffeehouse, tables are always respected by others to be particular tables for particular friends that come to share conversation *(kouventa)*. The focus here is not on the reciprocity of buying the drinks but on the sentiment of 'drinking together'. It is a particular type of male friendship where *kardiakoi filoi* (friends of the heart) will participate in *kerazma* or the buying of drinks.

These gatherings often aim at the achievement of *kefi,* the sense of high spirits and relaxation that arises when one is happily transported by the moment and the company. Drinking may contribute to the attainment of *kefi*, but becoming drunk is considered disgraceful.

Tsipouro

In the mountain villages of Northern Greece and the islands of the Sporades, *kerazma* may also be taken to a new level: that is, to the sharing of *tsipouro*. The partaking of *tsipouro* displays another side of *kouventa*, but the same rules apply. Friends come together, usually at lunchtime, and share the drink and its associated *mezes*, which include fish, sea food, or vegetables and salad: unlike an *ouzo meze*, no meat is served. The food presented is at the discretion of the cooks, who pride themselves on not serving the same dish twice within a meal. *Kouventa,* the sharing of conversation, means that a *tsipouro* meal is long, drawn-out, leisurely, opinionated and frequently animated.

A cousin to ouzo, *tsipouro,* which does not share its same strong anise flavouring, has only recently come to the attention of foreigners - mainly because until the eighties it was illegal to distil *tsipouro* except for home consumption. Some tavernas still brew the drink according to their own recipe and the addition of herbs and spices means that many different flavours are to be found among *tsipouro* varieties. It can be drunk straight, over ice, or with water, accompanied by appetizers. A visitor should try it and experience the true meaning of *kefi!*

Komboloi

By the way, the *Komboloi* (beads) that many Greek men hold in their hands sitting outside the *kafeneion* have no religious meaning. Playing with them is only a way of killing time: they are *worry beads,* not a rosary.

Some Common Greek expressions

The instinct to reassure and relax others is built into the Greek character, another manifestation of the affection that is related to warm and nourishing family ties. No one is expected to be perfect, and no one is allowed to worry too much. The expression *Den Berazei* (which is best expressed in English by the words *'Never mind'* or *'Don't worry about it'*) is one of the most common Greek expressions, as is *Mi se niazei* (same thing), or *Min anisiheis* (*'Don't be uneasy',* literally). One also hears the expression *'Siga siga'* frequently in Greece, which means something like *'Take it easy'* or *'Gently does it',* or *'Give yourself time'.*

Greeks have a similar expression for demurring when thanked for something or complimented: *Na 'sai kala* (or, in the plural/formal usage, *Na 'ste kala*), which means, literally, *'May you be well'.* When uttered in response to a compliment, it can be an expression of shyness or reluctance to hear praise.

The same words are used sometimes at the end of a telephone conversation, or at the end of a visit. Other words said to those who are departing are *Sto kalo* or *Na pas/pate sto kalo* (which means literally, 'Go to the good').

Thank you is also frequently deflected by Greeks with the word *Tipota* which means *'nothing'*, much like the English expression, *'Think nothing of it,'* or *'Don't mention it'*. Many will also respond to expressions of gratitude with the words, *Sto theo* (*'to God'*, meaning *'Thank God, not me'*, with the implication that everything comes from God). *Ta Leme* means *'We'll speak soon.'*

Hatching, Matching and Dispatching

'Hatching, Matching and Despatching' is concerned with name days; birth and baptism; engagement and marriage; death and mourning. Most of the Greek customs and traditions connected with these and still present in the twenty-first century stem from the Greek Orthodox religion: births, marriages, funerals, all naturally revolve around the Greek Orthodox Church.

Hatching: Childbirth

There are many traditions, customs and superstitions surrounding children and childbirth. Children are very important to Greek families and the birth of a child is a celebrated event regarded with great joy. Customary gifts are bestowed upon the newborn, often including silver or gold coins. This practice is called *'to asimo to pethi*, or *'to silver the child.'* Other gifts are sometimes given to ward off the evil eye, such as a *'mati'* - a small blue stone with a black eye in the centre, or a *'filakto'* - a small cloth pouch containing sacred items such as crushed dried flowers from the Easter service.

On the *First Day After Childbirth*, the Priest offers special prayers for the mother and child. These usually take place in the home. On the eighth day after birth, the *Order of Ablution* is performed. Ablution means to wash with water and so this is the prescribed washing of the infant with a prayer, prior to it being given a name later. For forty days a new mother remains at home to recuperate and to care for her child. However, if the child has not survived, the woman still remains at home to heal physically and emotionally. During the time of her confinement, the woman does not normally receive Holy Communion, unless she is in danger of death.

When a child is born, a name is not given immediately: the child is called *to moro (baby)* and doesn't have a name until it is baptized. For the first forty days after the birth of the child, no visitors are allowed into the house. After this, until the baptism, the child can only be visited in the day – never in the night. This is due to the fact that the child has not yet been blessed by the Church and is therefore unable to ward off evil spirits on a daily basis. When people do come to visit, they sometimes leave coins under the baby's or mother's pillow to bring good luck and fortune.

The mother must not go out at night at all and no clothes of anyone inside the household, but particularly the mother and child, must be hung outside at night, lest the spirits use this as a means to getting inside the house. The spirits' intention is to corrupt the child with bad feelings and give him a 'bad heart'.

Churching

On the fortieth day after childbirth, the mother is brought to the temple to be *Churched*; that is to say, to receive a blessing as she begins attending Church and receiving the Holy Mysteries (Sacraments) once again. The child (if it has survived) is brought by the mother, who has already been cleansed and washed, accompanied by the intended sponsors (Godparents) who will stand at the child's Baptism. They all stand together in the *narthex* before the doors of the *nave* of the temple, facing east. The Priest blesses them and says prayers for the woman and the child, giving thanks for their wellbeing and asking God's grace and blessings upon them.

Baptism and Chrismation

For families who are strictly Orthodox, the baptism will take place immediately after the 40 day period, but generally now, the baptism will take place anywhere between the child's first and second years. The Baptismal Day is one of the most important days in the life of a Greek Orthodox.

It is a rule of the Orthodox Faith that every person, child or adult, should have a Godparent *(nouno/nouna)* at Baptism. In Greek tradition, the *koumbaros* (best man) or *koumbara* (Bride's Maid) of the parents' wedding will baptize the couple's first child. To serve as a Godparent is both a special honour and imposes responsibilities which last a lifetime. Along with the parents, the Godparent is charged with the responsibility of assisting in the spiritual development of the child. Whether a blood relative or not, the Godparent becomes a part of the *spiritual family* of that Godchild.

The Godparent traditionally provides: a complete change of clothes for the child; one bottle of olive oil; a cross for the child; three white candles; one of each of the following - a bar of soap, hand towel, bath towel, sheet; *Martyrika (witness)* pins or ribbons that are given to those who attend a baptism.

The baby must be provided with three changes of clothing for the ceremony. On arrival at the Church, the baby is undressed and wrapped in a white towel. Then the Priest blesses the water of the baptismal font and adds olive oil brought by the godparent. He immerses the baby three times in the name of the Trinity: this is both the initiation into the Church and a sign of forgiveness of sins. The godparent wraps the baby in a white sheet and holds it during the *Chrismation.* This follows immediately after baptism and is by anointing with holy oil called *Chrism.* The *Chrism* is used to anoint different parts of the body with a sign of the cross. The forehead, eyes, nostrils, mouth and ears, the chest, the hands and the feet are all anointed. The Priest says the words, *'The seal of the gift of the Holy Spirit'* as he makes the sign of the cross at each point.

After reading the Gospel lessons pertaining to baptism (chosen from the *Lectionary*), the baby receives its first Holy

Communion. It receives the Sacrament from the Priest who blesses the baby with *'myrrh'* (olive oil blessed by the Patriarch) as well as the baby's clothes. With the Godparent holding the baby, the Priest cuts a lock of its hair to symbolize its belonging to Christ.

Then, the baby is dressed with white clothes and the Priest puts a gold chain with a cross, provided by the God parent, on the baby's neck. He gives a baptismal candle to the godparent and lights it, before leading a procession of the family, along with the baby, three times around the baptismal font. The newly baptised Christian is now a layperson, a full member of the people of God (the 'Royal Priesthood'). All Christians present are called to be witnesses to the Truth of this.

Finally, the baby is given a name. If it is the first child born to the grandparents, it normally takes the grandfather's name if a boy; or grandmother's if a girl. There are no middle names as such, unless the child is born on the day of an Orthodox Saint. Should this be the case and it is the first grandchild, two names may be given - that of the Saint and another. If it is not the first grandchild, only the Saint's name will be given as this is seen as a very good omen for the child.

At the end of the ceremony, the parents kiss the Godparent's hands and receive the guest's wishes: *Na sas zisei! (Long life to your baby!).*

The ceremony is followed by a celebration at the family's house or a restaurant. On the third day after baptism, the Godparent gives the child a bath (no bath must be given prior to this). Then for three consecutive Sundays after the baptism, the Godparent should take the baby in baptismal garments to the Holy Altar to receive Holy Communion, carrying also one of the baptismal candles.

Ritual Impurity

For the majority of girls born and raised in the Orthodox tradition, puberty marked the time when mothers used to expose them to the tradition of 'Ritual Impurity' and the teachings of 'Uncleanness'. Pious Orthodox mothers explained to their young impressionable daughters that while they were menstruating, they were in a period of uncleanness, and therefore, must never touch anything at all related to the worship of God. This, mothers informed their daughters, included reading the Sacred Scriptures, venerating icons, lighting candles or lanterns, baking the bread of offering, kissing the hand of a Priest, and especially not participating in any Sacrament - most importantly that of Holy Communion. For some girls, this was (and sometimes still is) calmly accepted as a fact of womanhood.

Matching

The Betrothal

Although Western culture, particularly with the advent of the European Union, is impacting on the culture of Greece, the old traditions, especially in small or more remote towns and villages, still exist.

Quite often two families will discuss their respective offspring as potential partners for each other and in fact introduce them to each other. They will then be allowed to get to know each other to see if they are compatible and if there is sufficient affection for the relationship to develop into something further. If this is the case, the couple will continue to court until such a time as they decide that the girls' family be approached by the boy to ask for their daughter's hand in marriage. If they agree, then the couple will make a verbal contract to be engaged and married. Although this is not always the case and a lot of couples just meet and choose each other as they do in Western societies, in some villages the purpose of the marriage may well be not for love, but as a sound business proposition.

When the details of the marriage contract are settled between the couple's fathers, the Priest is invited to bless the engagement rings and places them on the left ring-finger of the man and woman. The guests wish the couple well by saying: *'Kala stephana' (Good crowns! - Have a good marriage!)* and *'I ora I kali' (That the good hour -* the marriage *- comes!).* Afterwards, the bride's father gives the groom's father a tray of basil for good luck. Then he hands his future son-in-law a glass of coins to signify that he will now support and provide for his bride.

The betrothal is far more important than the actual wedding itself. This is the personal commitment that the couple make to each other. From now on, they refer to each other as husband and wife. To end a betrothal is seen in the same light as a divorce and can be felt to be shameful by the families concerned.

In major towns you will often see many older men with younger wives - older men are more secure financially. In rural communities it is more important that the man be young and strong.

On Skopelos, the traditional betrothal dress, now no longer worn, but seen on occasions at festivals, is distinguished from other traditional costumes by its very broad green border. It can be seen in the Folklore Museum. Even today, some brides have a dowry made by their mothers, grandmothers and aunts, consisting of sheets, towels and hand made embroideries, and the father of the bride offers a furnished home to his daughter and son-in-law as a wedding gift.

The Wedding

The Greek Orthodox wedding, regardless of where in the world it is held, follows a prescription established centuries ago. Nowhere in the ceremony do the bride and groom exchange or recite vows: instead the service is for the couple to announce their intentions to start a home together, based on their belief in God's blessing.

Preparation for marriage begins with counselling by the Priest for three sessions. This is the first of many allusions to the number three and it symbolizes the Holy Trinity. Only after these meetings will a Priest perform the ceremony.

In a traditional Greek Orthodox wedding, the engagement and the reception are included as part of the whole ceremony. Although in today's society the engagement on the day is more of a formality than an actual betrothal, it is carried out with as much seriousness as the vows and the prayers.

On the morning of the wedding the groom's male friends, the *vratimi*, set out to collect the *koumbaros (best man)*, or *koumbara (best woman.* The position can be taken by either or both). They used to hoist a white flag decorated with apples and herbs outside the house of the groom and escort him to the bride's house, but this no longer happens. In times past, the wedding would take place at the groom's house and the *'vratimi'* would load the bride's dowry into the groom's carriage for the journey: they used to fire their guns to ward away evil spirits. During the journey, the *vratimi* would bless the couple by showering them with cottonseed, rice, small coins and flower petals.

The Koumbaros/Koumbara

The *Koumbaros (koumbara* is interchangeable from now on) has a very important role as best man. He acts like a director or sponsor and instigates the actions of the ceremony. Along with the couple and the Priest, his role in the ceremony is a necessity and carries great weight. Often, he bears the main cost of the wedding celebration. It is not unusual to have several 'best men' in order to spread these costs. After the wedding he remains an important figure in the couple's life, eventually becoming Godfather to their first child.

Led by the *koumbaros*, the groom leaves his house, and walks to the bride's family home. The bride is dressed with the help of friends and women from her family, and kept hidden, for it is bad luck for the groom to see the bride before the ceremony. Once the father of the bride formally agrees to the marriage, the best man leads the groom to the Church. The *Koumbaros* must bring with him two large white candles tied in a bouquet of orange blossoms: they will be used in the traditional Orthodox Joining Ceremony. The groom stands outside the Church, supported by the *vratimi* and holding the wedding bouquet, to await his bride.

The *Koumbaros* then goes to the home of the bride: he feeds her a slice of cake and helps her to put on her shoes. Then he, the bride, her family and the bridesmaids walk to the

Church, accompanied by musicians, singing and dancing. When they arrive, the groom offers the bride the bouquet: when she takes it, everybody knows the wedding will go ahead.

A Greek Orthodox wedding has restrictions on when it may be performed: one such restriction is the period of the first fifteen days of August. Greek Orthodox weddings cannot be performed during periods of fasting, after Easter and Christmas and the day preceding a holy day. There are also superstition-based restrictions, one of which prohibits marriages in a Leap Year, which is considered to be unlucky. There are also restrictions that may apply to a particular Church, so the Priest must be consulted before setting a date.

Bridal Wear

Greek brides used to wear a traditional veil, either yellow or red in colour, representing fire. These coloured veils protected the bride from evil spirits. Brides also used other good luck charms on this special day. Some carried a lump of sugar to guarantee a sweet life. Others carried ivy, a symbol of endless love. The colour red is still important today, much as wearing 'something blue' in many Western traditions.

In the past, brides carried herbs or grains as a fertility rite: some contemporary Greek brides still include fresh herbs in the bouquet; rosemary, thyme, mint and basil are popular and aromatic. As the bride proceeds down the centre aisle of the Church, it is not uncommon for her to be 'spat' upon by the wedding guests for luck: keep in mind that no actual spitting happens, and the gesture is symbolic.

The Wedding Ceremony

The wedding ceremony of the Greek Orthodox Church is an ancient and meaningful service that has been celebrated in its present form for centuries. The service is abundant with symbols that reflect marriage: love, mutual respect, equality and sacrifice.

The format of the ceremony itself cannot be altered in any significant manner: no music or musicians may participate inside the Church. The only personalization the couple can do is in the selection of particular music and/or readings for the wedding reception. Although the bride and groom are free to invite guests of their choosing, the Church prefers that only those who have been baptized as Greek Orthodox enter the Church.

Generally in a tight-knit community, it is likely that the entire neighbourhood will be guests at the Church and at the wedding. The service takes about an hour and although the couple are already officially engaged, the ceremony is a combination of the *Service of Betrothal* and the ceremony of the *Sacrament of Marriage*.

The Betrothal Ceremony

The betrothal ceremony begins with the Priest lighting two white candles and handing them to the couple. The candles symbolize the light of Christ, a beacon to illuminate their way and a symbol of the couple's acceptance of Christ in their lives.

The Exchange of Rings

As the honoured director of the ceremony, the *koumbaros* leads the ring changing ceremony: during this the wedding bands are taken from the left hands of the Bride and Groom and placed on the right hand. Next, the Priest first blesses and then places the ring on the third finger, right hand of the bride and groom. (It is thought that it is the right hand of God that blesses and to which Christ ascended).The *koumbaros* then exchanges the rings three times on the couple. This is to invoke the presence of the Holy Trinity and to symbolize how the strength of one outweighs the weakness of the other, and the perfections of one make up for the other's imperfections, so that a married couple between them make a perfect whole. The Priest makes the sign of the cross

185

over the couple's heads and, three times, declares that they are betrothed. No vows are exchanged during the ceremony: in fact the couple do not speak at all because marriage is not considered a contract but a union of two people in love.

The Sacrament of Marriage

At this point the service continues with the Sacrament of Marriage. The couple join right hands, as the Priest blesses their union: their hands stay joined until the ceremony concludes. The open right hand is symbolic of strength, resource and purpose. The coming together of two right hands is thus representative that both bride and groom can depend on one another. It also symbolizes the resources that each will bring to the marriage, as well as the merging of their lives together into one.

The Stephanas

The most important moment of the ceremony is the placing of the *Stephanas* (Crowns) on the couples' heads. The crowns are always very beautiful and elaborate, made of silver, sometimes with flowers and pearls intricately woven into them. Traditionally, the crowns were woven with orange blossoms, sometimes interspersed with olive leaves. The *koumbaros* swaps the wedding bands back and forth between the couple's heads three times, to signify the Holy Trinity.

The crowns can be said to symbolise many things. Most believe that it crowns the couple as King and Queen of their own little kingdom, their home. Others say that it evokes the crown of thorns worn by Jesus and others that it signifies the couples' triumph over passion and are a reward for their virtue.

The crowns are joined together by a ribbon, symbolising the unity of the couple forever from this moment forth. After the ceremony, the crowns are removed and placed on the altar.

The Common Cup

The crowning ceremony is followed by readings which include retelling the first miracle of Jesus - converting water into wine by at the wedding of Canaan in Galilee. Wine is then given to the couple as a remembrance of the miracle. The Bride and Groom take three sips of wine from the same cup, which is also symbolic of the life they will share. The cup represents life and symbolises the couple's mutual sharing of joy and sorrow. As they drink wine from the common cup, they are reminded that from that moment they will share everything, doubling their joys and dividing their sorrows. The drinking of wine is separate and apart from Holy Communion, which takes place before the wedding day.

There is a tradition of the bride stamping on the groom's feet at some point during the wedding ceremony: success in this venture is said to guarantee a wife the upper hand throughout her marriage. The problem is, in some Greek families, she tends to dominate throughout the duration of her son's marriage as well!

The Walk of Isaiah

The bride and groom kiss the Bible, then the Priest, the groom and the bride join hands and make three circles around the altar, followed by the *Koumbaros*, who walks behind the couple to hold the crowns in place. They all stop after each quarter turn, so that guests can shower them with good wishes in the form of rice, flowers and sugared almonds. In this way they recognize the Trinity and express their happiness at the union of the two families. The ceremony is called the *'March of Isaiah'* and they are the first steps the couple make together into their new life together.

Once the ceremonial walk is concluded, the Priest again blesses the couple and removes their crowns: he beseeches God to bless the couple with a long, happy life together. The Priest then separates the hands of the couple, reminding them that as God has joined them, so He alone can separate them.

After the ceremony, the bridal couple stays in the Church. All the guests kiss them and wish them *Na zisete!* (Long life to you!)

Unlike wedding ceremonies in most non-Orthodox Churches, marriage in the Orthodox Church is not a contract - a legal agreement with the exchange of vows or promises - between two people. Rather, marriage is the setting up, by two people, of a miniature Church within the greater Family Church, with the spiritual purpose being the mutual salvation of the husband and wife: each is to help and encourage the other in saving his or her soul; each exists for the other, as a companion, a helper, a friend.

The Orthodox wedding ceremony is a public affirmation of the commitment the couple made to each other at their engagement and reaffirmed in the wedding ceremony. It is a joyful affair, celebrated by the whole community and often, on the mainland, involving a thousand guests.

Here on Skopelos, we have no Aphrodite's Palace - a large, purpose built place in which to hold weddings where the guests are invited in such numbers - so large numbers are invited to the Church and a few families only go to the reception.

Although marriage is seen as a permanent commitment in life and in death, remarriage and divorce are permitted in certain circumstances.

Koufettas

In traditional Greek weddings, *'koufetta'* are placed in odd numbers in little bags. The fresh almonds have a bittersweet taste, reminding us that life is both bitter and sweet: the hardness of the sweet represents the endurance of marriage. The sugar coating is added in the hope that the life of the newlyweds will have more sweetness than bitterness. The odd number is indivisible, symbolising how the husband and wife will share everything and remain undivided. White symbolizes purity. The egg shape represents fertility and the new life which begins with marriage. Sugar-coated almonds, known as Jordan Almonds are sweets also typically served at Greek wedding receptions, carried to guests on a silver tray. The belief holds that if an unmarried woman takes them off the tray and puts them under her pillow, she will dream of the man that she will marry that night.

Walnuts

On Skopelos, an old tradition was to end the wedding ceremony with honey and walnuts offered to the bride and groom from silver spoons. Walnuts are chosen because they break into four parts; symbolising the bride, the groom, and the two sets of family.

The Reception

After the ceremony, everybody goes to the wedding reception, which is usually a restaurant rented for the night, where they dance, eat and drink. The reception includes the traditional *money dance* in which guests pin money to the couple's clothes, or put money into a money bag. The *Kaslamantiano* circle dance is performed by all and the bride and groom dance the *Isaiah dance* together. Traditional Greek food is on the menu.

In another ancient tradition the couple eats a small cake made of traditional ingredients of honey, sesame seeds and quince. A new trend features tossing money to the musicians, but the tradition of smashing dishes on the floor for good luck is dying out.

Despatching

Death and Mourning

In Greece, some beliefs about death and the afterlife date back to antiquity. *'Charos'* was the ferryman of the dead in classical mythology. When someone has a life-threatening illness Greeks often describe this as a person's *'fight with Charos'*. The afterlife is known as *'Hades'* after the god of the underworld in classical mythology. In antiquity the deceased was provided with items for the journey to and life in the underworld. Even now, small personal items that belonged to the deceased are placed in the person's coffin.

However, for most Greeks the beliefs, rituals and traditions surrounding death and mourning are founded in the Greek Orthodox religion, which has a total belief in life after death and the resurrection of the dead.

Followers believe in eternal life: thus the Church strongly emphasises a positive outcome in death - that the deceased is alive with God. Death is a *sleep*, rather than the end. In fact, the English word *cemetery* comes from the Greek word *kimitirio*, literally meaning *sleeping place*. While death is the separation of the soul (the spiritual dimension of each person), from the body (the physical dimension), the physical body will be reunited with the soul at the *Last Judgement*.

This notion of the eternal life of the soul and the integrity of the body underpins many of the traditions surrounding death and mourning. For example, cremation is forbidden as it represents the destruction of the eternal physical body. Organ donation, too, was originally prohibited. However the Church does support the use of transplants and Church leaders have recently shown a more supportive attitude towards organ donation. The Church has no objection to autopsy.

Suicide, the taking of one's own life, is regarded as self-murder and as such, is a sin. More importantly, it may be evidence of a lack of faith in a loving, forgiving, sustaining

God. If a person has committed suicide because of a belief that such an action is rationally or ethically defensible, the Orthodox Church denies that person a Church funeral, because such beliefs and actions separate a person from the community of faith. The Church shows compassion, however, on those who have taken their own life because of mental illness or severe emotional stress, when a physician can verify a condition of impaired rationality.

Any parishioner in good standing with the Orthodox Church is entitled to a funeral service: however, Orthodox Christians who have expressed in their wills the desire to be cremated may not have a funeral in the Church.

Imminent Death

If an elderly person is in palliative care, or so unwell that death appears imminent, the family will usually want a Priest to administer communion and/or confession. The Priest is expected to respond quickly: as well as administering the Sacraments he will support the family members.

Trisagion

The prayer service held by the Priest just after death and in the presence of the deceased is called the *Trisagion*. On the night before the funeral the *Trisagion* is usually held again, either at a Church or in the chapel of a funeral home. This is also an occasion for viewing the deceased. The *Trisagion* is thereafter repeated, either in Church or at the grave, usually on the third day, the ninth day, the fortieth day, six months, and one year after the death.

The Vigil

Traditionally, Greek women - who historically have functioned as the keepers of the home, family, birth, and death - are designated responsible for death-related customs: in the past, there would be vigils in family homes where for

24 hours women would sing ritual *mirologia* (funeral dirges) over the body of the deceased. Although this ritual wailing is not followed by Greeks today, the vigil, along with many other traditional beliefs and customs remain important on Skopelos.

In many homes the women of the family actually dress, bathe and prepare the bodies of close relatives for burial: the hands and feet of the deceased are tied together with ribbon. The body is displayed in the home of the deceased prior to the funeral in a ritual known as the *viewing*. Flowers brought to the house are laid on the body until only the head is exposed. The entire community is invited to attend the viewing and funeral, while the other successive events primarily include those family and friends closest to the deceased. These events collectively represent a movement from intense mourning within a religious context to the after-meal's more social atmosphere with lots of fond reminiscing about the deceased.

Mourning Customs

The Church's officially designated period of mourning is forty days. Upon the death of a family member, women prepare and distribute important death-related foods such as *kollyva* (which represents the soul of the deceased and symbolises everlasting life, made of wheat representing the life cycle of death and regeneration) and *paximathia* (dry twice-baked biscuits), purchased from Greek cake shops or home-made. Relatives and friends visit the home of the grieving family both before and after the funeral, bringing drinks and food to share with family members and other guests: brandy, wine, coffee, and *paximathia* are the food and drinks most commonly associated with the period of mourning.

The body is always buried with the other family members, on top of the previous member's grave. A daughter who has been married will be buried with her husband's family, as she becomes part of that family when she marries him. A single daughter of marriageable age who dies is often even today dressed in a wedding dress before being placed in the coffin. She is buried wearing a wedding crown (*stephania*) and a wedding ring. The family looks after the grave as if it is the new home of the departed, keeping it clean at all times and laying fresh flowers regularly. Sometimes candles are lit.

The wearing of black as a mark of respect depends on how close the family members were to the deceased. The immediate family members of the deceased traditionally wear black clothing for at least forty days. During this time they do not participate in social occasions - parties or family celebrations - and they do not dance or listen to music. Many individuals choose to extend this period to one year or even longer, and in some cases, widows or widowers continue to wear black for the rest of their lives.

In the past, widows would cut their hair short at this time. Traditionally, women in the immediate family wear black for a year. If a husband dies, the wife is supposed to wear black forever to respect her husband, unless she is young enough one day to marry again. Otherwise, the wife is expected to grieve for the remainder of her life. The only time she may go away from black is if she attends family weddings or baptisms, as black is bad luck at these joyous occasions. Then she may wear grey or dark blue instead. If a wife or female member of the family dies, the husband or relative wears a black armband. In some villages, a black material is hung over the doorway of the house to show that someone has recently died. On Skopelos, Greek men do not shave for a period of forty days after the death of a close family member.

Funeral and Burial

On Skopelos, the funeral must take place quickly, as there are no refrigeration facilities on the island. The date and time of the funeral is arranged directly with the local parish Priest.

Funerals are held on weekdays, rarely on Saturdays and never on Sundays. Funeral notices are placed in the local Greek newspapers - mostly in *Neos Kosmos* - either by family members or the funeral directors. Or posters with blue or black borders are placed on walls and telegraph poles at strategic points around town announcing the *kideia* (funeral), or the *mnimosyna* (memorial service).

Funeral Service in the Church

The Orthodox funeral service emphasizes the reality of death and the new life of the deceased. It is a positive service featuring prayers for forgiveness and repose of the departed's soul. Priests wear white to symbolize the joy of the resurrection. Funerals take place within the Church and are only allowed at a cemetery or mortuary chapel with special permission.

The deceased and the family arrive at the Church where the Priest begins the service by meeting the family, friends, and casket at the front door. Chanting, he leads them into the sanctuary for the service. The family sits or stands in the front row before the icon of Christ in the *iconostasion*. The body of the dead person, is carried - feet first - into the Church for the burial service and set in the centre of the *nave* - facing the altar, which faces Constantinople and the sunrise, symbol that after the night of death, there will be a re-awakening. The open casket is arranged so that the eyes of the deceased look east towards the altar, the direction for which Christ will rise again.

The coffin is opened and an icon of Christ or the patron Saint is placed in the hands, a wreath (with the *Trisagion* printed on it) is placed on the forehead and the hand-cross is placed in the coffin near the head of the departed. Candles are distributed to the worshippers who, receiving the light from the Priest, hold them lit throughout the service until near the end.

The Greek Orthodox funeral ceremony takes between thirty and sixty minutes and is not part of a larger service. The Priest leads the bereaved in hymns, scripture, readings and prayers, asking God to give rest to the departed soul and forgive all sins. The Priest then invites the visitors to 'Come and kiss (pay respects) the one that was with us a short time ago.'

After the *Dismissal* and *'Memory Eternal,'* friends come to say a last goodbye to the departed. Everyone moves to the front of the Church where they bow in front of the open casket. They may kiss the hand-cross which is set on the side of the coffin or the icon placed in the hands of the deceased. The closest relatives should be given an opportunity to spend several minutes with the departed alone. They sit near the casket or by the door of the Church and guests express their sympathy to the family.

To conclude, the Priest pours oil and dirt on the body in the form of a cross, saying, *'Wash me with hyssop and I shall be pure, cleanse me and I shall be whiter than snow.'* The casket is closed and the service ends.

The coffin is then carried all the way to the cemetery, or to the hearse, which on Skopelos is a small blue van. The choir sings the *Trisagion*, and the bells are rung slowly. The funeral cortege proceeds to the cemetery, situated on the old road to Raches (which is off the ring road), where a short grave-side service of *entombment* is sung by the Priest. Family members may stay and witness the lowering of the casket if they desire.

The dead are buried with their heads pointing east, so that they will be able to witness the angel's trumpet blast to signal the *Second Coming of Christ.*

The Rite of Blessing of the Cross
Since pre Christian times, it has been customary to mark the place of burial by the erection of a grave mound. The Christian Church has adopted this tradition, beatifying

the grave mound with the Holy Life-giving Cross, which may be depicted on a gravestone or elevated over it. The cross on the grave mound is placed at the feet of the buried Christian, so that he will be facing the Crucifix. The Priest then performs The Rite of Blessing of the Cross. Those present may place a flower on the casket before it is lowered or while it is being lowered into the ground.

The Makaria (Mercy Meal)

Although it is not a religious custom, family members traditionally host a wake after the funeral - in their home, or at a cafe. On arrival at the wake all guests are offered brandy, and either before or after the meal Greek coffee and *paximathia* (dry biscuits) are served.

Afterwards, close family mourners share a meal called a *Makaria* to celebrate the life of the deceased. It provides an opportunity for the relatives and friends to refresh themselves and remember their loved one in an informal setting. Traditionally fish is served as a sign of fasting and mourning that the departed has left this life.

Memorial Services

Memorials and funerals are equally significant in Greek culture. This is evident in the number of notices for memorial services placed in Greek newspapers. At memorial services family members and loved ones pray for forgiveness and mercy for the soul of the deceased. At the *Last Judgement*, to be held at the time of Christ's second coming, the soul of the deceased will be cast into either an ultimate state of blessedness or damnation. Memorial services enact the belief that prayer can intercede in the granting of forgiveness, thereby providing rest to the soul of the deceased.

The most widely observed memorial service, *Mnimosyno*, is held on the Sunday closest to the fortieth day after the death. According to Orthodox belief, Christ remained on earth for forty days after the Resurrection.

This memorial service, at which the Priest prays for forgiveness for the deceased, is part of the regular Sunday Church service. Relatives and friends attend the service and family members sit in the front row. The family provides a tray of *kollyva* – boiled wheat prepared with sugar, walnuts, cinnamon and other spices. Using icing sugar and almonds, the *kollyva* is decorated with a cross and the deceased person's name and placed on a table with candles at the front of the Church.

At the end of the service the *kollyva* is distributed to the congregation and people attending the memorial service are invited to join the family for a meal. The meal shared on this occasion is similar to the one served at the time of the funeral.

Memorial Service Dates

Memorial services may also be held three months and six months after the death, on the anniversary of the death, on the third anniversary and on the Saturdays dedicated to the souls - *Psychosavata* - which occur four times a year and are dependent on the dates of Lent and Easter. Memorial services cannot be held on the following days:

♦ From the Saturday of Lazarus until the Sunday of St Thomas (dates vary depending on Easter)
♦ Christmas Day
♦ The Feast of the Parish Church
♦ On the Dormition of the Virgin Mary (15 August)

And on the feast days of the Lord:

♦ Circumcision of our Lord (1 January)
♦ Epiphany (6 January)
♦ The Presentation (2 February)
♦ The Annunciation (25 March)
♦ The Ascension, (40 days after Easter, or Pascha)
♦ Pentecost (50 days after Easter, or Pascha)
♦ The Transfiguration (6 August)

Exhumation

Unless it is an old family plot, the burial site is only rented from the Church. After a period of time (not less than 3 years) the body is exhumed, washed with rose water or wine and certain bones (the skull and long bones) are placed in a casket and returned to the family, who may then put it in the ossuary or take it to the family land for reburial. An ossuary, also referred to as a bone house, is a facility for the storage of human bones. While the idea of an ossuary makes some individuals squeamish, ossuaries have been a part of human life for thousands of years. Ossuaries can range from complex underground crypts to simple wooden boxes. They play a vital role in several world religions which practice exhumation of bodies after burial. Many countries have ossuaries that people can visit, some of which include architectural features made from bone including chandeliers, wall decorations, and flooring. Most ossuary buildings contain individual boxes of human bone, also called ossuaries. There is a small ossuary chapel in the graveyard at Skopelos *Chora* and an old ossuary at the Monastery of Taxiarchos near Glossa.

Greek Expressions of Sympathy

Greek phrases used by family and friends at this time include:

- *Zoi se sas* : May life be granted to you (said to family members at the funeral).
- *Syllypitiria* : My condolences (said only at the funeral).
- *O Theos na ton/tin synghoresi* : May God forgive him/her (said to family members at the funeral and at memorial services).
- *O Theos na ton/tin anapafsi* : May God rest his/her soul (said to family members at the funeral and at memorial services).
- *Zoi se mas* : May life be granted to us (said amongst mourners and to family members at the funeral and at memorial services).

Traditional Crafts

Handicrafts have their roots in the rural crafts—the material-goods necessities—of ancient civilizations, and many specific crafts have been practiced for centuries; while others are modern inventions, or popularizations of crafts which were originally practiced in a limited geographic area. In Greece, many traditional crafts contribute to a sense of personal history and personal identity. Learning and practising traditional skills in companionship with others is experienced as binding the self symbolically to family and the wider community.

There are still many trades being practiced and handed down from father to son: for example, there are many carpenters on the island, possibly due to the island's history of boat building, and some are still making the traditional couches and trunks. A sector of the population still takes its income from fishing: fresh fish is sold from small boats (*caiques*) on the waterfronts of both Skopelos and Loutraki.

There are many islanders that have continued their traditional family trades and crafts, not only as a means of income, but to ensure the trade is not lost. Most of the current traditional craftsmen were apprentices who learned their trade under the watchful eye of an old craftsman, many of whom were their fathers and grandfathers. Despite the difficulties that the old professions have encountered - for example, the naval carpenters had no work when the shipyards closed and the old ceramic workshops were industrialised, trades and crafts continue.

For women, the arts of cross-stitching, knitting and weaving with a loom are intrinsically embedded in the Greek culture. This tradition goes way back in time and used to be a woman's duty, as well as a favourite pastime. They were activities that many mothers would do collaboratively to bond while they were creating their daughter's dowries. Often, girls started at a young age in order to fill their dowry chest. The

199

time of pride was when they would show off their creations to their guests on their wedding day, a sign that the girl would be a good and qualified housewife.

Times change, but the long-standing traditions of pottery, metalworking, rugmaking, woodcarving, and textile production can be seen in shops and workplaces all over the Sporades.

Embroidery

Greek embroidery is noted for its exquisite variety of colour, symbolism and varying techniques. The most notable classic techniques are *grafta,* which involves patterns drawn freehand onto the fabric, and *Metrita-xombliasta*, made by counting the threads in the fabric. Both these techniques and others are employed to create exquisite embroidered pieces.

Many embroidered pieces such as Church decorations, pillows, valances and hems, are drawn from the Byzantine tradition. They feature decorative motifs with complex floral designs, mermaids, double-headed eagles, snakes, winged snakes, animals, birds and female figures at prayer. Many 20th century framed embroideries or decorations feature proverbs or figures drawn from history or the mythology of ancient Greece.

The women of Skopelos traditionally gathered in the narrow streets or courtyards to pass their time embroidering together. However, as life in the village catches up with the rapid pace of contemporary society, this handmade craft is being replaced by machine-made replicas imported from China and Greece to meet the demand of tourists.

Lace making

Lace making in the Greek islands can be traced back to ancient times, but was reintroduced to the villages from the West during the Renaissance. A true lace is created when a thread is looped, twisted or braided to other threads independently from a backing fabric. Originally linen, silk, gold, or silver threads were used; as in the headdress of the traditional costume of Skopelos. Now lace is often made with cotton thread, although linen and silk threads are still available.

Some lace work, such as **krossia** (tassels) and **desies** (ties) is made using the hands alone. Other types of lace work are made with small tools, such as shuttles, sock needles, smaller lace needles or bobbins. Examples of this form of art can be seen in the home and in traditional costume, and are used to decorate weavings and embroideries.

Greek lace making includes *'kopaneli'* (the border lace), *'asprokentito'* (the cutwork), *'macroulos'* or *'traversa'* (the long, thin pieces). Of particular note is the **Kopaneli**, which dates from Byzantine times. It involves the technical interweaving of many silk threads on a vertical layout that are rolled around 14 narrow and long wood sticks that are called kopanelia. Some of the most common motifs are the meander, spiral, roses, grape vines, and pine cones. Knotted lace includes macramé and tatting. Tatted lace is made with a shuttle or a tatting needle. Crocheted and knitted lace can also be found on the island.

Weaving

From the Homeric, through the Classical and into the Byzantine period, the loom was prevalent in Greek homes. This continued even through the Turkish occupation. The 18th and 19th centuries saw the art of weaving flourish and production of wool, cotton and silk increased significantly.

Culture and tradition show that weaving was one of the oldest crafts of the Island, and is an important element of Folk Art. At work on the *telaro* or *argastir* (loom), women wove the family's clothes and cloth for use in their homes. The raw materials were wool, flax, silk and cotton, which in many cases they themselves had produced, processed and dyed.

Greek weavings are characterised both by richness of colour and the arrangement of decorative designs into bands. The oldest and most common designs are geometrical, featuring variations and combinations of the rhombus as their basic motif. Other common patterns involve stylised floral and animal motifs, human figures and scenes inspired by religion or history.

Flokati rugs have been woven in Greece since the 5th century. Originating high up in the Pindos Mountains, and made from thick sheep's wool, Vlach shepherds used the flokati for clothing and sleeping during cold winter months. The shaggy textured rugs are not actual sheepskins; although made entirely of wool, it has been carded and spun into a yarn which is then soaked in the waters of a fast-running stream. The wool fibres swell in size during this process, providing the body of the rug with a thick and luxuriant texture.

As with other woven products, although the looms still exist in some older houses of Skopelos, the skilled workers are no longer to be found to make them.

Wood carving

Triantafyllos Boundalas was born in Skopelos 1927, into a family of naval carpenters and shipbuilders whose art has been handed down from generation to generation. His great-grandfather was born in the Kostantza in the Black Sea: a master craftsman, he had two shipyards, in Kostantza and in Vraila, and made many boats. His grandfather was also a good shipbuilder. His father went to America taking with him his wife and son. He developed his own shipyard and later returned to Skopelos where he continued working in the local shipyards.

Triandafyllos started learning the trade at the early age of 15 years. He loved the craft, even though his family had originally intended him for the Priesthood. When the shipyards began to close in Skopelos, and wooden ships were succeeded by metal ones that were cheaper and easier to build, Triantafyllos turned his attention to model boats.

All the model boats he makes are precision made copies of real boats and are able to float on the sea. The creation and manufacture of a faithful model boat takes 8 months or more.

This traditional art is continued by his son Yannis Boundalas and his wife Ourania at their workshop off the ringroad of Skopelos *Chora.*

Pottery

The art of village pottery making has not changed all that much in the last few thousand years; often, the clay is still dug from the surrounding hills, the wheels are in most cases powered by foot and the kilns still fuelled with wood. Only men were allowed to make pots in Ancient Greece, though women were permitted to paint them; but on the island there are potters of both sexes.

Skopelos has a number of shops and workshops selling handmade Greek and local pottery. One of them, Rodios, was established by Nicholaos Rodios, who moved from Kythnos to Skopelos in 1900 and became a renowned artisan. He patented his technique in 1930 qnd his work has continued through the generations since, with the family producing pottery which is clearly based on the classical art form and having a lustre, brilliance and black colour so good that it is difficult to distinguish it from ancient works of art. The present scion, Nikos Rodios, uses the same traditional production methods, including a foot-pumped wheel, and extends the old archaic shapes into more modern art forms.

China Plates

China plates are to be found decorating many of the exterior walls of churches and chapels of the island, many of them English iron ware brought back by sailors and merchants from their voyages. Plates, dishes and tiles were also brought back from Turkey, the Black Sea, Italy and other European countries; all dating to the eighteenth century. Because of this, some excellent examples of Ottoman and European pottery have survived on the walls of the Orthodox Churches and monasteries. Unfortunately, many of these ceramics have suffered serious damages from the passage of time, people's ignorance and natural elements.

Pomegranates

Replica pomegranates are to be found in most jewellery and china shops on the island; the fruit was notable in Greek mythology because of its association with Persephone, the goddess of the Underworld. In one version of the myth, Persephone was kidnapped by Hades and taken off to live in the Underworld as his wife. Her mother, Demeter (goddess of the Harvest), went into mourning for her lost daughter and thus all green things ceased to grow. Zeus, the highest ranking of the Greek gods, could not allow the Earth to die, so he commanded Hades to return Persephone. It was the rule of the Fates that anyone who consumed food or drink in the Underworld was doomed to spend eternity there. Persephone had no food, but Hades tricked her into eating six pomegranate seeds while she was still his prisoner and so, because of this, she was condemned to spend six months in the Underworld every year. During these six months, when Persephone is sitting on the Throne of the Underworld next to her husband Hades, her mother Demeter mourns and no longer gives fertility to the earth. This became an ancient Greek explanation for the seasons.

Alternatively known as the 'fruit of the dead', in ancient times pomegranates were offered to Demeter and to the other gods for fertile land, for the spirits of the dead and in honour of compassionate Dionysus. In modern times the fruit still holds strong symbolic meanings for the Greeks. It is used when preparing *Kollyva*, which consists of boiled wheat mixed with sugar and decorated with pomegranate seeds, and which is eaten by Greeks to commemorate the dead.

On important days in the Greek Orthodox calendar, such as the Presentation of the Virgin Mary and on Christmas Day, it is traditional to have at the dinner table '*polysporia*', also known by their ancient name '*panspermia,*' in some regions of Greece. When one moves into a new home, it is conventional for a house guest to bring as a first gift a pomegranate, which is placed under/near the *ikonostasion* (home altar) of the house, as a symbol of abundance, fertility and good luck. It is also traditional in Greece to break a pomegranate on the ground at weddings and on New Year's Eve. Pomegranate decorations for the home are very common in Greece and are also sold in most home goods stores in one form or another.

Making Knives

Most Greek men carried or possessed a knife and the tradition of handmade knives was strong until recently. Now Christos Patsis is the last manufacturer of these handmade knives. He loves his work and wants to teach it to his son so that the profession is not lost from the island. According to Christos, 'The technique of the manufacture of knives in Skopelos is passed from generation to generation and the cutler wrote his name above the name of his island (when signing his work)'. The knife blade is wrought on the anvil in stainless steel, while the handle is made from goat horns that have been left to dry for 3 years. The horns are heated in the fire and shaped, before being placed in a vice and left to dry. The handmade knives of Christos Patsis are rare and coveted. He makes about 300 pieces during the winter to sell during the summer.

Lantern making

Prior to the advent of electricity, lanterns were of necessity placed outside each house, Church and monastery;

they were placed on horse carriages and carts and on boats. Some places still retain the original traditional lanterns made by the Lithadiotis family. Three generations ago, the grandfather of Giorgos Lithadiotis made lanterns for prospective bridegrooms; as tradition demanded that the groom presented his future bride with a lantern upon acceptance of his proposal. The Kanari Lithadioti lanterns were tasteful and well worked with various decorations using different techniques using copper or lead. The support columns and the glass panes were rounded as opposed to those of others that were square shaped. 'The materials', says Giorgos 'were made by the men themselves. They worked with a brazier and charcoal and made them out of tin, and opalina for the glass- using a variety of ways and techniques to colour the glass'.

Greek Music and Dance

Music and dance are major forms of group and self-expression, and within Greece, genres vary from Byzantine chants to the music of the urban working class known as *rebetika*. Distinctively Greek styles of music, dance, and instrumentation have not been displaced by the popularity of Western European and American music. Some of the most commonly used instruments are the *bouzouki, santouri* (hammer dulcimer), *lauto* (mandolin-type lute), *clarinet, violin, guitar, tsambouna* (bagpipe), and *lyra* (a-stringed Cretan instrument), many of which function as symbols of national or regional identity. The popular composers Mikis Theodorakis and Manos Hadjidakis have achieved international fame.

Rembetiko

The typical music style on Skopelos is called *'Rebétiko'* or *'Rembetika'*, and its roots are found in the Greek music of the middle 19th century on the West coast of Asia Minor and Constantinople.

It developed in the poor areas of Greek cities like Athens or Siros, after the expulsion of the Greeks from Asia Minor. Its popularity arises from the fact that it is the Greek version of the American blues.

It has its roots in poor and seedy urban areas. However, although *'Rembetika'* is the name of the typical Greek music in general, it is now considered as distinctive of Skopelos island.

The Skopelian Giorgios Xintaris is one of the biggest exponents of *Rembetika,* and he can usually be seen performing in typical taverns and *Rembetika* clubs with his son, or other musician friends. The cadence of this beautiful music sounding in the taverns at night usually communicates a very special atmosphere.

When high season begins, this '*rebeti*' artist usually plays in an open air restaurant at the top of Skopelos *Kastro*. Although he is one of the last remaining icons of **Rembetika** on the island some very famous modern day singers such as Eleni Tsaligopoulou and Eleutheria Arvanitaki began their careers in Skopelos' **Rembetika** clubs, which maintains interest in the older tradition. Other tavernas also offer live performances; and those that do not usually play Giorgios Xintaris records, among with other **Rembetika** music, at late evening.

Another '*rebeti*' singer on Skopelos is Kostas Kalafatis, who was born in Thessaloniki. He was taught Byzantine music by his father and has been a singer since a young boy, when he sang in the Orthodox Church. This influence and his Asia Minor origin, make up the essence of his voice.

At fourteen years of age he bought his first guitar and started at the age of 16 playing and singing in bands. For 35 years he has shared his knowledge of the Greek **Rembetiko** (urban and folk song genres) working mostly in Thessaloniki, Patras and the island of Skopelos where he has lived for the last 30 years.

Kalafatis expertly interprets **Smyrneiko, Rembetiko** and popular Greek song. He plays guitar and also a variety of stringed instruments of the Eastern Mediterranean such as the bouzouki, lute, oud and baglama. He also contributed as a composer on his latest CD entitled '*Thessaloniki Patra Skopelos*', which includes a remake of old songs and some contemporary compositions of his own and other composers.

Although Skopelos island has not the reputation of offering many night activities, the available options are enough to satisfy the demands of tourists staying for a while. And in fact, the music of **Rembetika** played by Giorgio Xintaris and other gifted musicians, gives Skopelos the edge over other islands offering only disco and 'pop'.

The Bouzoukia

The **Bouzoukia** are not places that typically or traditionally promote family atmosphere and solidarity. Single, divorced, or even married Greek men and women frequent these places alone and in groups. The dances performed here become more an expression of individualism. The *zeibekiko,* also known as the 'drunken man's dance' is the favoured expression for the male who dances solo or alone. The male dancer is never in a fully upright position and is often hunched forward, darting into space in front of him. Aggression is also part of the agile performance. This is most evident when the male dancer hits parts of his body, such as the heels of his feet, or when, during his dance performance, someone transgresses into his space, which is considered to be an invitation to quarrel.

Often male friends squat down and clap for those dancing *zeibekiko,* expressing male solidarity represented by the human circle formed around the dancer. Greek males are also able to share in the expression of the solo dancer by the act of 'giving a gift' to him. In the past one very popular physical expression of 'gifting' was plate breaking, performed to help heighten the dancer's experience of *kefi* and to corroborate his sense of emotion. Nowadays this is discouraged and instead, flowers or money may be thrown.

Greek women may dance solo within a circle of female friends during the *rebetiko* dance called the *tsiftetel* – a kind of belly-dancing which is the female representation of *kefi.*

Dancers may throw money to the floor, displaying the willingness to part with money because of the deep feelings of *kefi.* Larger amounts of money are thrown if *kefi* is further inspired by the musicians. Other forms of 'gifting' that are related to money, include dancers spitting on the bill and placing it on the musician's forehead, at the back of the ear, or into the musical instrument itself.

Dance

Greece is one of the few places in Europe where the day -to-day role of folk dance is sustained. Rather than functioning as a museum piece preserved only for performances and special events, it is a vivid expression of everyday life. Occasions for dance are usually weddings, family celebrations, and *paniyiria* (Patron Saints' name days). Dance has its place in ceremonial customs that are still preserved in Greek villages, such as dancing the bride during a wedding and dancing the trousseau of the bride during the wedding preparations. Carnival and Easter offer more opportunities for family gatherings and dancing. Greek taverns providing live entertainment often include folk dances in their programme, whilst nightclubs and *Bouzoukia* are places where Greek dancing reigns supreme.

Greek folk dancing was an important expression of national identity throughout the centuries of Ottoman occupation. Greek national dances have also served to strengthen cultural identity in modern times, especially in Greek *diaspora* communities abroad. Through performance, ordinary people retain their cultural heritage and collectively remember it. Dancing also commemorates the dancers of old as national heroes and celebrates the value of nationhood.

Kefi and Dance

The 'good mood' of *kefi* symbolizes masculinity. It is adopted as a programme for action against work, domestic obligation or dealing with the state that weighs down and pollutes the heart. *Kefi* is present when Greek males celebrate and drink together. It is connected to drunkenness, but does not refer to the drunken state. It refers to the emotional state heightened by alcohol, primarily governed by social occasions that feature alcohol around a table with song and dance.

Greek songs provoke a particular emotion that inspires a man's *kefi*. A man will have a favourite song that represents, for him, a strong personal meaning triggered from an event in his life. From listening to this song while in a state of *kefi*, he responds to it by dancing. The male dancer in a state of *kefi* will dance in a kind of horizontal dance (leaning backward), which represents surrender to the emotional power that the song is giving him.

In popular culture, one dance of this type is the *syrtaki* or what is now known as *Zorba's dance*. The character of Zorba as portrayed by Anthony Quinn represents the ultimate male expression of *kefi.*

Circle Dances

Most Greek dances are **circle dances**, which start with the right foot and move counter-clockwise. Each dancer is linked by a handkerchief or by holding hands, wrists or shoulders. In mixed dances, the man will lead the dance, which allows him in most regions to improvise or break away allowing him to express himself. Until recently, men and women rarely danced together although chains of men and women danced together at the same time, the women in the inner circle and the men in the outer circle. The order of dance varies from region to region. In general, especially at occasions like weddings, the men are commonly at the beginning in descending order of age, followed by the women also ranked according to seniority. Sometimes the married men come before the bachelors and likewise for the women. The oldest inhabitant always leads the dance. In the islands the circle is usually formed of groups of families, the husband leads the wife who is followed by the eldest son, his wife and their children etc. Occasionally the local Priest will lead the first dance, symbolising a blessing.

The **Kalamatiano,** a lively, 12-step, open circle dance, is usually the first dance to occur at celebrations. There is plenty of time to get comfortable with the steps because bands often like to play 15- to 20-minute marathons of this music. *Tsamiko* is, by contrast, a much slower, open circle dance. Traditionally, the person leading the circle will perform various tricks (*fygoures*), while the rest of the circle follows a simple 12-step routine. Though this dance is not very fast-paced, it is always touching to experience the emotion and pathos of the leader, especially if it is an older man or woman.

Thessaly and the Sporades retain a strong tradition of song-dances where the dancers sing the music, often without instrumental accompaniment . Most of the dances are slow and controlled. The main dances are *Sta Tria, Kalamatianos, Klistos, Svarniara, Karagouna, Tai-Tai* and *Pilioritikos*.

Sacred Dancing

The *Dance of Isaiah* is a sacred dance performed during religious rituals in the Greek Orthodox Church. It is a circle dance performed as part of a ritual for those Christians who are being initiated from one religious state into another. For example, the circle dance is performed during the *ghamos* or marriage ceremony of the Greek Orthodox Church, when the bridal party and the Priest enact the *Dance of Isaiah* during the Sacrament of Marriage. The *Dance of Isaiah* is also performed as part of *hirotonia* or the Sacrament of Ordination. Ordination occurs on three occasions: when a lay person is ordained to Deacon, when a Deacon is ordained to Priest, and when a Priest is ordained to Bishop. Thus, Greek clergymen will enact the sacred dance of the Church when initiated through holy rank.

In both the Sacraments of Holy Matrimony and Holy Orders, the Christian can only perform the *Dance of Isaiah* three times. If a Christian marries, he can only dance the *Dance of Isaiah* twice more. If a Deacon has married, he has danced it once in Holy Matrimony and is only allowed to dance it twice more in Holy Orders, which means that the highest rank he can attain in Holy Orders is Priesthood. However, an unmarried Deacon can perform the *Dance of Isaiah* three times for Holy Orders and attain the rank of Bishop.

The Loiza Festival on Skopelos

Every summer, in Glossa village, on the northern side of Skopelos, there takes place the **Loiza Festival**, dedicated to one of the most famous and beloved music composers in Greece, Manos Loizos. It usually takes place at the end of July and the beginning of August and includes various cultural events such as musical concerts, photograph exhibitions, theatrical performances, fairy tale reading, traditional dancing performances and exhibitions of local or international organizations.

The Loizia Festival has been organized by the Cultural Association of Glossa Skopelos since 1983, one year after the death of the composer. Manos Loizos (1937-1982) was born in Alexandria, Egypt, and died in a hospital in Moscow. He lived and made his career in Athens. He cooperated with famous singers, while his songs had a political view. He was part of the Greek Communist Party and fought for the rights of the working class. His songs were beloved by the Greek people and they are sung till today, especially during the festival, when they are accompanied by traditional dancing.

High Days and Holidays: The Orthodox and Secular Year

The festive cycle of the Orthodox Church calendar begins on September 1st the start of the Ecclesiastical year and ends on August 31st, with the feast day honouring the Holy Belt of Virgin Mary.

Each day is sacred: each is a saint's day, so at least one saint is venerated daily. In addition to the specific dates mentioned, there are literally scores of local festivals, or *paniyiria*, celebrating the patron saint of the main village Church. With hundreds of possible name-saints' days (calendars list two or three, often obscure, for each day) you're unlikely to travel around Skopelos for long without stumbling on something.

Paramoni

It is important to remember the concept of the **paramoni,** which is the *eve* of the festival. Most of the events listed below are celebrated on the night before, so if you arrive on the morning of the date given you will very probably have missed any music, dancing or drinking.

The following is an accumulation of some of the most significant and important festivals and celebrations that are still followed avidly in Skopelos today. The actual rituals and procedures can vary from region to region and even from village to village, but overall, this will give you an insight into the more common traditions not only on the island, but in Greece itself.

September 1 - Pomegranates and the first day of the year.

On the 1st of September the grape harvest begins and that is considered to be the beginning of the New Year in the Orthodox calendar. So, early in the morning, the housewives fill their pots with water from a spring and head back home, or nowadays take a bottle of water and go outside the house.

Upon re-entering the house they will drop a pomegranate and step on it. This brings good luck for the new year. Then they say loudly 'Good morning house' and step inside with the right foot first. Water is then spilled in the four corners of the house and the lady of the house says 'As the water spills and rolls so will the good times roll in this house'.

According to Greek mythology pomegranates symbolize death and fertility: they can be seen in many different guises in the shops of Skopelos, from silver, to pottery, to glass; as painted decoration, as ornament and as jewellery. They are considered to bring good luck.

September 8 - Birth of Mary - Gennisis tis Panayias

September 8th celebrates the Birth of the Virgin Mary, who intercedes between God and Man. The source for the story of the birth of the Blessed Virgin Mary is the **Protoevangelium of James**, an apocryphal gospel written about A.D. 150. From it, come the names of Mary's parents, Joachim and Anna, as well as the tradition that the couple was childless until an angel appeared to Anna and told her that she would conceive.

The angel directed them to name the child Mary, which in Hebrew means 'lady and hope.' The one who was to be the Mother of God was born into a righteous family, known more throughout the generations for its goodness than for its royal blood. The importance of this feast, the first in the Church calendar year, is that it was the first step in preparing mankind for its promised salvation.

The traditional date of the feast falls exactly nine months after the feast of the **Immaculate Conception of Mary**. Perhaps because of its close proximity to the feast of the **Assumption of Mary**, the **Nativity of the Blessed Virgin Mary** is not celebrated today with the same solemnity as the Immaculate Conception. It is, nonetheless, a very important feast, because it prepares the way for the Birth of Christ.

September 14 -

The Feast of the Exaltation of the Cross -Ipsosi to Stavrou

September 14th commemorates both the finding of the True Cross in 326 A.D. and its recovery from the Persians in 628 A.D., and is considered to be one of the **Twelve Great Feasts** of the Church year. It is always a fast day, even if it falls on Saturday or Sunday, and the eating of meat, dairy products and fish is prohibited, in remembrance of the suffering and death of Christ on the Cross.

The Feast of the Cross has a one-day **Forefeast**, when the Cross is brought out from the sanctuary into the centre of the Church; and an eight-day **Afterfeast**. The Saturday and Sunday before and after September 14 are also commemorated with special Epistle and Gospel readings about the Cross at the Divine Liturgy.

The Cross will remain in the centre of the Church throughout the Afterfeast, and the faithful will venerate it whenever they enter or leave the Church. Finally, on the **Apodosis of the Feast**, the Priest and Deacon will cense around the cross, there will be a final veneration and then they will solemnly take it back into the sanctuary through the Holy Doors. This same pattern of bringing out the Cross, veneration, and returning the Cross at the end of the celebration is repeated at a number of the lesser Feasts of the Cross through the year.

The Cross is the sign of God's love for man, the harbinger of the coming transfiguration of nature. Thus, this is also considered an important date for farming activities in Greece. The Priest gives basil leaves to the faithful and farmers take a mixture of all the seeds they intend to sow, to have them blessed by the Priest.

October 28 - Ochi Day (No Day)

The national holiday on October 28th commemorates the negative reply of Metaxas (a Greek General, appointed

Prime Minister of Greece between April-August 1936 and dictator during the 4th of August Regime, from 1936 until his death in 1941) to Mussolini's demands for an Italian invasion of Greece in 1940. It was a 'No!' that brought Greece into the war on the Allied side; for a time, Greece was Britain's only ally against Hitler. This day is celebrated across Greece with remembrance services, military parades and folk dancing. On Skopelos, the day belongs to the school children, who gather at the cenotaph to be reminded of their history and then march down the Paralea to the applause of their families and friends.

November 8 - Feast of the Archangels - Taxiarches

November 8th celebrates the archangels Gabriel and Michael with ceremonies across Greece in Churches and Monasteries named after these religious figures, also known as the *Taxiarches.*

November 17 - Epanastatiki Organosi dekaefta Noemvri

The **Athens Polytechnic uprising** in 1973 was a massive demonstration of popular rejection of the Military Junta, a regime which abolished civil rights, dissolved political parties and exiled, imprisoned and tortured politicians and citizens based on their political beliefs. The uprising began on November 14, 1973, escalated to an open anti-junta revolt and ended in bloodshed in the early morning of November 17 after a series of events starting with a tank crashing through the gates of the Polytechnic.

This day is currently observed as a holiday in Greece for all educational establishments; commemorative services are held and students attend school only for these, while some schools and all universities stay closed during the day. Here on Skopelos, students honour the tradition by having a holiday after the services and 'cocking a snook' at authority by shouting, singing and 'revving' their scooters - under the indulgent eyes of the townspeople. Since 1973, police, armed forces or anyone in politics are not allowed onto educational premises without permission. Pupils have been known to lock out their teachers by padlocking the doors to the school. When this happens, the school remains closed until pupils relent!

November 21 - The Presentation of the Theotokos

The **Entry of the Most Holy Theotokos into the Temple** (its name in the East), or *The Presentation of the Blessed Virgin Mary* (as it is known in the West), is another of the Twelve Great Feasts celebrated by the Orthodox Church on 21st November. In the Orthodox Church the feast always falls during the **Nativity Fast**, but on the day of the feast the fasting rules are lessened somewhat so that fish, wine and oil may be eaten.

The feast is associated with an event recounted not in the New Testament, but in the apocryphal *Infancy Narrative of James*. According to that text, Mary's parents, Joachim and Anne, in thanksgiving for the gift of their daughter, brought her when still a child to the Temple in Jerusalem to consecrate her to God. Mary remained in the Temple until puberty, at which point she was assigned to Joseph as guardian. Later versions of the story tell us that Mary was taken to the Temple at around the age of three in fulfilment of a vow. Tradition held that she was to remain there to be educated in preparation for her role as Mother of God.

This date is the nameday of unmarried girls called Maria. Married Marias have their name day on August 15th. As Mary is the patron saint of the armed forces, this is also Greek *Armed Forces Day.*

December 6 - Feast of St Nicholas - Aghios Nikolaos

Saint Nikolaos means 'victory of the people' and the state Church of Skopelos *Chora* is dedicated to him. Also called Nikolaos of Myra, he was a 4th-century saint and Greek

Bishop of Myra (part of modern-day Turkey) in Lycia. Because of the many miracles attributed to his intercession, he is also known as Nikolaos the Wonderworker. He had a reputation for secret gift-giving, such as putting coins in the shoes of those who left them out for him, and thus became the model for Santa Claus, whose modern name comes from the Dutch Sinterklaas, itself from a series of elisions and corruptions of the transliteration of 'Saint Nikolaos'.

In Greece, Saint Nicholas does not carry an especial association with gift-giving, as this tradition is carried over to St. Basil of Cesarea, celebrated on New Year's Day: here, St. Nicholas is the protector of sailors. He is considered the patron saint of the Greek navy, military and merchant alike, and his day is marked by festivities aboard all ships and boats, at sea and in port.

December 6-9 - The Nikolobarbara

The day is also associated with the preceding feasts of St. Barbara (4 December), St. Savvas (5 December), and the following feast of St. Anne (9 December); all these are often collectively called the **Nikolobarbara**, and are considered a succession of days that heralds the onset of truly wintry cold weather in the country. Therefore by tradition, homes should have already been laid with carpets, removed for the warm season, by St. Andrew's Day (30 November), the week before the *Nikolobarbara*. Hence the presence of the itinerant carpet sellers on the island at this period.

December 25 -The Nativity - Gennisis tou Christou

In Greece, **Christmas** is preceded by a 40 day fast beginning on November 15th: This is a time of reflection, self-restraint and inner healing in the Sacrament of Confession. Christmas tends to be a quiet, solemn, season.

Ceremonial pastries are baked during this time for the big family meal, served after Church services on Christmas

Day: **Melomakarona** are honeydipped biscuits often stuffed with nuts; **Kourambiedes** are biscuits dusted with powdered sugar; **Loukmades** are fried dough balls dipped in honey.

There are similarities, as well as differences, between the Eastern and Western celebration of Christmas. The Eastern Christmas has a very strong family and social appeal just as it does in the West. It brings people of all generations together to celebrate the Birth of Jesus Christ. Unlike the West however, where Christmas ranks supreme, in the East it is **Easter**, centred on the cross and the resurrection of Christ, which is the most important festival of the year. The Church places enormous significance on the death and resurrection of Christ, rather than on His birth, and celebrates Easter above all else. Also, Eastern Orthodox Christmas lacks the commercial side that is so typical to the West.

However, there are still many traditions associated with Christmas and these customs begin on Christmas Eve. On Skopelos, early in the morning, children knock on doors of houses and shops in the neighbourhood, jangling triangles and singing songs - **kalanta**. The songs are considered to bring a blessing on the house. The children are given sweets and money.

Usually, on **Christmas Eve**, observant Orthodox Christians fast till late evening, until the first star appears. When the star is seen, people lay the table ready for the Christmas supper. During the Christmas season Greek cooks prepare **loukanika** (sausages) and **lountza** (smoked fillet), **hiromeri** (smoked ham), and **zalatina** (brawn). The Greeks also eat rose water flavoured shortbread and syrup-drenched honey cakes called **kourambiédes** and **melomakárona**, respectively.

On **Christmas Day** people take part in *Divine Liturgy*. Then a great feast is held indoors where everyone joins in to eat, drink and enjoy themselves. Roasted pig was an obligatory dish in the Orthodox tradition, but it has been superseded by stuffed roast turkey for Christmas Day, doubtless influenced by the customs of Western Europe. Turkeys are stuffed with a mixture of minced beef or lamb, rice, and pine nuts and served with a variety of salads and potatoes.

The Christmas dining table is decorated with traditional cakes and sweets and the *'Christopsomo'* – The *Christ Bread*. On Christmas Day, the male head of the household traditionally crosses the bread with a knife, offering each person at the table a piece and wishing them *'Chronia polla!'* or *'Kala Christouyenna!'* (Merry Christmas.) More and more often, reflecting the commercialisation of Western tradition propagated through American television, small presents are given today.

Incidentally, the word **Xmas**: this abbreviation for Christmas is of Greek origin. The word for Christ in Greek is *Xristos*. During the 16th century, Europeans began using the first initial of Christ's name, 'X' in place of the word Christ in Christmas as a shorthand form of the word. Although the early Christians understood that X stood for Christ's name, later Christians who did not understand the Greek language mistook 'Xmas' as a sign of disrespect.

Greetings for Christmas are: *Kala Christouyena!* and *Christos Gennatai ! Doxasate!*

Kalikantzara

Kalikantzara are little devils from the underworld, which are small and black, with pointed ears, horns, curly tails, goats' legs and human hands. During the *Twelve Days of Christmas*, from today until Epiphany, these goblins emerge from the ground to make mischief, until they are banished by the Priest casting a cross on the waters of the sea on January 6th.

Besides this ecclesiastical purification there are various Christian precautions against the *Kallikantzaroi*: marking the house-door with a black cross on Christmas Eve; the burning of incense and the invocation of the Trinity. Other means of aversion are the lighting of the **skakantzalos** (*Yule*) log, the burning of something that smells strong, such as coffee grounds (sometimes the Greeks will also burn old shoes, the smell of which keeps the wicked elves away); and - perhaps as a peace-offering – the hanging of pork-bones, sweetmeats, or sausages in the chimney.

December 26 - St Stephen's Day - Synaksis tis Panagias

The day after Christmas (*Boxing Day or St. Stephen's Day*) is called **Synaksis tis Panagias** (*The Gathering of the Holy Family*) in Greece. As its name implies, it is a quiet day at home for families.

January 1 – Ag. Vassilios- Protochronia

New Year's Day, on January 1st, is a secular celebration, but today is the Saints' Day of several Saints and martyrs, including Aghios Vassilios – Basil the Great - one of the founders of the Church.

On New Year's Eve, the children of Skopelos once more go from house to house singing New Year Carols - **Kalanta** - and banging on metal triangles. In the past, the children would carry a toy boat with them, but now boats are only seen in some shop windows or as part of the street light decorations. In Ancient Greece, boats on wheels were the traditional way of transporting Dionysus, the god of wine and feasting.

At the moment of the change in the year, all the lights are switched off in the house, all the taps turned on and all the windows opened to let in the fresh air. Some women drink a glass of water as the clock strikes twelve, having previously placed it next to jewellery or money. On New Year's Day the first person across the threshold should be the master of the house, the eldest son, or another lucky child, if there is to be a good, prosperous new year. They enter the house with the right foot first, carrying a small icon of a saint, or smashing a pomegranate inside the door, whilst wishing everyone *'Kali protochronia'* (*Happy New Year.)*

Generally, people celebrate New Year's Day by having parties, visiting relatives and gambling. While they are out, they leave a tray with sweets and water for **Aghios Vassilios**, who is believed to visit the house and leave gifts for the children, thereby becoming the *Santa Claus* of the Greeks in recent years, as this is the main day Greeks receive their Christmas presents. On this day, Godparents give presents to Godchildren. It is unlucky to break glass objects and mirrors, to quarrel, to cry, or to lose things today, lest such mishaps will happen all year long.

The most important custom is cutting the *'vassilopitta'*. This is a big, round cake, like a brioche, which is dedicated to *Aghios Vassilios*. The cake can be decorated with icing sugar, representing wishes and has a coin buried into it on the underside by the woman of the house. The family gather round the table and the father of the house carries out the following ritual:

With a knife, he makes a cross three times on the cake, wishing everyone a *'Happy New Year'*, before cutting it into pieces. He starts by naming each piece according to the recipient: the first piece for Jesus Christ; the second for Ag. Vassilios; the next to the house; the fourth piece symbolizes material possessions and is given to the poor; then a piece is given to the animals; then to each member of the family in turn - first the grandparents, then the parents - himself and his wife - then the children. Other relatives are served next and then friends, so that all will be blessed both spiritually and physically during the coming year. Before those pieces are eaten, each person dips his piece in wine and invokes St. Basil. The family member who finds the coin in their piece of bread will have good luck and prosperity for the coming year. The coin is used to buy a candle that is lighted in Church on Christmas Day. After the dinner, the family lifts the table three times for good luck. After the meal, the covers are removed and family and friends play card games through the night.

January 6 – Epiphany – Aghia Theophania (Phota)

On the 5th of January, the first sanctification of **Theophania** (*the Epiphany* or *Enlightenment*, meaning the manifestation of God to man) takes place in Church on the eve of the holiday. **Theophania** is the Feast which revealed the Holy Trinity to the world through the Baptism of Jesus by St. John the Forerunner, and the Holy Spirit descended upon the Son in the form of a dove. From ancient times, this Feast was called the **Day of Illumination** and the **Feast of Lights**; colloquially *phota*.

The Priests, each accompanied by two choir boys, holding a cross and a basil branch, visit every house in the parish and bless it, the surrounding land and its occupants. This exorcises the **Kallikantzaroi**, who have nowhere to go but into the water - the sea, a river or even a reservoir.

In celebration of this, on Skopelos on the 6th of January, a long procession is formed and follows whatever road that leads to the sea. Up in front of the procession are the cherub icons, followed by the Priests dressed in their best holiday splendour, then the VIPs, followed by all the people. The Priests then perform the ceremony of **'blessing the sea.'**

They throw a cross into the water, in memory of the Priests who gave the icons to the protection of the sea during the Turkish Occupation, and by this action the devils are sent back to the underworld. Then, volunteers - mostly the younger people of the village - jump into the usually icy water and compete in retrieving the cross. The one who brings the cross up to the surface will enjoy good luck and health for the entire year. The fishing boats send up flares and sound their klaxons, after which the whole town then repairs for coffee in the cafes.

Epiphany - the day when Jesus was baptised - is the official end of the *Twelve Days of Christmas*. It also celebrates the arrival of the three kings and their giving of gifts to the Holy Family. Therefore January 6th is the day for the proper exchange of presents and gifts are given today in the Orthodox world. The day-long festival also features the blessing of small boats and ships, and later on affords entertainment, music, dancing and food to all those present.

In Greece, greenery and nativity scenes put up at Christmas may be taken down at Epiphany, but usually they remain up until Candlemas on February 2.

January 8 - Rule of Women - Gynaikokratia

Although not widespread on Skopelos, this is the day when women take over the cafes while the men stay home and (supposedly!) do the housework: often there is an evening meal organized in one of the restaurants, although this may devolve into a celebration of the more generally known *International Women's Day.*

January 30 – The Three Hierarchs – Oi Treis Ierarches

Three of the most important of the Early Church Fathers were Basil the Great, Gregory the Theologian and John Chrysostom, all celebrated on this day: they were highly influential Bishops of the Early Church who played pivotal roles in shaping Christian theology. All three have separate feast days in January: Basil on January 1st, Gregory on January 25th, and Chrysostom on January 27th; but disputes raged in eleventh century Constantinople about which of the three hierarchs was the greatest. Some argued that Basil was superior to the other two because of his explanations of Christian faith and monastic example; supporters of John Chrysostom countered that the Golden Mouthed Archbishop of Constantinople was unmatched in both eloquence and in bringing sinners to repentance; and a third group insisted that Basil's close friend, Gregory the Theologian, was preferred to the others due to the majesty, purity and profundity of his homilies and his defence of the faith from heresy.

Then the Three Hierarchs appeared together in a vision to St. John Mauropous, Bishop of Euchaita, in the year 1084, and proclaimed that they were equal before God 'There are no divisions among us, and no opposition to one another.' As a result, a common feast day commemorating all three in common was instituted around 1100. They became the patron saints of Education: Greek children go to Church in the morning and then have the rest of the day off from school.

February 2 - The Presentation of the Lord - Hypapante

The *Presentation of Jesus at the Temple*, which falls on 2nd February, celebrates an early episode in the life of Jesus. In the Eastern Orthodox Church, it is one of the twelve *Great Feasts*, and is sometimes called **Hypapante** (*'Meeting'* in Greek). Other traditional names include **Candlemas**, the **Feast of the Purification of the Virgin**, and the **Meeting of the Lord.**

It has a *forefeast* of one day, and an afterfeast of seven days. However, if the feast falls during **Cheesefare Week** or **Great Lent**, the *afterfeast* is either shortened or eliminated altogether.

The holy day is celebrated with an all-night vigil on the eve of the feast, and a celebration of the *Divine Liturgy* the next morning, at which beeswax candles are blessed and then distributed among the congregation. This tradition is also associated with the *Churching of Women* – the ceremony wherein a blessing is given to mothers after recovery from childbirth. The ceremony includes thanksgiving for the woman's survival of childbirth, and is performed even when the child is stillborn, or has died unbaptized. The rite is associated with Candlemas because it was the custom for women to carry lighted candles into the Church to receive the blessing.

Carnival – Apokries

Before the season of Lent, there are the **Apokries:** Carnival is the three week period before *'Saracosti'*, (Lent) during which people stop eating meat or animal products. According to the etymological interpretation of both the Greek and the Latin terms (**carne vale** or **apo crea**) mean *'goodbye to meat'*.

For the duration of Lent and through Holy Week, weddings, parties, festivals and celebrations come to a stop. Because there are many days of deprival through the fasting season, and Greeks being the party people that they are, they use the three weeks prior to Lent to 'lift up' their spirits.

The Triodion Period –
The Sunday of the Publican and the Pharisee

The three-week period of *Apokria* consists of three feasts that are mostly celebrated on the Sunday of the week. The first one is called **'Protofoni'** or *'First Voice'*. The Sunday of the Publican and the Pharisee is the first Sunday of a three-week period prior to the commencement of Great Lent. It marks the beginning of a time of preparation for the spiritual journey of Lent, a time for Orthodox Christians to draw closer to God through worship, prayer, fasting, and acts of charity. It is also on this day that the **Triodion** is introduced, a liturgical book that contains the services from this Sunday, the tenth before **Pascha** (Easter), to Great and Holy Saturday. The only day of fasting this week is Friday since it precedes **'Psihosavato'** – 'All Souls Day' and Lenten dishes are prepared.

The Feast of the Prodigal Son - Kreatini

The second feast is **'Kreatini'** or *'Meat Filled'* because during this week, it is allowed to eat meat on Wednesday and Friday. The Thursday of this week is known as *'Tsikno Pompti'* or *'Burnt Thursday'*. It is traditional on this day to cook foods and let them char or burn so that the smell is carried out through the village. Charcoal pits burn bright on this day as most homes have barbecues and people of all ages visit each other. It is also a night filled with laughter and practical jokes, the first masqueraders make their appearance and the first carnival parties are held. Bars, clubs and restaurants are packed and for twelve days parties are 'gate-crashed' by marauding revellers.

The theme of this Sunday is repentance, and the focus on the parable of the Prodigal Son leads Orthodox Christians to contemplate the necessity of repentance in their relationship with their Heavenly Father.

All Soul's Day - Psihosavato

'Psihosavato' or *'All Soul's Day'* is one of the days that the dead are remembered in Church services and memorials. On the Saturday before this Sunday, the first of three Saturdays of the Souls are held. This is a special commemoration on this and the next two Saturdays, when the Church offers a Divine Liturgy and Memorial Service for the departed faithful. This is considered a universal commemoration of the dead. It is closely related to the theme of the **Sunday of the Last Judgement** since the services focus on the Second Coming of Christ and the resurrection of the dead. Through the memorial services, the Church is commending to God all who have departed and who are now awaiting the Last Judgement.

Families will give the Priest lists of names of the deceased and he will read them out loud in Church as part of the service. During the special services *'Kollyva'* are handed out to all those in attendance On the evening of this day, people will dress up in their masquerade costumes and go from house to house as this also marks the eve of the final week of *Apokries* or Carnival.

Sunday of the Last Judgement - Meatfare Sunday

The Sunday of the Last Judgement is the third Sunday of a three-week period prior to the commencement of **Great Lent**. On this day, focus is placed on the future judgement of all persons who will stand before the Throne of God when Christ returns in His glory. This Sunday is the last day on which flesh (skin and meat) from a vertebrate, which is an animal with a spine/backbone (mammals, birds, fish, etc.), and shellfish can be eaten until *Pascha*. Dairy products are allowed on each day of this week, even Wednesday and Friday.

On the Sunday of this week, men and boys on Skopelos take part in the *Trata Festival*. This old custom is a performance parodying maritime life, exclusively organized by groups of men or young boys. Various groups of participants gather together in the courtyard of the farmer's Co-operative or in other places and make boats, called *tratas*, from rubbish. At midday, when the boats are ready, they make their appearance. The men drag them through the streets and squares creating a lot of noise, speaking and behaving in a provocative way, participating in dances, singing songs, telling dirty jokes and making rhyming verses of situations and events depicting the life of the local community. By the afternoon they end up in the harbour side and sink the boats into the sea. The sole purpose of the exercise seems to be to get as drunk as possible whilst having a good time without the presence of women!

The festival comes down to modern Greece from the ancient worship of Dionysus, who always arrived from the sea: He was often depicted as a male god wearing female clothing. Symbolically, the deity is carried through the streets in his ship, and he is honoured by the singing of bawdy songs and drinking. It is the type of behaviour the god appreciates - the dirtier and drunker the better! It is a time of dancing, masquerade and wine, which loosens inhibitions and brings a mellow, cheerful mood that reaches its peak a few days before people begin the long Lenten fast.

Sunday of Forgiveness – Tirini (Cheesefare Sunday)

The Sunday of Forgiveness is the last Sunday prior to the commencement of **Great Lent**. Orthodox Christians are encouraged to enter this period in repentance and confession by attending these services, coming for the *Sacrament of Confession*, and dedicating themselves to worship, prayer, and fasting throughout Lent. On the *Sunday of Forgiveness* focus is placed on the exile of Adam and Eve from the Garden of Eden, an event that shows how far Man has fallen in sin and separated himself from God.

At the onset of **Great Lent** and a period of intense fasting, this Sunday reminds believers of the need for God's forgiveness and guides them in returning to Him in repentance. Another name for this day is *'Tirini'* or *'Cheese Filled'*. As the name suggests, cheeses are eaten throughout this week and in most villages, lots of pasta too: it is the last day that dairy products can be eaten prior to the commencement of Great Lent.

The Sunday before the last day of Lent, here on Skopelos the islanders also celebrate the **Vlaki Wedding**. This is an old custom and it is mostly organized by groups of women, traditionally the guardians of fertility and fecundity rites. In the past, to please the god and further his magic, the ancients carried out ritual weddings, symbolically celebrating the coming together of male and female in procreation. This was a joyous occasion complete with singing, dancing and a procession through the community to show off the happy couple. A successful Carnival predicted a good harvest.

Today in *Chora*, people dress up, many in traditional Skopelitan clothes, and join in a wedding procession in a celebration called **Tis kales**: as this is carnival, where anarchy prevails, the groom is a woman dressed as a man and the bride is a man dressed as a woman. The event begins in the morning and lasts until evening. A procession, accompanied by local musicians playing traditional folk music, begins at the top of the ring road midway through the morning, with more and more people joining as it parades through the town, past the Churches of **Farnouremini, Panagia Papamelitiou**, to **Ag Spiridon**, to the Milos platia, to the **Three Hierarchs (Ag. Ioannis)**, to **Christos** and then to the Paralea. It stops in the squares and everybody dances in double and triple circles, while they are treated to the traditional sweets – including *Ambrosia* (rice pudding) and wine offered by the local women. Eventually, in the early evening, everyone meets at the *Demotiko Kafenion* on the paralea for dancing, drinking wine and singing ribald songs. Glossa and Elios also have processions – involving many cars driving around, some pulling **tratas**, loud music and singing.

Throughout the entire *Apokries*, people go to visit each other at their homes, play games, sing songs and tell jokes. Prudity and modesty are put aside and good fun with good company prevails. Balloons and streamers are everywhere and it's not uncommon to walk down the street and get a face full of paper confetti. It's a time of happiness and celebration.

Adults and children alike, dress up in costumes of one kind or another: old women will hang veils over their faces or smear themselves with ashes from the fireplace just to frighten the younger children. At night, the masqueraders take to the streets, singing, playing practical jokes and just plain having fun: the bars, clubs and restaurants at this time of year are full.

The last night of *Apokria* is the most celebrated and often bonfires are lit on the beaches. The revellers sing songs and dance around them. When the flames die down, some of the braver folk will jump over the fire to *'burn the fleas off'*.

It is also said that on this last night of *Apokria*, the younger members of the family should genuflect before the elders and ask for forgiveness for whatever sins they might have committed. This leaves their hearts 'Clean' to celebrate the next day, which is **Clean Monday**.

Clean Monday - Kathari Deutera - Koulouma

Clean Monday is the first day of *'Sarakosti'* or the Season of Lent, when everywhere in Greece groups of people gather together in the *kaliva* - country cottages - or by the sea side for a family picnic. The picnics are simple affairs with everyday utensils and colourful tablecloths laid next to pits that have been dug to house hot charcoals to cook over. The families eat traditional local delicacies, they drink wine, dance and sing. Children and adults play games and fly kites, the traditional activity for **Clean Monday**: all their sins and unhappiness are projected onto the kite and cast to the winds, so that they may begin Lent in a cleansed state.

For the Greek Orthodox observer, the day marks the beginning of the *Great Fast*: a special flat bread called *lagana* is baked for the occasion. Other foods for this day are *'Nistisima'* or Lenten and contain 'no blood': fresh and pickled vegetables, salads of all kinds, shellfish, octopus, squid and *taramasalata* as well as *Halva* make up the menu. Meat, fish and dairy products are not allowed.

In every little village, not just on Skopelos, but everywhere in Greece, Churches with minimal attendance for the rest of the year will be visited by crowds of Greeks. Churches are adorned with two flags, the Greek national flag and the yellow flag with the double headed Eagle, representing the symbol of the Old Byzantine Empire, in a more complex celebration of a broader national identity.

Lent - Saracosti

At the end of the day of *Clean Monday*, the housewives wash all the grease from their kitchens, pans and utensils, before putting them away until after the Lenten fast is over. For those who fast, Lent passes very slowly. In the past, people would cut out a figure of a woman who had no mouth (because *Lady Saracosti* never stops fasting) and whose hands were joined together in prayer. She had seven legs, one for each week. Every Saturday they cut off one leg, the last one being removed on Saturday of Holy Week.

First Sunday of Lent - The Triumph of Orthodoxy

The Feast - or Triumph - of Orthodoxy is another moveable feast, celebrated on the first Sunday of Great Lent (six Sundays before *Pascha*) in the liturgical calendar of the Eastern Orthodox Church and Greek- Catholics (Eastern Catholics of Byzantine rite). The Feast is kept in memory of the final defeat of Iconoclasm and the restoration of the icons to the Orthodox Church.

On Skopelos many people take an icon to the Church of **Panagia Livadiotissa**, situated behind the Asklepion site, on the Spitalia side of the bay. After the service everybody walks in procession to the **Christos Church** with their icons and then back again.

Second Sunday of Lent – Sunday of St Gregory Palamas

Today, the Orthodox Church commemorates Holy Father Gregory Palamas, Archbishop of Thessaloniki, the Wonderworker. The feast day of Saint Gregory Palamas is November 14, however, he is commemorated on this Sunday as the condemnation of his enemies and the vindication of his teachings by the Church in the 14th century was acclaimed as a *Second Triumph of Orthodoxy*.

Third Sunday of Lent -
Sunday of the Veneration of the Holy Cross

On the Third Sunday of Lent, the Orthodox Church commemorates the Precious and Life-Giving Cross of Jesus Christ. Services include a special veneration of the Cross, which prepares the faithful for the commemoration of the Crucifixion during Holy Week.

Fourth Sunday of Lent - Feast of John (Climacus) of Sinai

On March 30 and on the Fourth Sunday of Lent the Church commemorates Father John Climacus. He is called Climacus due to his authorship of the great spiritual work **The Ladder of Divine Ascent**. His commemoration is designated by the Church on one of the Sundays of Lent as his life and writings affirm him as a supreme bearer and proponent of Christian asceticism. The ascetic example of this great Saint of the Church is to inspire believers during their Lenten journey.

Fifth Sunday of Lent - The Sunday of Saint Mary of Egypt

On the Fifth Sunday of Lent the Orthodox Church commemorates Mary of Egypt, who fasted alone in the desert for 47 years. The feast day of Saint Mary of Egypt is April 1, however, she is also commemorated on this Sunday due to her recognition by the Church as a model of repentance.

February 14 - St Valentine's Day

In the Eastern Orthodox Church, **Saint Valentine the Presbyter** is celebrated on July 6, and **Hieromartyr Saint Valentine** (Bishop of Interamna, Terni in Italy) is celebrated on July 30. Notwithstanding that, conventionally, members of the Greek Orthodox Church named Valentinos (male) or Valentina (female) celebrate their name on February 14, according to the *Typikon*. The Western Valentine's Day itself in Greece is not a very big holiday, but even on Skopelos the shops boast cuddly teddy bears, heart shaped toys and other Valentine compliments. The day is important as it is one when people should forgive and forget any sins or slights against them.

However, there is a long association in Greece with the customs and traditions which underpin the Western traditions: in Ancient Athens, from the middle of January to the middle of February (on our calendar) was known as the month of *Gamelion* (actually the fifth month on the Athenian calendar). This entire month was dedicated to the sacred marriage of Zeus and Hera, referred to as the **hieros ghamos**, or literally *'holy or sacred marriage'*. Despite Zeus' constant infidelities, it seems that the Greeks nonetheless revered the union between their king god and his queen, as well as Aphrodite, the Goddess of Love and Eros, her helper – now more commonly known as Cupid.

Later, in Ancient Rome, the **Lupercalia** was celebrated on February 15. This festival honoured Faunus or Lupercus, a god of fertility and farming, and was celebrated with annual sacrifices and feasts. One of the aims of the festival was to purify the land and the young women of child-bearing age (February comes from the latin **Februare** meaning to purify). During the *Lupercalia*, two Priests, called *luperci*, sacrificed two male goats and a dog at the sacred cave where Romulus and Remus were supposedly nursed by the she-wolf. After a feast, the *luperci* dressed in the goats' skins and ran through the city streets, whipping people (mostly young girls and women) with thongs cut from the sacrificial skins. This act was thought to purify the girls, ensure their fertility, and lessen the pain of eventual childbirth. Names were also drawn from an urn to pair up young men and women as part of the festivities. This was intended to lead to marriages and subsequent births.

On February 14 496 AD, the feast of St. Valentine was first declared, and the *Lupercalia* was outlawed as a pagan ritual; however, throughout Greece, young men still consider this a lucky day to propose to girls or to get married. On Skopelos, it was the custom to give your loved one a rice pudding today, as a way of declaring yourself.

Ευτυχισμένη μέρα του Αγίου Βαλεντίνου!

February 25 - Aghios Rhiginos: the Patron Saint of Skopelos

The evening before this date, a ceremony takes place in the Church belonging to the monastery of Rhiginos. The next day a second ceremony is held early in the morning, which

235

lasts several hours. When the liturgy is finished a procession begins from here, ending at Christos Church in the *Chora*. For the entire day it is possible to visit the Church, the shrine and the monastery: a candle may be lit and many people leave flowers.

March 1 - Martis

On March 1st, it is customary for mothers to braid bracelets for their children. These bracelets are called *'Martis'*. They are made of red and white string and are tied onto the wrists of the children. The superstition is that the children wear these bracelets so that the sun of early spring doesn't burn their cheeks. The bracelet is red and white, symbolic of rosy cheeks yet a white complexion.

Devout young people also wear the bracelets as a reminder of the death and resurrection of Christ. The bracelets are worn until the Midnight Mass of the Greek Orthodox Easter. When the traditional bonfires are lit, the bracelets are removed and thrown into the fires.

March 25 - Annunciation of the Virgin Mary – O Evagelismos/Greek Independence Day

March 25th marks the celebration of the *Annunciation of the Virgin Mary* or *'O Evangelismos'*. The feast marks the visit of the angel Gabriel to the Virgin Mary, during which he told her that she would be the mother of Jesus Christ, the Son of God. More importantly, since it occurs nine months before the birth of Jesus on Christmas Day, the Annunciation marks the actual *incarnation of Jesus Christ* - the moment that Jesus was conceived and that the Son of God became the son of the Virgin.

March 25th is also Greek Independence Day. In 1821 the Bishop Germanos of Patras raised the Greek flag at the Monastery of Agia Lavra in Peloponnese and began another revolution against the Turks. The people of Greece shouted

'**Freedom or Death**' and fought the War of Independence for 9 years, until a small part of modern Greece, including the Northern Sporades, was finally liberated and it was declared an independent nation. The day is celebrated with pride not just in Greece itself, but in every Greek community around the world. This passing on of Greek traditions to the next generation is an important responsibility for most Greek families.

In Skopelos, as in in every town and village throughout Greece, there is a school flag parade. All the schools take part and march along the paralea, with the chosen honour student carrying the flag. There is also a big armed forces parade in Thessaloniki, in the north of Greece and in Athens. After the liturgy on this day, special prayers are said to God for the liberation of the Greeks. Although this day falls within the Lenten period, the Church allows fish and seafood to be eaten because of the celebration of Liberty.

April 23 – St George - Aghios Georgios – Patron Saint of Greece

April 23rd (or the Tuesday after Easter) is the feast of **Aghios Georgios** (Saint George). St George is the patron saint of Greece and of shepherds, so this is a big rural celebration, with much feasting and dancing at associated shrines. If April 23rd falls before Easter, that is, during Lent, the festivities are postponed until the Monday after Easter.

Easter Preparations

The season of Lent and Easter is a time when all village housewives will 'spring clean' their homes and properties. Houses and streets are given new coats of white wash and homes are cleaned from one end to the other. This is also the time of year that the men will begin the chore of tilling their land, pruning their fruit and olive trees as well as sowing their summer vegetables. In days gone by, Easter was one of the holidays that every member in the family got a new outfit and a new pair of shoes - Christmas being the other. Even today, it is still customary for families to buy new outfits and shoes for Easter and wear them to Church for the Resurrection and on Easter Sunday.

The Godparents - **Koumbari** - of children will also purchase them gifts of clothing and bring them to the house at the end of Holy Week. The mothers will make the Godparents 'Easter Baskets' filled with home-made Easter biscuits, **Tsourekia**, **Avgoules** and dyed eggs.

Lazarus Saturday

Lazarus of Bethany or *Lazarus of the Four Days* was a believer in Jesus, whom, according to the Gospel of John, Jesus raised from the dead. During the preceding week of the commemoration of this event, the hymns in the Lenten **Triodion** track the sickness and then the death of Lazarus, and Christ's journey from beyond Jordan to Bethany. The scripture readings and hymns for Lazarus Saturday focus on the resurrection of Lazarus as a foreshadowing of the Resurrection of Christ, and a promise of the General Resurrection. On the Saturday before Holy Week, the Resurrection of Lazarus is celebrated. On Lazarus' Saturday, children are given traditional bread rolls, called *'lazarakia'*, which have the shape of a man wrapped in a shroud - the fore runner of the gingerbread man.

The miracle of the raising of Lazarus, the longest coherent narrative in John aside from the *Passion*, is the climax of John's *signs*. It explains the crowds seeking Jesus on Palm Sunday, and leads directly to the decision of Caiaphas and the Sanhedrin to kill Jesus. This day, together with Palm Sunday, holds a unique position in the Church year. They are days of joy and triumph between the penitence of Great Lent and the mourning of Holy Week.

Easter

Easter, or as the Greeks call it *'Pascha'*, is the most important religious festival in the Greek Orthodox Calendar.

In the Orthodox religion, *every* Sunday is dedicated to the resurrection of the Lord, but 100 days are dedicated to Easter: 50 days before the festival and 50 after it to commemorate the glory of God. Easter is therefore considered the **'Feast of Feasts'**.

Holy Week - Megalo Eudomada (Bright Week)

Palm Sunday – To Vagion

'To Vagion' *(Bay Leaf Sunday)* or *Palm Sunday* precedes Holy Week and commemorates Jesus Christ's entrance into Jerusalem following His miracle of raising Lazarus from the dead: it is one of the most joyous feasts of the Orthodox year. Having anticipated His arrival and having heard of the miracle, the people when out to meet the Lord and welcomed Him with displays of honour and shouts of praise. Churches are decorated with palm and bay branches; sometimes the palm leaves are shaped into a cross, or the crest of the moon, or a star. A basket containing the woven palm crosses or the sprigs of bay is placed on a table in front of the icon of the Lord, which is on the *Iconostasion*, and blessed during the service.

After the liturgy, pieces of palm leaves that have been braided and tied into crosses, or bay sprigs are handed out to all those in attendance. These take their place in the *Iconostasio* when they get home. They are considered to be lucky as people believe in the power of life and fertility that they pass on to women, animals and plants.

On Skopelos, bay leaves - ***daphne*** - are given to everyone in the congregation. A custom unique to the island is that the future mother-in-law of the bride-to-be gives a piece of jewellery or a coin to the Priest on the day before the service, which is then given to the engaged girl with her bay leaves on the day.

Palm Sunday is a day of fasting from meats and dairy products: traditionally, fish are eaten. This is also the Name day celebration for all those named *Vagianos*. The Christian symbolism of Easter was first underlined by Apostle Paul. When Christians began to celebrate Easter, they retained some of the features of the Jewish Passover, while at the same time, adding others. This can be seen from the *paschal lamb* and the red eggs.

Every evening throughout **Holy Week** (*Great Week*), all the Churches are decorated with purple bands. Priests dress in dark vestments and Church bells keep tolling. Weddings, christenings, balls and celebrations are not to take place during this week: people only gather in Church to commemorate the **Passion** of Christ.

The first of the Bridegroom services begins this evening, continuing through the evening of Holy Tuesday. Each evening service is the Matins or *Orthros* service of the following day (e.g. the service held on Sunday evening is the *Orthros* service for Holy Monday). The name of the service is from the figure of the Bridegroom in the parable of the Ten Virgins found in Matthew 25:1-13: the Priest will process with the icon of the Bridegroom, which is then placed in the middle of the *solea* of the Church and remains there until Holy Thursday.

Service of the Bridegroom - Akolouthia tou Nimfiou

The Christ of the Passion is the divine Bridegroom of the Church. The imagery connotes the final union of the Lover and the beloved. The title Bridegroom also suggests the *Parousia* (Passion). In the patristic tradition, the parable of the wise virgins is related to the Second Coming; and is associated with the need for spiritual vigilance and preparedness, by which believers are enabled to keep the divine commandments and receive the blessings of the age to come. The *troparion* 'Behold the Bridegroom comes in the middle of the night...', which is sung at the beginning of the *Orthros* of Great Monday, Tuesday and Wednesday, relates the worshipping community to that essential expectation:

watching and waiting for the Lord, who will come again to judge the living and the dead.

Great Monday - Megali Deutera

Today commemorates Joseph the Patriarch, the beloved son of Jacob in the Old Testament. The two important themes of today are preparedness and hypocrisy, in the parable of the wise and foolish virgins and the event of the cursing of the fig tree, said to have occurred on the morrow of Jesus' triumphant entry into Jerusalem. The fig tree is symbolic of Israel become barren by her failure to recognize and receive Christ and His teachings. The cursing of the fig tree is a parable in action, a symbolic gesture. Its meaning reflects that Christ's judgement on the faithless, unbelieving, unrepentant and unloving will be certain and decisive on the Last Day.

Great Tuesday - Megali Triti

On Holy Tuesday the Church calls to remembrance two parables, which are related to the Second Coming. The one is the parable of the Ten Virgins (Matthew 25:1-3); the other the parable of the Talents (Matthew 25:14-30). These parables point to the inevitability of the *Parousia* and deal with such subjects as spiritual vigilance, stewardship, accountability and judgement. Today during the Bridegroom service, the beautiful **Hymn of Kassiani** is sung.

On Great Tuesday, housewives make sweet rolls called **'koulourakia'**.

Great Wednesday - Megali Tetarti

On Holy Wednesday the Church invites the faithful to focus their attention on two figures: the sinful woman who anointed the head of Jesus shortly before the Passion, and Judas, the disciple who betrayed the Lord. The former acknowledged Jesus as Lord, while the latter severed himself from the Master. The one was set free, while the other became a slave. The one inherited the kingdom, while the other fell into perdition. These two people bring into focus concerns and issues related to freedom, sin, hell and repentance. Today at many Orthodox parishes the *Sacrament of Holy Unction* is offered: the long service consists of seven Epistle and seven Gospel readings.

On Wednesday, women clean the house, then in the evening they go to Church for the blessing of the Holy Oil. In Greek-speaking Churches this is performed annually for the whole congregation during Holy Week on the eve of Holy Wednesday. It is connected with the Sacrament of the healing of the sick. Everyone is encouraged to come forward for anointing with the special oil whether they are physically ill or not.

Holy Thursday - Megali Pempti

Today begins with the **Divine Liturgy of St. Basil** early in the morning. Later on, the women of Skopelos will begin their Easter preparations by dyeing their eggs: the egg is a symbol of life and red the colour of life (as in blood).Traditionally, Greeks dyed only red coloured eggs to symbolise Christ's blood, but now many people use an assortment of colours. In Byzantine times, it was the custom to bake ring-breads with a red egg in the middle. This tradition continues today and ring-breads are still sold in supermarkets and bakeries across the island.

On Holy Thursday Night, the Priest will read twelve excerpts of the Four Gospels relating to Christ's Passion in a long and solemn mass. After the first six are read, a large wooden cross with a carved statue of Christ is brought out and placed in front of the altar. With this symbol of Christ's hanging, the next six excerpts are read. Since this day is symbolic of Christ's death, the women will express mourning as they decorate the *Epitaphios* with garlands of white and purple flowers in all the most important Churches of the island. Flower shops are open until after midnight and the women work through the night. The *Epitaphios* symbolises the **Tomb of Christ**. It resembles a large table with a domed canopy built over it and it is adorned with intricate filigree that carpenters have painstakingly carved out. In each of its four corners, wooden handles extend so that it can be carried. During the **Lamentation Service**, the Priest and choir chant Byzantine hymns around the *'Epitaphios'*. The Priest will remove the symbolic wooden figure of Christ from the wooden cross in front of the altar. This figure is then covered with a sheet and kept in sanctuary for 50 days when it will be taken out for **Pentecost** and then returned to its original position. It is replaced by a special cloth that has been elaborately embroidered with the image of Christ, which is placed in the centre of the *Epitaphios* as a symbol of his dead body.

Good Friday - Megali Paraskevi

After the service on Friday morning, it is the custom for the islanders to make a tour of the Churches to admire the *Epitaphioi* and congratulate the women who have decorated it. The parishioners file past the symbolic tomb and kiss this cloth. Young children and maybe some not so young, crawl under the *Epitaphios* to the other side: this is done so as to be given a blessing.

Throughout Greece, **Good Friday** is known as the day of mourning. It is the only day of the year that the Divine Liturgy will not be celebrated. The drama of the Death of Christ is followed with great devoutness. Sweet things are not eaten, for the love of Christ, who was given vinegar to drink. Soup made with sesame-paste, lettuce or lentils with vinegar is the food eaten on this day for the devout. It is considered a great sin to work with a hammer or nails or sew on this day. There are three services: the Imperial Hours in the morning, Vespers in the afternoon, and the Great Friday evening service. In addition, some parishes offer a Holy Friday youth retreat.

On Great Friday noon, all Greek flags fly at half mast. On Great Friday evening, the **Service of the Epitaph**, which symbolizes the funeral of Christ, is held. Afterwards, the *Epitaphios* is taken out of the Church and carried by men through the town in a slow procession of Priests and altar boys carrying gold crosses and Icons. Then everybody follows the procession of the **Epitaph**, carrying brown lighted candles. The procession begins and ends at the Church, following a fixed itinerary through the town. Each procession meets the congregation from the next Church along the route, until all the Churches process together along the *paralea*, before returning the biers to the Churches from which they came: the chants are sad and solemn and the Church bells will ring slowly and rhythmically as they do when signalling a funeral. After the procession returns to the Church, the followers walk past (and under) the *Epitaphios*, kissing the image of Christ which is laid upon it, in order to receive a special blessing.

Holy Saturday - Megalo Savato

The Holy Saturday morning service is the first announcement of the Resurrection: the reading is taken from the Old Testament. Shortly after the hymn, the Priest decorates the Church by throwing bay leaves and/or flower petals.

On Holy Saturday afternoon, Greek Television shows the arrival of a Greek Military Jet carrying the Eternal Flame from Jerusalem. Multitudes of Priests wait with their lanterns at the airport for its arrival to take this 'light' to their Churches.

Everyone in Greece, young and old, attends the Resurrection service for Easter, dressed in formal attire. Shortly before midnight, the Churches are filled to overflowing and most of the congregations stand outside in the courtyards. Facing the altar, they silently pray while holding unlit white candles, *lampada*. Just before midnight, the Church will turn off all its lights - except for the Eternal

Flame that is inside on the Altar. Everything is dark and the congregation is silent, symbolising the darkness and silence of the tomb.

The Resurrection Mass concludes as the clock strikes midnight: the Priest lights his candle from the Eternal Flame and sings out *'Christos Anesti'* -'Christ is risen'. Holding his lighted candle out, he offers the flame to those of the congregation that are closest to him. After lighting their own candles, they pass the flame back to others so in a few minutes the entire Church and courtyards are filled with flickering candle light. While doing this, the Byzantine Chant *'Christos Anesti'* is sung by all in attendance. The ceremony of lighting candles from the flame of the Holy Light is the most significant moment of the year: as they pass the flame, people kiss in a deeply symbolic moment; in the moment of conquering death, there is a certain meaning to kissing older people at that point, who you know you'll be burying soon; and to be kissing the children who are coming up, who will be replacing you in the next generation. All around, people exchange wishes for the day, telling each other *'Christos Anesti!'*. To which the reply is *'Alithos Anesti!'* – *'He is truly risen!'* Everything comes alive: Church bells peal joyously, all the boats in the harbour sound their horns and set off flares; buildings are floodlit, farmers fire their shotguns into the air and town people set off fireworks.

Then they carefully carry home their lighted candles. Before entering their houses they make a cross with the smoke of the candle on top of the door: this sign stays there all year through and means that the spirit of the Resurrection has been brought into the house. The burning candles are then used to light the lantern before the icon stand. This light must be kept burning throughout the year.

Following the Midnight Easter Service held on Saturday night the Greeks have the traditional *Anastasimo* meal, the first meal of the Resurrection, which consists of a special paschal soup (known in Greek as *'margeirista'*) made from the intestines and other organs of lamb. The soup is eaten in the early morning following the midnight service, along with the sweet bread called *tsorekia* (flavoured with the spice *machlepi*, which is made from a ground seed from Syria), *koulourakia pascalina* (bread rolls), the *kalitsounia* (cheese pies), and a salad of greens. The red-dyed boiled eggs, which have been prepared on Holy Thursday, are cracked by faithful Greek Orthodox accompanied with the words *Christos Anesti!* and the reply *Alithos Anesti.*. Afterwards, children and adults will challenge friends with the question *'Na Tsoungrisoume?'* - 'Shall we crack them?' This tradition is still very much enjoyed throughout Greece. Dyed eggs are held in the fist with one end exposed. The other person does the same, and then they are tapped together. The breaking of the eggs is meant to symbolize Christ breaking from the Tomb. Whoever ends up with the cracked egg is the loser. The last person with the un-cracked egg at the end has a special blessing for the year to come.

Easter Sunday - Pascha Lambri - Kyriaki tou Pascha

The day begins with the *Agape Service*. In the New Testament, *agape* stands for the fatherly love of God for humans, as well as the human reciprocal love for God. The term necessarily extends to the love of one's fellow man. The Church Fathers used *agape* to designate both a rite (using bread and wine) and a meal of fellowship to which the poor were invited: all celebrants leave the Church with a small token of food.

Easter Sunday is a holiday that is spent with family, relatives and friends. The meal is usually a communal affair with roasting lamb turning over barbeques or open pits, grilled offal, Easter rolls and bread, and red wine. Lamb is served in honour of the Lamb of God who was sacrificed and rose again on Easter.

Some women will bring pots of *'Lambriotis'*: this is a dish of stuffed goat or lamb that has been cooking overnight in the ovens. A large loaf of leavened bread is always present on the Easter table together with traditional sweet rolls (*koulouria*), sweetened bread (*tsoureki*), and little filled cheese envelopes. Of course, no Greek party would be complete without the traditional music and dancing. Tables are decorated with colourful cloths and fresh spring flowers as well as baskets of dyed eggs for *'Tsoungrisma'*. Since this is the biggest celebration of the year for the Greeks, there is also lots of *Ouzo, Retsina* and *Tsipouro* to drink.

Easter Monday - Deutera tou Pascha

The entire week of Easter Monday through to the following Friday is a holiday. Each day a different Monastery is visited honouring a different Saint. Friends and families gather together for dinners and dances. The celebration of the Resurrection continues until the **Holiday of the Virgin Mary** on Friday night, when the biggest parties are held.

Easter is a time that all the dead are memorialised. From the time of **Carnival** and **All Soul's Day** through **Good Saturday** and the **Resurrection,** all Greeks go to the cemeteries to visit their deceased loved ones. It is customary to take flowers and light the lanterns on the memorials of the dead.

For the next six weeks, each Sunday commemorates Doubting Thomas; The Myrrh bearing women; the paralysed man; the Mid Pentecost; The Samaritan Woman; and the blind man respectively; interrupted by Mayday and culminating in Pentecost.

May 1 - Protomayia

The 1st of May is traditionally seen as a celebration of spring and fertility and it's considered *'Labour Day'* for the Greeks, as it is also International Workers Day, a holiday first popularized by the Soviet Union. Worker's groups and unions may be active today; major strikes are sometimes scheduled for May Day.

Greek families will take their picnics out to the country where the children will play and pick wild flowers – the first spring blooms. The flowers are then braided carefully into wreaths of all sizes to be taken home and adorn front doors. Some islanders, particularly taxi drivers, even hang them on the grills of their cars. The wreaths used to remain in place until the **Feast of St. John on August 29th**, when they were burned. Today, however, they tend to stay in place all year round.

Ascension Day - Analepsis

This holy day is celebrated on the fortieth day after the Resurrection of Christ, on the Thursday of the sixth week of *Pascha*. *Analepsis*, meaning the 'taking up', and its other name the *Episozomene*, the 'salvation from on high', denote that by ascending into his glory Christ completed the work of Man's redemption. Ascension is one of the Twelve Great Feasts of the Orthodox liturgical year. The feast is always observed with an All-night vigil. The day before is the *Apodosis* (leave-taking) *of Pascha* (the last day of the Feast of Easter).

Ascension has an afterfeast of eight days. The Sunday after Ascension is the **Sunday of the Holy Fathers** of the First Ecumenical Council at Nicaea.

This Council formulated the Nicene Creed up to the words, 'He (Jesus) ascended into heaven, and sits at the right hand of the Father; and shall come again, with glory, to judge the living and the dead; Whose kingdom shall have no end.' The afterfeast ends on the following Friday, the Friday before Pentecost. The next day is appropriately a *Saturday of the Dead* (general commemoration of all faithful departed).

Certain customs were connected with the liturgy of this feast, such as the blessing of beans and grapes after the *Commemoration of the Dead* in the Canon of the Mass, the blessing of first fruits, the blessing of a candle, the extinguishing of the **Paschal Candle**, and triumphal processions with torches and banners outside the Churches to commemorate the entry of Christ into heaven. In England it was once common for Churches to 'beat the bounds' on this day, and some continue the custom: members of the parish walk round the parish boundaries, marking boundary stones (e.g. by writing on them in chalk) and hitting them with sticks. Some of these customs can be observed on Skopelos, but the author has only seen the beating of the bounds once.

All Soul's Day - Psihosavato

The Saturday before *Pentecost* is another *'Psihosavato'* or *'All Soul's Day'*. Sweet cereal porridge, sweet bread, and other foods are consecrated in the Church and then brought to cemeteries where they are distributed to the poor.

Pentacost - Aghiou Pnevma/ The Holy Trinity - Aghia Triada

The Monday of **Aghio Pnevma** (the Holy Spirit, Whit Monday in UK) marks the descent of the Holy Spirit to the assembled disciples, fifty days after Easter. (The name comes from the Greek *pentekoste*, meaning fiftieth). It is also called Whitsun, but does not necessarily coincide with the Whitsun Bank Holiday in the UK. The symbols of Pentecost are those of the Holy Spirit and include flames, wind, the breath of God and a dove.

In the Eastern Orthodox Church, Pentecost is one of the Great Feasts and is considered to be the highest ranking Great Feast of the Lord, second only to Easter. The service is celebrated with an All-night Vigil on the eve of the feast day, and the Divine Liturgy on the day of the feast itself. Orthodox Churches are often decorated with greenery and flowers on this feast day.

The feast itself lasts three days. The first day is known as **'Trinity Sunday'**; the second day is known as **'Spirit Monday'** and the third day, Tuesday, is called the **'Third Day of the Trinity'**. The Afterfeast of Pentecost lasts for one week, during which fasting is not permitted, even on Wednesday and Friday.

Pentecost is often regarded as the birthday of the Christian Church, and the start of the Church's mission to the world, although theologically, Orthodox see the Church as having existed before the creation of the world. Usually a modest liturgy is celebrated at rural chapels of the Holy Spirit, gaily decked out with pennants, as Pentecost is a happy festival.

All Saints' Day - Agion Panton

The Sunday after Pentecost marks the close of the *Paschal* season. It is set aside as a commemoration of all locally venerated saints. The icon of the **Sunday of All Saints** depicts Jesus Christ seated above the Throne of heaven surrounded by the Saints. The rows of Saints include the Archangel Michael and other Angels, the Theotokos and John the Baptist, the Apostles, Bishops, Great Martyrs, Ascetics and Monastics. To the side of the Throne are Adam and Eve, bowing in reverence to Christ. At the lower left of the icon is the Patriarch Abraham, at the lower centre is the Good Thief who was crucified with Christ, and on the lower right is the Patriarch Jacob. In addition to this special day, Saturdays throughout the year are also days for general commemoration of all saints.

June 21

June 21 is the day to celebrate the Summer Solstice. It is the moment at which the sun is in the highest place, the longest day of the year and the shortest night. June is the sixth month of the current Gregorian calendar and the first month of summer. It is a time when the children of Skopelos rejoice as their long summer vacation from school begins. Originally dedicated to the Goddess Hera, patron of the female sex, and sacred to all gods and goddesses who preside over love, passion, and beauty, this month is considered an excellent month for marriages.

The goddess of the Summer Solstice was Hestia, the goddess who watched over domesticity and the family. She was given the first offering at any sacrifice made in the home. As a hearth goddess, Hestia was also known for her hospitality. If a stranger came calling and seeking sanctuary, it was considered an offense against Hestia to turn the person away. This was the beginning of the custom that made Greece a byword for hospitality until modern times.

June 24 - The Nativity of St John the Baptist

24th June celebrates one of the oldest festivals of the Christian Church. It comes three months after the celebration on March 25 of the Annunciation, when the Archangel Gabriel told Mary that her cousin Elizabeth was in her sixth month of pregnancy, and six months before the Christmas celebration of the birth of Jesus. It is the **Nativity of Ag. Ioannis Prodromos**, and is a day of rest: like Christmas, it is celebrated with three Masses; a vigil, at dawn, and at midday.

The Eastern Orthodox faithful believe that John was the last of the Old Testament prophets, thus serving as a bridge between that period of revelation and the New Covenant. They also teach that, following his death, John descended into **Hades** and there once more preached that Jesus the Messiah was coming, so he was the Forerunner of Christ in death as he had been in life. According to Sacred Tradition, John the Baptist appears at the time of death to those who have not heard the Gospel of Christ, and preaches the Good News to them, that all may have the opportunity to be saved. Orthodox Churches will often have an icon of St. John the Baptist in a place of honour on the iconostasis, and he is frequently mentioned during the Divine Services. Every Tuesday throughout the year is dedicated to his memory.

St John the Baptist was the first Monk, which is why he is the patron-saint of monks and the monastic life.

July 3 - Aghios Yakinthos

Aghios Yakinthos, or Saint Hyacinth, is the patron saint of love, youth and lovers: he is therefore the **real** Saint Valentine of Orthodoxy. He was born in 98 AD in Caesarea in Ancient Cappadocia and was martyred at 20 for his Christian faith. Nowadays in Greece Aghios Yakinthos is celebrated not in order to replace the imported St Valentine, but to form the opposite pole to the complete commercialisation of the day of love.

July 6 - St Valentine's Day

In the Eastern Orthodox Church **Aghiou Valentinou the Presbyter** (St Valentine) is celebrated on July 6. The saint was a Priest who lived in Rome during the reign of Emperor Claudius Flavius. At that time it was forbidden to be a Christian and therefore Christians had to perform their Sacraments in secret, including marriage ceremonies. So St. Valentine would take Christian couples down into the catacombs in the middle of the night and marry them without anyone knowing. In the year 269 AD the emperor ordered General Asterius to persuade Valentine to deny Christ. Instead, he healed the general's daughter from a blindness that had afflicted her for two years, sending her a letter from prison which he signed '*From your Valentine*,' an expression that is still in use today. He then baptised the general and his entire household. The emperor was enraged and had them all tortured and put to death.

August 6 - Transfiguration - Metamorfosis tou Sotiros

August 6th is the Feast of the Transfiguration, one of the Twelve Great Feasts, one of the central events recorded in the gospels. Christ took Peter, James, and John up to a high mountain and was '*transfigured before them.*' There also appeared to them Moses and Elijah. The two stand for the law and the prophets, as well as for the living and dead, for Moses died and his burial place is known, while Elijah was taken alive into heaven in order to appear again to announce the time of God's salvation in Christ the Messiah. Thus, in appearing with Jesus on the mount of Transfiguration, Moses and Elijah showed that the Messiah is Son of God, the Lord of all Creation, of the Old and New Testaments, of the living and the dead. The feast day is celebrated throughout the island: both grapes and wheat may be consecrated as an expression of thanksgiving. In Skopelos, people take part in a traditional evening concert, dressed in national costume and singing and dancing on the *paralea*.

August 15 - the Dormition of Mary - Apokismisis tis Panagias

The **Dormition of the Theotokos** on August 15th, commemorating the death of the *Theotokos* (Mary), and her bodily resurrection before being taken up into heaven, is the third most important religious holiday in Greece, after Easter and Christmas. This is when the tourist season here on Skopelos reaches its peak. Everyone goes to their ancestral home for the Festival and all the businesses will be closed on that day. The entire country is virtually shut down as the Greeks head for the islands and everyone takes advantage of the long weekend to rest or to light a candle for *Panagia* (the Virgin Mary) whose ascent to the heavens is commemorated during this day.

The **Feast of the Dormition** is preceded by a two-week fast, referred to as the *Dormition Fast*. From August 1st to August 14th (inclusive) Orthodox fast from red meat, poultry, meat products, dairy products (eggs and milk products), fish, oil, and wine. The *Dormition Fast* is a stricter fast than either the *Nativity Fast* (Advent) or the *Apostles' Fast*, with only wine and oil (but no fish) allowed on weekends.

This is a very important religious feast and it is celebrated with pilgrimage. The day is marked with family reunions, and since most Greeks are travelling to their home towns, ferries and flights are very crowded and the transportation system generally can seem to get jammed around August 15th. August is the most crowded and most expensive month across the whole of Greece. The weather is very hot (with temperatures reaching 100^0 F / 37.8^0 C on some days), the beaches crowded and the festivals in full swing.

August 31 – Cincture (Belt) of the Theotokos

According to Sacred Tradition of the Orthodox Church, at the time of her Dormition, the *Theotokos* was buried by the Twelve Apostles in Jerusalem. Three days later, Thomas the Apostle, who had been delayed and unable to attend the funeral, arrived and asked to have one last look at the Virgin Mary. When he and the other Apostles arrived at Mary's Tomb, they found that her body was missing. According to some accounts, the Virgin Mary then appeared and gave her belt (*cincture*) to Thomas, before ascending into heaven. Made out of camel hair, the belt is presently kept in a silver reliquary at the Greek Orthodox Monastery of Vateopedi on Mt. Athos.

Saint's Day Festivals - Glendi

The saints are divided into six main categories: 1) The Apostles 2) The Prophets 3) The Martyrs 4) The Fathers & Hierarchs 5) The Monastics 6) The Just. In Iconography they are usually dressed accordingly. On top of the above festivals and holidays, each Church holds a special celebration on the feast day of whichever of the above is its patron – for example, Ag. Ilios (Elijah) and Ag. Paraskevi (Preparation), to name but two. Often, this day is the only day the Church may be used, especially if it is a family Church or a Church isolated in the countryside. You will know if there is to be a celebration, as the Churches are decorated with flags and preparations are often being made for the after service party.

The Name day - To Yeorti

A **Name Day** is the day of the year in which one's patron saint is commemorated. Most Orthodox are named after a saint, although in Greece and Cyprus many names derive from antiquity, and there may not be a Christian saint by the same name. In such a case the person may choose to celebrate on **All Saints' Day.** Some name days are very important in the Greek calendar and many children are named after these Saints: on these days, a national holiday takes place.

Generally, the name day is more celebrated than the birthday, and in the not so distant past, people were not so sure of their date of birth, whereas the name day was certain. In fact, it remains more important, because the birthday simply marks the passage of time, whereas the Name day links each Greek Orthodox to one of the citizens of Heaven who has already shown his or her love for mankind by granting the use of their name.

The celebrant provides five special loaves called *prosphoro* to their Church on the eve of the saint's day. The bread consists of two loaves baked together, one placed on top of the other: each loaf is stamped with a seal. The double loaf represents the divine and human nature of Jesus Christ. Traditional Greek homes reserve a pan that is used only for making *prosphoro.* The small round loaves of white bread, which are spiced with cloves and bitter orange-blossom water, are then blessed by the Priest, and one of the loaves is sent to the *yortaris,* or feast giver, while the other loaves are cut into pieces and offered to the congregation and to the poor.

The traditional format of a name day celebration is an *open house*: no specific invitations are extended and all well-wishers are welcomed. This is not uniformly observed: a family or person may choose to celebrate with invited guests only, at home, at a restaurant, a bar or a club, or not celebrate at all (e.g. following a recent bereavement). Name day celebrations are similar to birthdays, except for expected differences (for example, there is no cake with candles on a name day). Children celebrate their birthdays and name days equally festively; as the person grows up the emphasis shifts decisively to the name day and birthdays become lower-key, family affairs.

Part of the *glendi* (celebration) involves the celebrant offering sweets to those around him at home, at school, or at work: friends and family visit uninvited and offer their wishes (***Xronia Polla!*** *Long life to you, live many years*!) as well as small presents.

Legends and Superstitions

A superstition is a belief based on fear and not on the laws of science, which tell us that everything which happens has known cause and effect. Instead, superstition tells us that certain things happen because of luck or chance. Many people do not fully believe in superstitions, but follow some because they think it may be safer to do so.

Historians believe that superstitions have probably existed as long as people have existed: thousands of years ago people didn't always understand why things happened, so they made up ways to explain them: it is now believed that these old explanations have become our superstitions. Below are some of the superstitions that exist now or have existed in the past, on the island of Skopelos.

Vaskania - The Evil Eye

Fear of the Evil Eye is by far the most famous of all Greek superstitions, with very old roots in Hellenic culture from the time of paganism. Paintings of Greek *triremes* over two thousand years ago have an eye painted at the front of the trireme in an attempt to ward off the Evil Eye, which is known widely throughout Greece and the Greek Islands. It is said to be able to strike anywhere without notice: If you receive a compliment, and then develop a painful headache immediately after, then this occurrence is attributed to the Evil Eye.

In order to avoid suspicion that you might possess the Evil Eye, you should go out of your way to be seen as generous, giving to those in need without begrudging the gift given. It is thought best to avoid complimenting people on their possessions and to deny any recent improvement in one's financial status, so that you do not attract the Eye

The Greek Orthodox faith accepts the cultural belief in the Evil Eye, which is referred as *Vaskania*, but prefers to attribute its cause to the Devil, or the very human emotions of admiration (lust or pride) or envy. The Church believes the Eye is harmful to both the one casting the spell and the one receiving it, and invokes an ancient prayer to heal both parties. The Church encourages people who believe they've received the Evil Eye to seek help from their faith, claiming prayers from God are the most effective way of breaking the spell.

Common practice in Greek society has it that people are taught the prayer by a Priest and will use it themselves to 'treat' cursed friends and relatives, sometimes even over the phone. Some believe that for a woman to be able to do the prayer she must be taught it by a man.

On Skopelos, there are people who are said to know how to remove the Eye from someone who is affected, even though the Greek Orthodox Church strictly forbids this. The Church sees this as dangerous ground, and believes only a Priest has the power to read a person in an attempt to remove the Eye: the Church fears that attempts to remove the Eye can result in possession. Believers of the Evil Eye should understand that the person who is attempting to remove the Eye should be using the method that the Church uses, and not some custom that has been passed down generation to generation. However, many Skopelitian old ladies regard themselves as having the power of healing against the Evil Eye and openly practice its removal, against the wishes of the Church.

The Eye is cast away through the process of *xematiasma*, whereby the healer silently recites a secret prayer passed over from an older relative of the opposite sex, usually a grandparent. Such prayers are revealed only under specific circumstances, for according to superstition those who reveal them indiscriminately lose their ability to cast off the evil eye.

If consulted, the healer will take a teacup and pour water into it and then sprinkle a few drops of olive oil into it.

The victim takes the cup and swirls the contents around before putting the cup on the table and turning it around three times. The handle should face to the East when the cup is at rest. The healer will make the sign of the cross on the victim's face and hands using the oil and holy water, while reciting a secret, silent prayer.

The prayer is only ever revealed in special circumstances, because those who utter it without discretion will lose the power to cast out the Evil Eye. It is said that if evil is indeed present, both the healer and the victim will find themselves yawning. After making the sign of the cross a further three times, the healer spits into the air three times, all symbols of the Holy Trinity to defend against the Eye, and the Evil is vanquished.

Another simple test used to check if the evil eye was cast is that of the oil: two drops of olive oil are placed into a glass of water. If the drops remain separated, the test concludes there is no evil eye, but if they merge, there is. This is often performed by a grandparent.

Mataki - Charms

To ward off the Evil Eye several things can be done: the most popular form of protection against the Eye being a charm. Coloured blue - the colour to ward off Evil - it is painted with an eye that supposedly deflects the evil. These charms are available in a variety of forms, from personal jewellery to different sized and shaped pieces to hang inside cars or on walls. Some people cement Evil Eye charms into their driveways. Although the Greek Orthodox Church states the only form of protection is a crucifix or a religious icon from a Church or monastery, the Evil Eye charm is very popular and visible all over Skopelos. Blue beads can also be worn instead of the eye charm in the form of a necklace or bracelet.

Unfortunately people who have blue eyes are thought to be exceptional givers of the Evil Eye. In such circumstances, believers of the Evil Eye are wary of compliments received from a blue eyed person.

Garlic will also negate the effect of the Eye, especially if a single clove grows into the shape of a small head of garlic. This clove does, however, need to be carried at all times, worn in the clothes, which is not always easy and practical. (This probably accounts for the popularity of the charm to ward off the power of the Eye instead.) Garlic is believed to ward off demons and evil spirits in the same manner that incense does: demons and evil spirits are believed to fear it. If you find garlic hanging in Skopelos' businesses or houses, it is there for the purpose of warding off evil.

When receiving an extravagant compliment it is advisable to whisper *skorda* (the Greek word for *garlic*) immediately after accepting the praise. This should reduce the risk of attracting the Evil Eye. It's also said one should spit three times while saying *skorda*, before asking the one paying the compliment to do the same. This strange practice could be deemed unsociable and unhygienic, so it is comforting to know the general consensus seems to be that the word *skorda* alone offers sufficient protection.

Precious and semi-precious stones and crystals are commonly used in amulets and talismans, each stone having its specific significance and power. For example: *amber* wards off evil spirits and protects against rheumatism; *aquamarine* brings love, hope to the oppressed and protects travellers; *diamond* repels wild beasts and evil men, and ensures fidelity in a lover; *emerald* strengthens the memory and prevents possession by evil spirits; *garnet* brings good health and protects against nightmares; *lapis lazuli*, like all blue stones, protects against black magic and wards off melancholy and insomnia; *onyx* protects a marriage from intruders; *pearl* improves the skin, cures fevers and brings tranquility; *sapphire* brings peace and happiness and protects the eyes; *topaz* helps to locate buried treasure; and finally, *turquoise* brings peace to married life.

Different symbols and shapes are also considered to have different magical properties. For example, the shape of a bee brings success in business; a black cat is one of the best all around good luck charms known to witchcraft, but a white cat crossing your path is unlucky; anything egg shaped brings good luck and is a powerful fertility charm; a fish brings a large family, especially if cast in gold or mother of pearl; a stone arrowhead is a powerful force against evil spirits; anything in the shape of a sacred oak tree, or a piece of oak itself, is lucky; the shape of a pig is a potent bearer of fertility; the pomegranate is a lucky fruit and may be used as a good luck charm; and the form of a serpent brings long life and wisdom.

Some of the oldest houses on Skopelos have a door knocker in the shape of a woman's hand, often holding a ball, representing the globe: this is a relic from the Muslim occupation often called *khamsa*, the **Hand of Fatima**, the compassionate daughter of the Prophet Mohammed, who was the only woman allowed to touch his head. Miracles have been attributed to her; for example, it is said that when she prayed in the desert, it started to rain. Her hand is therefore lucky as another powerful charm against evil spirits and the Evil Eye.

Talismans - 'Filahta'

Filhata are holy items and are regularly used in Greece generally. Most commonly you will see these charms pinned to the backs of small children's and infant's clothing. But you will also find that many of the older people carry them in their pockets and purses or have them discreetly pinned to their clothing too.

There are numerous items that are used for *Filahta* that are thought to guard you from the Evil Eye. Of course, there are the simple gold crosses or medals of Saints, but there are also small pieces of cloth sewn into sachets, holding an array of mysterious contents. These sachets can be filled with pieces of olive branch or basil that have been used by a Priest

261

in some ceremony, dirt from the grave of a Saint or perhaps burnt candle shavings from a Church altar. Anything can be used for these charms, but the rule is that it has to be something from holy ground or something that has been blessed. Any one item, or a combination, are sewn into a very small, triangular sachet and sometimes adorned with beads in the sign of the cross.

Talimans – 'Gouria'

Some charms may have more pagan origins and these cannot be bought, but must be given in order for them to be lucky. Sometimes people have glass pomegranate charms or ones made from silver or gold, but *gouria* can be almost anything that has been given to give the recipient good luck. Jewellers cash in on this tradition and produce *gouria* every year, so that they can be given as Christmas or New Year's gifts.

In March, many devout young people, pregnant women and children feel the need to protect themselves from the vagaries of fate. You will often see them wearing thin red and gold cords around their left wrists during this month. At Easter weekend, these are taken off and burned with ceremony in the Church.

Spitting

It is customary for Greeks to spit to ward off evil. If a Greek hears bad news they may spit on themselves three times to ward off the possibility of anything bad happening to themselves. They may even raise their shirt and spit between their clothes towards their chest. The person does not actually spit on themselves, what they say is *'Ptew, Ptew, Ptew'* with very little spit actually being thrown about. Skopelitian fishermen may spit into their nets so that they will ward off any evil not allowing them to get a good catch. Likewise, a student may feel that he has written a wonderful report and spit on it before handing it in for marking. The spit will chase the bad spirits away and avoid a jinx.

Also, if someone compliments a Greek, to avoid the Evil Eye they may spit onto themselves, and may say to the person *'Ptew, Ptew mi me matiasis'*, which basically says, *'I'm spitting on myself so that you do not cause the Evil Eye to come upon me.'* Spitting is believed to be very effective against The Evil Eye.

In most cultures, the primary victims of the Eye are thought to be babies and young children, because they are so often praised and commented upon by strangers or by childless women. It has become a particular custom in Greece to exorcise babies by the use of spitting, including in baptisms in the Greek Orthodox Church ceremony. When a child is baptized the Priest will blow into the air three times to glorify the Trinity, and both the Priest and godparent spit three times in order to ward off the devil.

The Danger of a Parent's Curse

Traditionally Greek families tend to be very close, and there usually exists strong bonds between all members of the near family and the extended family. Greeks place a very high respect on elders and younger children will often call elders who are not blood relatives 'Aunt' or 'Uncle' out of respect.

Parents have an even greater respect placed upon them. It is customary for Greek children to ask the blessing of the parents, for example in marriage. The Greek Orthodox Church places a great value in parents, and in the upbringing of their children into a Christian life. As such, it is believed that disrespect towards a parent that has done a great deal for the child is shameful.

Each man or woman is considered to have two fathers: the physical father, and God. The same can be said indirectly that each man or woman has two mothers: one being the patron saint of Mothers, the Virgin Mary and the earthly mother. Therefore disrespect of your physical parent is thought to transcend to disrespect towards God.

It is believed by some that a curse of a parent will take effect as it will fall on the ears of God, who will pull his protection away from the disrespectful child. This is called in Greek a *Parahorisis*. There are two forms of *Parahorisis*: one is for the Good, as is the case with gifts from God such as being able to prophesy, or able to smell myrrh. The other form of *Parahorisis* is the feared form which can result in the worst case of *Possession*.

Either way, it is believed by some that a curse will take effect if it said by a parent. For example, if a parent curses a child never to be successful in their life, if the child never amounts to nothing it will be attributed to the curse. The most dangerous curse is said to not be from a father, but from a mother. The mother is said to have a special bond with the child as the child is carried in the mother's womb for many months. If the mother curses the child it is believed that the child must have been extremely disrespectful, and will be punished. In fact, in no circumstance is disrespect towards either parent acceptable. It is believed that disrespect will be paid for in this life as much as in the next.

Priests

It is customary for Greeks, upon seeing a Priest, to go up to them and kiss their hands or even the clothes that they are wearing. However, just as in ancient times, it is considered a bad omen to see a Priest walking in the street. Upon seeing one, Greeks may spit three times into their shirt. It is also considered bad luck to see a Priest in the morning. If you do, you must tie a knot in your handkerchief until the day is ended. In this manner any bad luck will be tied until a time when the chance of something bad happening will not be as likely.

Fairies

Does any fragment of ancient Greek mythology survive in the beliefs of the people of Skopelos today? The answer is, 'Yes, the nymphs.' *Nymphi (nymph)* and *Neraida (fairy)* both have the same meaning: their very name is as old as *Pontus*, their father, and *Doris*, their mother. Fairies are none other than the modern forms of the *dryads, oreads, naiads, neraidas, fates, furies, graces* and *muses* of the ancient myths. They are the nymphs that sang and played with *Pan* and *Hermes, Apollo* and the *satyrs*, but now they play and dance and sing with common shepherds, fishermen and hunters. This is why the island of Skopelos is so fertile: on the two high mountains of Palouki and Delfi, full of streams and springs, the fairies now dance and play and radiate a subtle charm.

Fairies are the virgin divinities of the earth. They know no heaven, for they take the place of the lower, earth-dwelling gods of the ancient mythology. They were never born; they never grow old; yet they are not immortal. Their beauty is everlasting and their dance eternal. They were created out of the earth and always live upon it, the anthropomorphic spirits of hills, streams, trees and ocean.

However, their power is not unlimited. They can be frightened and driven away by the firing of a gun. They dare not touch the mortal who wears a *Filahta* charm: the cross, a sign of the cross, and prayer are protections against them. And if a mortal seizes a fairy's handkerchief or veil, a strand of hair or a bit of clothing, the fairy becomes a helpless mortal woman, bound to serve the human being who thus has captured her.

If the fairy article returns to the possession of its rightful owner, the woman regains her fairy attributes and power, but should the article be burned to ashes, communication between her and the fairy world ceases and she is doomed to die a mortal's death.

265

Occasionally, as in the case of the water fairies, they offer gifts to their prospective captives. By accepting these gifts, mortals place themselves under the fairies' dominion, from which escape is possible only by burning the gifts. Fairies have destroyed the happiness or wrecked the life of many a youth who, having seen them, cannot put the memory of them from his mind, or who, having possessed one of them, has lost her forever.

The springs from which fairies drink are called *magemenes, bewitched.* The mortal who drinks from such a spring becomes *magemenos, fairypossessed,* and, forgetting home and family, wanders aimlessly like one mad.

There are many old tales of fairies and their interactions with humans on Skopelos, which has a fairy tradition much like that of Ireland. The dolls to be found hanging on the walls of many tourist shops, with long hair and dresses, are representations of these fairies or nymphs of the waters.

The Sorceress

The mediator between the fairy and the mortal worlds is the sorceress, usually an old woman with a practical knowledge of healing and much supernatural lore. She not only cures physical ills, but she ministers also to the troubled mind. By conjuring, murmuring mystic words, and applying magic herbs, she can release a *magemenon, bewitched mortal,* from evil spirits. The sight of an old sorceress with her bag of magic, wandering over lonely hills in search of herbs, used to be familiar to every villager in Greece. These awesome women lived a hermit's life, seeking the unfrequented ways, speaking little, mingling with their fellow beings only when summoned to aid.

Vampires

Greece is one of the oldest sources for the contemporary vampire legend. Ancient Greek writings record the existence of three vampire-like creatures - the *lamiai* (who kill children by sucking their blood), the *empusai*, and the *mormolykiai* (hobgoblins who cannibalize their own children). Also known in Greece was the *strige*, a vampire witch. *Strige* was derived from the Latin *strix*, which originally referred to the screech owl and later to a night flying demon that attacked and killed infants by sucking their blood.

The Ancient Greeks soon lost their fear of the *lamiai* and, even in ancient times, they had simply become a tool for parents to frighten their children. However, when a child dies suddenly from an unknown cause, a saying still popular in Greece suggests that the child has been *strangled by the lamiai*.

The *lamiai, empusai,* and *mormolykiai,* though known for their drinking of blood, were not vampires in the same sense as those of Eastern Europe: they were spirit beings rather than revivified corpses. The ancient Greeks, however, did have a class of *revenants*, (beings that return from the grave), which would develop into the modern perception of true vampires.

Originally, there were three circumstances that would predispose an individual to become a *revenant*: first, there could be the curse of a parent or someone who an individual had failed; second, one might become *undead* because of an evil or dishonourable act, most notably against one's family, such as the murder of a kinsman or adultery with a sister- or brother-in-law; third, the dead might join the *undead* by dying violently or by not being buried.

The ancient Greek revenant was essentially benign and returned primarily to complete some unfinished family business. On occasion it committed an act of vengeance, but always one that most would consider logical. It did not enact chaotic violence.

Gradually, the view that vampires were characteristically vicious came to dominate Greek thought about the *revenants*: ideas about the nature of the vampire became focused in its bloodthirstiness and its wanton nature. The most common name for the undead vampire in Greece seems to be *vrykolakas*. On the islands the vampire has such names as *vurvukalas* and *vrukolakas*. On Crete, the vampire is called the *kathakanas*.

The popular belief in *vrykolakes* was taken into the doctrinal perspective of the Greek Orthodox Church as it became the dominant force in Greek religious life in the first millennium AD. In the face of persisting accounts of the undead, the Church developed an explanation, claiming that the devil inhabited the body of the dead and caused it to move. It went on to propose that the dead might become *vrykolakes* if they died in an excommunicated state; if they were buried without the proper Church rites; or if they died a violent death. To these it added two other causes: stillborn children or those who were born on one of the great Church festivals. These causes expanded the earlier Greek notions of those who died under a familial curse or in great sin.

According to Greek beliefs, those most likely to become undead vampires also included those who have eaten the flesh of a sheep which was killed by a wolf; and those over whose dead bodies a cat or other animal has passed.

From at least the 17th century to the early 20th century, it was a common belief in Greece that the undead vampire was essentially a corpse possessed and animated by a demon. It was sometimes believed that the vampire only had to return to a grave on Saturday and that he could go about even during the day time, though in most tales he is most active at night.

Becoming a Vrykolaka

An interesting description of a process by which a victim of vampire also becomes a vampire occurs in the writings, published in 1898, of a Priest on the island of Crete concerning the *vrykolakes*:

'It is a popular belief that most of the dead, those who have lived bad lives or who have been excommunicated... become *vrykolakes*; that is to say, after the separation of the soul from the body there enters into the latter an evil spirit which takes the place of the soul....it keeps the body as its dwelling place, and it runs swift as lightning wherever it lists....And the trouble is that it does not remain solitary, but makes everyone, who dies while it is about, like to itself, so that in a short space of time it gets together a large train of followers. The common practice of the *vrykolakes* is to seat themselves upon those who are still asleep and by their great weight to create an agonizing sense of oppression. There is great danger that the sufferer might himself expire, and himself too be turned into a *vrykolakas*....This monster, as time goes on, becomes more audacious and blood-thirsty, so that it is able to devastate whole villages.' (Found in *'Modern Greek Folklore and Ancient Greek Religion'* by John Lawson)

The Callicantzaros

One other type of vampire existed in Greece: the *callicantzaros*. These were related to the extraordinary sanctity ascribed to the Christian holy days at Christmas time. Children born during the week between Christmas and New Year's (or Epiphany of Twelfth Night, the evening when the Three Wise Men are supposed to have arrived at Bethlehem to present their gifts to the baby Jesus) are considered unlucky. They were described as *feastblasted* and believed to be destined to become vampires after their death.

The *callicantzaros* had an effect upon everyday life, as any person born during the forbidden period was viewed with some degree of hostility. Parents would fear that these children would act out vampiric fantasies as they grew up and would harm their brothers and sisters.

There were several ways to deal with vampires: Usually the first means resorted to was to exhume the corpse and have a Priest exorcize the demon from it. If this method failed, the corpse might be exhumed and reburied on a desert island - it was often believed that the vampire could not cross sea water. The ultimate way to get rid of the vampire was to cremate the corpse.

Belief in vampires was well documented into the 1960s, especially in poor rural communities. Today, Greece stands as one of the oldest and most important centres for vampire lore. Its idea of the vampire, having passed through a complicated process of development, remains strong today and continues as a resource for understanding the impact of the vampire myth. In addition, Greece also has contributed significantly to the emerging image of the modern fictional vampire.

General Superstitions

Sneezing

In Greek superstition, if you sneeze, it means that someone is talking about you. If you want to know who it is, there is a way you can find out. Ask someone around you to give you a three-digit number. Count each digit together and then count down the alphabet. Whatever letter it falls on, is the initial of the person that is talking about you.

For example, 534 is the number given. Add it together 5+3+4=12. Count down the alphabet to 'L', which is the twelfth letter. That is the first initial of the person that is talking about you. For the number 999, add together 9+9+9=27. In the English Alphabet there are only 26 characters so we add 2+7 together and get 9. Now count down to the ninth letter which is I. The person who is talking about you is thought to have a name beginning with I.

Touch Red / Piase Kokkino

It might be considered a form of ESP or maybe just coincidence, but sometimes two people have the same thought and speak the same words at the same time. Take, for example, two girlfriends going out shopping together and stopping to admire a dress in a window. They both say 'That's beautiful' simultaneously.

Greeks believe this to be an omen that those two persons will get into a fight, unless they say 'Piase Kokkino' or 'Touch Red' to avoid the argument. Both persons have to touch something that's red, right then and there. Any item will do, clothing, food – anything.

The Use of Salt

Salt is considered to have great powers as a purifying force. As such, it can be used to ward off demons and evil spirits by throwing it over your left shoulder. Similarly a new house can be purified by sprinkling it with salt to remove any demons or lurking evil spirits.

Salt can also be used to remove an unwanted guest, or a guest that has overstayed their welcome, from your house. To remove an unwanted guest, salt can either be sprinkled on the chair of the unwanted guest, or thrown behind them. It is said that if the guest sees you throw the salt the power of the salt is weakened, and is not as effective.

In some areas of the island, another superstition tied to salt is that it should be covered in the darkness of the night. If the moon or the stars shine upon it, it is believed that the carrier of the salt will develop warts or a rash on their body.

Plants & Cuttings

If you have tried to take a cutting and root it without success, maybe you are doing something wrong. Skopelites believe that in order for a cutting to root, it has to be stolen. You have to nonchalantly cut off a piece of the desired plant and take it home without telling the owner. According to superstition, it will then root easily.

Cactus

No Greek home would be complete without at least one cactus positioned somewhere near the front entrance. In a big 'Feta' can or garden pot, a cactus with its thorny spikes takes it place, proudly warding off the Evil Eye from the property.

Knives

Never hand someone a knife. Set it down and let them pick it up, or else you will get into a fight with that person.

Money

Greeks believe that money attracts money, so never leave your pockets, purses or wallets completely empty and never completely empty your bank account. Always leave at least a coin or two. It is also considered good luck that when you give a gift of a wallet or a purse, that you put a coin or two in it before giving it to the recipient.

Itchy Hand

If you have an itchy hand it foretells that you are either going to receive or give money: if you're right hand is itchy it indicates that you will get money; if you're left hand is itchy it indicates that you will give money.

The right hand is thought to be holy and the left unholy. This is why you receive from the right, as in the case of money it is usually believed better to give, than receive. The use of the 'right' can be further be seen in the Orthodox Church: the Son of God sits to the right of the Father; Orthodox laity cross with the right hand, etc. If both hands are itchy then you will both give and receive money.

Crows

Crows are birds of ill omen and might predict a death or accident. If a Greek sees a crow, he will tell it to have a good day, stay well and bring good news. They actually say *'Sto kalo...sto kala, nea na mou feries.'*

There are many, many other superstitions, far too numerous to mention here, but these are ones you might come across while on holiday. If you don't know what is happening, you might well be bemused. As it is, knowing a little more about what 'makes the islanders tick' can only serve to enhance your holiday: hopefully now you won't be so confused if you see people scurrying around looking for something red to touch - especially as the nearest red object might be something of yours.

Kafemandeia - Reading the Coffee Cups

Coffee Readings are psychic readings done by using a cup of coffee as though it's a crystal ball: both tealeaves and coffee cup readings are known as *kafemandeia* (in Greek) or *tasseography*, or *tasseomancy* in English. This type of fortune telling - *I Tyhi Mas Sto Flitzani (Fortune in a Coffee Cup)* - has been practiced for centuries and originated in China.

Older ladies on Skopelos will on occasion meet, drink, then spontaneously turn their coffee cups upside down at the end of a meal or afternoon 'tea', and a member of the gathering will then start reading them: it goes with the dramatic Greek nature to be both curious (and often anxious) about the present and future, as well as to enjoy making Cassandra-like predictions about how events or situations will unfold. The trick is not to take it all too seriously, but also to consider the possibility that some, if not most of it may be likely, indicative of something important or true; certainly everyone who has had their cup read comments that what it reveals often is uncannily spot-on.

Fortune telling begins as soon as the coffee is brought to the table – you can see if romance is in store for you by how many bubbles there are on top. If you spill the coffee in the saucer when you're drinking it then you're about to come into some money (No cheating here please, because otherwise you get bad luck.)

Ground Turkish coffee is mostly used when cup readings are done. Make it as follows:

1. Prepare coffee: one heaped tea spoon to every coffee cup measure of water
2. Stir in a wish, then boil twice!
3. Scoop froth into cup, then pour coffee
4. Sip at leisure

5. Cover cup with saucer, thumb on top, shake, then flip over
6. Leave to drain on saucer
7. Drain excess over tissue paper before starting to scry (read and interpret)
8. Scry clockwise, finishing back at the cup handle

The patterns formed on the inside of the cup trigger psychic insight; and are interpreted according to what they mean to the seer. It is often believed that the drinker of the coffee should not read their own cup. If you do, write down any impressions that pop into your mind, then go back to your notes after a few days - you will begin to notice happenings taking place and understand what each symbol or pattern means.

It is important to mention here that for the reading to be meaningful, or indeed accurate, the coffee must be sipped or drunk while relaxing: if a cup of coffee is drunk in a hurry, without the intention of having it read, or while not in a relaxed state, it *can't* be read. The grains do not appear to form any meaningful patterns - merely chaotic brown dots or mud in a cup!

Interpreting coffee symbols

Many interpretations for symbols exist, but one common thread is the colour of the symbols. Since most cups used are white or ivory and the grounds are dark, strong contrast exists for the symbols. White is considered a *good* symbol foretelling of generally positive things for the drinker, while the grounds themselves are considered to form *bad* symbols.

Symbols can be many things, including people, animals, and inanimate objects. Usually, the fortune teller will group nearby symbols together for a prediction. After a reading, the drinker will be asked to *'open the heart'*.

This is done by placing the right thumb at the inside bottom of the cup and twisting clockwise slightly. This will leave an impression behind that the fortune teller will interpret as the drinker's inner thoughts or emotions.

Some images will simply reveal something that is already known, consciously or unconsciously, whilst other symbols are said to foretell events beyond individual knowledge or expectations.

Some symbols and their meanings include:

- **Rings:** A deal completed, a proposal, an engagement.
- **Circles with a dot inside:** Desire for children will be fulfilled.
- **Fire Works:** Quarrels, unpleasant personal problems.
- **Squares:** New home.
- **Lines:** Journey, a project. If lines are clear, they will go smoothly.
- **Candle:** A wish fulfilled, help from above. Fulfil your promise.
- **Mounted horseman:** A new man, good news, engagement.
- **Cat:** Moody person (white is good, black, be wary), a deceitful friend or relative.
- **Dog:** loyal friend or relative.
- **Cross:** Victory over an ordeal.
- **Ladder:** Social advancement, promotion, change.
- **Open window:** Lucky break.
- **Bowl:** Summer.
- **Peacock:** Splendour, luxury, something to be proud of.
- **Butterfly:** Flirting.
- **Fish:** Money - specific sum - depending on size of fish!
- **Bird:** Good piece of news.

- **Rat:** Robbery, theft. (If there is a dot inside, stolen item will be returned.)
- **Apple:** Achieving knowledge, completing school, getting a diploma.
- **Flying birds:** Good news.
- **Kite:** Wishes will come true.
- **Raven:** Death or bad news.
- **Knots:** Anxiety or stress.
- **Spider:** Success in finances.
- **Star:** Good luck.
- **Umbrella:** Protection against obstacles.

Important Guidelines

Generally, the bottom part of the cup represents people, situations, or ideas from the past, the middle part on the sides of the cup represents the present whilst the top part indicates what's approaching in the future. Where a symbol appears on the cup can create different meanings.

Readings take three parts. The first reading coming from the very bottom of the cup: If it is covered by thick and dark grounds, it is unlucky. But don't worry though, because if they are slightly up the side it means bad times are on their way out. If there are hardly any grounds on the bottom of the cup, the future is rosy and the outlook bright.

The second part to look at is around the handle, where you'll learn for example that a line sweeping around the cup, means a journey. The length of this line shows you the distance of your journey. Two lines parallel show that you're doing this trip with somebody else. If you can make out a letter of the alphabet the person whose name starts with that letter is thinking of you. The shape of a dog means some news of a good and faithful friend. A snake stands for a wish coming true. If you see the shape of a cockerel this means good news is on the way: An arch or a doorway predicts an important meeting or interview.

If going through the coffee-reading process seems like too much hard work, don't despair. There will always be a friendly coffee-reading neighbour, or a professional fortune-teller a stone's throw away - ask in the coffee shop if they know anyone!

And Finally... Greek Etiquette

Meeting Etiquette

Greeks are warm and hospitable people. When meeting someone for the first time, they shake hands firmly, smile, and maintain direct eye contact. Good friends – male and female - often embrace; they may also kiss each other on each cheek. Male friends often slap each other's arm at the shoulder. Members of the family or friends greeting people at the airport or port after a period of absence, often give them a flower to welcome them home.

Gift Giving Etiquette

In general, Greeks exchange gifts with family and friends for 'name days' (birth date of the saint after whom they are named) and Christmas. Some Greeks celebrate birthdays, but in general, celebrating name days is more likely. Gifts need not be expensive: since gifts are generally reciprocated, giving something of great value could put a burden on the recipient since they would feel obligated to give back something of equivalent value.

When invited to dinner at a Greek home, take something small: a floral arrangement may be sent in advance of the actual event. Gifts should be wrapped and are usually opened when received.

Special candles made for Easter called *labatha* are often given as gifts to children from their parents or God-parents, or can be given within the family. The candles can be lavishly decorated with favourite children's heroes or storybook characters, flowers or keepsakes and may be as much as three feet tall, but the candle itself is usually white. They are only used for one Easter midnight service.

Invited to a Greek home

If you are invited to a Greek home, remember to bring something for the hosts. Flowers or chocolate is the most common; or something you have made yourself – a jar of marmalade, for instance. If the occasion is a name day, you must bring a present, which you deliver when you enter the house. The present will be put together with the rest of the presents on a table - unopened. The recipient will open the gifts when all the guests have left.

Dining Etiquette and Table manners in the Greek Home

When accepting an invitation to a Greek home, arriving 15 to 30 minutes late is considered punctual! Visitors should dress well; this demonstrates respect for the hosts. An offer to help the hostess with the preparation or clearing up after a meal is served may not be accepted, but it will be appreciated. Expect to be treated like royalty! Compliment the house.

Rules are uncomplicated and most are connected with universal good manners:

- ♦ Remain standing until invited to sit down. You may be shown to a particular seat.
- ♦ Table manners are Continental - the fork is held in the left hand and the knife in the right while eating.
- ♦ The oldest person is generally served first.
- ♦ Do not begin eating until the hostess starts.
- ♦ Keep your elbows off the table and your hands above the table when eating.
- ♦ Accepting a second helping compliments the host.
- ♦ Expect a great deal of discussion. Meals are a time for socializing.
- ♦ It is considered polite, unless the occasion is very formal, to soak up gravy or sauce with a piece of bread.
- ♦ People often share food from their plate.
- ♦ Finish everything on your plate.

♦ Put your napkin next to your plate when you have finished eating.

♦ Indicate you have finished eating by laying your knife and fork parallel on your plate with the handles facing to the *right*.

♦ The host gives the first toast.

♦ An honoured guest should return the toast later in the meal.

♦ The most common toast is *'to your health'*, which is *'stinygiasou'* in informal situations and *'eis igían sas'* at formal functions.

Eating times

Lunch is generally eaten at about 2.00pm and dinner no earlier than 9.00pm. This is why if you walk around looking for a restaurant patronised by the 'locals' as a sign of quality, it is very likely to be deserted before 9.00pm. It is not unusual to arrive at a restaurant at midnight, especially in summer.

Ordering and eating out

For Greeks, a meal is a social occasion and it's hard to imagine a Greek meal without noise. When families and friends sit down to eat, the decibel level goes up. To those unfamiliar with traditional Greek meals, the sights and sounds of people talking, clinking glasses, and reaching across the table from all different directions can be alarming, but it is this traditional Greek way of serving and eating food that turns everyday meals into celebrations of tastes and people.

Foods are often shared by all at the table, so accordingly, food is ordered for the 'table', not for the individuals. You order a bit of everything, spread it around the table, or more often cover the table with different dishes and everybody picks at everything. At a traditional Greek meal, diners may take helpings of food onto their plates from serving dishes, but, more often than not, serving oneself means leaning over and around to take a fork- or spoonful directly from serving dish to mouth. A typical table will include everything from appetizers to one or two (or more) main dishes, sides, and beverages. Long reaches, clashing forks, and bumps and spills are all part of the process. It creates a babble of talk and laughter, and leaves no room for a quiet meal of 'eating what's on your plate.'

If or when more food is needed, more is ordered. There is also quite an element of status involved in the ordering and it is not uncommon for Greeks to order far too much, either to show off their status or show their generosity. This unfortunately can lead to a fair amount of food being wasted.

You can of course stick to the Western habit of not sharing food but ordering for each person; Greeks are used to foreigners and their habits, but you will miss out on an enhanced eating experience.

At the end of the meal, you may well be offered another drink or sweet *'on the house'*. You don't have to eat or drink it, but you do have to say **efaristo** - thank you. Then either leave it on the table, or in the case of accepting a drink, meet the eye of the giver - that is the waiter, or the owner, or whomever - and 'toast' them.

If a Greek unconnected with the establishment sends you a drink, the procedure is the same. Under no circumstances should you send a drink back; you are implying by doing so that he cannot afford to treat you – wait for another occasion to reciprocate.

Table manners

Table manners are pretty lax. The main bad manner would possibly be ordering for yourself when in company. Use of the fingers instead of forks and knives is very common. After all, food is there to be touched and eaten, not picked at. Eating meat (especially lamb or goat) with a fork and knife is considered a little silly because you are missing out on the most sensual part of the experience. When pouring wine, don't fill the glass to the brim: when drinking it, leave a little in your glass until it is refilled.

Paying the bill when invited out by a Greek

If invited out for dinner or a drink by a Greek, don't EVER try to make him split the bill in half, or pay it for him, as this can lead to awkwardness and embarrassment. As with ordering, paying a bill has a lot to do with offering hospitality. I have never seen older Greeks sharing the payment of a meal (at least not in a way that could have been visible to others). One will pay for all and there is often a hefty argument about who will have the privilege of paying.

Eating and waiting alone at a taverna in Greece

A single person sitting at a table in a *taverna*, can wait quite a long time for the waiter to appear. In Greece it's very unlikely that anybody eats alone: he/she must be waiting for someone. For the waiter it will be very impolite and bumptious to ask for the order before all the guests have arrived. This has changed in the major tourist places, and especially for tourists, but you can run into this phenomenon in villages on Skopelos.

By the way, the fact that trunks of trees in or near tavernas are often painted white (limewash) is primarily to fight the ants. The preponderance of basil plants in restaurants is to keep flies away.

GMT Time

In Greece the stranger must learn to live with the GMT-time, and in this case GMT is an abbreviation for *'Greek Maybe Time'*. The Greek people have a very different attitude to time: when a meeting is scheduled for 10.30, it will happen between 10 and 11, depending on the traffic, how many people the other man had met and felt he should talk with, and many other small things. Greek people don't generally live by the clock. If they do, they also have a different opinion about when it's morning, afternoon and evening: You say Good Morning until 12. If you have agreed to meet in the 'afternoon', the earliest meant by this will be 6.00 pm! In Greece, the evening meal begins no earlier than 9.00 pm. Also no one will think anything of it if you telephone at 10.00 pm in the evening.

Ores kineese esihias - The 'hours of popular quiet' (Siesta)

'Siesta' time, between 3.00 pm and 5 pm is held as sacred. It is very bad manners to disturb someone during these hours. It is not only considered very bad manners in Greece to make noise during the period from around 2 to 5 pm (and especially after 3 pm), but there is a law against it (though broken sometimes by those doing construction or using *rototillers*, because work is often excused if the workers have no other time to do that work).

On Skopelos, it is common to have the largest meal of the day in the early afternoon, as is practical and common in cultures dominated by agriculture. Then during the heat of the day, people have a nap. (Studies have indicated that those who nap have less risk of heart attack.) So if a visitor to Greece is staying in a rooms' complex that is near the houses of local Greeks, it is not appropriate to sit outside talking loudly and playing a radio or live music at that time. The same need for quiet holds for those renting apartments in Greek towns or cities.

During the hot summer months the midday meal and nap may get pushed forward until it cools off a little, with the meal even as late as 4 pm, and the nap to 5 pm or so. Few rules are 'set in stone' in Greece, but to be on the safe side, in the heat of summer, one should be aware that many Greeks are perhaps still napping until 6:30.

Many visitors to Greece learn to do as the Greeks do, and find that this way of patterning one's day makes perfect sense, given the climate. A by-product of the siesta is that having slept all afternoon, most Greek children are running around or out with their families until ten o' clock (22.00), which is children's bedtime.

The Evening Volta

One very memorable tradition on Skopelos is the evening walk. Families or mothers and daughters, friends etc. walk together along the *paralea*, catching up on each other's lives and local gossip. Young men group together in hopes of catching young ladies' eyes, and everyone enjoys a good breath of fresh air.

Giving Lifts

That is, offering to take someone somewhere in your car. On Skopelos, sections of the community are extremely widely scattered; some people are elderly, have no means of transport, or infirm and therefore cannot easily get into town. Older people will therefore quite often see one or two people in a car with seats to spare and think nothing of asking for a lift. It is not dangerous and they will be very grateful. If you see someone in the middle of nowhere, it costs nothing at all to offer them a ride. They may not accept, but they will be gratified by your good manners.